The Gods That Failed

HOW BLIND FAITH IN MARKETS HAS COST US OUR FUTURE

By The Same Authors

The Age of Insecurity

Fantasy Island: Waking up to the Incredible
Economic, Political and Social Illusions of the Blair
Legacy

This book is dedicated to our families. Larry would
like to thank his wife Carol and his daughters
Ursula and Eowyn. Dan would like to thank his
wife Sarah and his sons Aloysius, Aidan and Fergus.

The Gods That Failed

HOW BLIND FAITH IN MARKETS HAS COST US OUR FUTURE

LARRY ELLIOTT AND DAN ATKINSON

THE BODLEY HEAD
LONDON

Published by The Bodley Head 2008

2 4 6 8 10 9 7 5 3 1

Copyright © Larry Elliott and Dan Atkinson 2008

Larry Elliott and Dan Atkinson have asserted their right under the Copyright,
Designs and Patents Act 1988 to be identified as the authors of this work

This book is sold subject to the condition that it shall not,
by way of trade or otherwise, be lent, resold, hired out,
or otherwise circulated without the publisher's prior
consent in any form of binding or cover other than that
in which it is published and without a similar condition,
including this condition, being imposed
on the subsequent purchaser.

First published in Great Britain in 2008 by
The Bodley Head
Random House, 20 Vauxhall Bridge Road,
London SW1V 2SA

www.rbooks.co.uk

Addresses for companies within The Random House Group Limited
can be found at: www.randomhouse.co.uk/offices.htm

The Random House Group Limited Reg. No. 954009

A CIP catalogue record for this book
is available from the British Library

ISBN 9781847920300

The Random House Group Limited supports The Forest Stewardship
Council (FSC), the leading international forest certification organisation.
All our titles that are printed on Greenpeace approved FSC certified paper
carry the FSC logo.
Our paper procurement policy can be found at www.rbooks.co.uk/environment

Mixed Sources
Product group from well-managed
forests and other controlled sources
www.fsc.org Cert no. TT-COC-2139
© 1996 Forest Stewardship Council

Typeset in Dante MT by Palimpsest Book Production Limited,
Grangemouth, Stirlingshire

Printed and bound in Great Britain by
Clays Ltd, St Ives plc

Contents

Introduction: The view from Mount Olympus 1

1 Under the Volcano: 1929–1973–20?? 11
2 Northern Rock: Just like a rolling stone 42
3 Let's Go Round Again: The free-marketeers' Sixty Years' War 73
4 Sunday, Monday, Happy Days: The Goldilocks economy 114
5 The Rainy Season: Rising damp in Middle Britain 135
6 'Never Break the Chain': Debt and delusion in the British economy 158
7 Here There be Monsters: The perils lurking in the uncharted waters of the financial markets 188
8 Last Tango on Wall Street: The fall of the 'American miracle' 221
9 Thunder in the West: Scanning the horizon for the perfect storm 251
10 After the Gold Rush: How the New Populism makes the financial system safer, gives ordinary people a bigger slice of the cake and puts the New Olympians back in their cage 279

Afterword 311
Index 315

Introduction:

The view from Mount Olympus

'It was a credulous age, perhaps the most credulous ever.'

    – Bernard Levin; *The Pendulum Years*; Jonathan Cape; 1970

March 2008 was no time to be a welfare scrounger in Gordon Brown's Britain. That month saw a much-trumpeted move, the latest of many since Labour came to power in 1997, to end the so-called 'sick-note culture'.

On March 17, Dame Carol Black, the government's national director for health and work, declared that absence and worklessness related to sickness were costing the country £100 billion a year, and it was announced that ministers were to look at replacing the doctor's sick note with a 'fit note', detailing what people can do rather than what they cannot when they are on leave for health reasons. This was of a piece with the 'tough love' approach of Mr Brown and his predecessor Tony Blair to those on welfare benefits. It was all about reminding those who wanted to get their hands on public money that rights came with responsibilities.

Funnily enough, four days later the chief executives of Britain's five largest banking institutions – Barclays, HBOS,

HSBC, Lloyds TSB and Royal Bank of Scotland – met the Bank of England. In the jargon of the City, they wanted Bank governor Mervyn King to widen the types of collateral against which the Bank would lend to the clearing banks. In plain English, this meant the banks wanted Mr King to lend taxpayers money against much flakier assets than would normally be considered acceptable.

Justifying this was the notion that the 2007–2008 'credit crunch' had drained liquidity from the system and drastic measures were needed to refloat the wholesale money market. Behind the crunch was the fear that banks had made too many loans that would not be repaid but that, because of fancy financial engineering, no one knew which institution was holding these 'securities', thus which institutions were at risk of collapse. It was safest for each bank to assume that all the others were in danger, and decline to lend to them. So lending dried up.

Over the previous three decades, banks had shrugged off controls on lending, allowing them to create as much debt as they liked and, when they had created too much of it, to raise interest rates, thus making even more money. Were the Bank of England to accede to the bankers' latest request, this process would be complete. The banks would be able to offload their previously unacceptable assets on the Bank in return for cash. Profits would be privatised, losses increasingly socialised.

No, March 2008 was no time to be a benefits scrounger in Gordon Brown's Britain – if you were an ordinary person. But the banks, it seems, were arranging for themselves a welfare state with Scandinavian levels of generosity.

It was the same story across the Atlantic. Over the weekend of March 15 and 16, America's central bank, the Federal Reserve Board, launched a rescue for Bear Stearns, the country's fifth-largest investment bank, brought to its knees by the credit crunch, having seen two associated hedge funds invest in subprime lending. To smooth a takeover by the bank JP Morgan Chase, the Fed assumed up to $30 billion of Bear's more doubtful assets. Were this act of corporate welfare not sufficient, the Fed also announced that it was to provide emergency liquidity to the market and, for good measure, it cut the main US interest rate on March 18 by 0.75 percentage points to 2.25 per cent.

What was perhaps most extraordinary about all of this was not the bailing out of City and Wall Street types who had spent decades, like surly teenagers, insisting that they wanted only to be free from the stuffy, paternal state institutions to which they now turned for help. Rather it was the failure of those same institutions to insist on any *quid pro quo* from the City or Wall Street. In the real world, when a wild-child son or daughter comes home, tail between their legs, their 'boring' parents usually require them to clean up their act in return for financial support and use of their old bedroom. Not so in the world of banking and finance, where not only was there little suggestion of tougher controls in the wake of a crisis created by the banks' own stupidity, but the British Treasury ruled them out in remarks to the press over the weekend of March 8 and 9 2008.

But then, there is plenty of evidence that, in Britain at least, those in government could see little wrong with the system as it was.

Gordon Brown had been prime minister for barely two weeks when he killed stone dead the idea that Manchester – or, indeed, anywhere else – would be the site of Britain's first Las Vegas-style 'super-casino'. In a deliberate and, apparently, successful attempt to distance himself from his predecessor, Tony Blair, Mr Brown made it clear that he thought there were better ways of bringing jobs and regeneration to one of the country's blighted inner-city areas. As a statement of vague intent, Mr Brown's change of direction may well have been welcome. But vague intent was all it was. The contention of this book is that Britain does indeed have a gambling problem, but that tackling the casino mentality requires more than saying no to banks of slot machines and roulette tables in east Manchester. Real change would involve action against the casinos 200 miles to the south and 3,000 miles to the west of Manchester – the City of London and Wall Street.

This the new prime minister had no intention of doing either on July 11 when he signalled the government's gaming U-turn nor six months later when his political honeymoon had been cut short by what even the arch-speculator George Soros described as the most serious financial crisis since the Second World War. In any event, Mr Brown still approved the creation of 16 smaller casinos dotted around Britain, all of them considerably bigger than the discreet gambling joints found in the plusher parts of Mayfair.

Our previous book, *Fantasy Island*, looked at the legacy of Tony Blair. *The Gods that Failed* uses a wider canvas, setting Britain's increasingly rickety economy against a global backdrop of slowing growth, rising inflation and traumatised financial markets.

The argument in the pages that follow is simple. The world economy has been taken to the brink by a mania for speculation. This speculation has been fostered by the excessive power of the financial markets. They have taken advantage of the gradual erosion of any serious control over their activities and indulged in riskier and riskier activity.

Democratically elected governments have, over the past three decades, willingly ceded control of the world economy to a new elite of freebooting super-rich free-market operatives and their colleagues in national and international institutions. We call these people the New Olympians, so named because of their remoteness from everyday life and their lack of accountability and because of the faith to which they subscribe.

We contend that these Olympians gained this control on a prospectus every bit as false as much of the promotional material for the 'exotic securities' of which they are so fond and which have recently wreaked such destruction in world markets. The charge sheet is as follows:

They promised economic stability, and have delivered chaos and volatility.
They promised an economic order based on enterprise, thrift and personal

effort and have delivered one based on chronic indebtedness and wild speculation.

They promised a 'transparent' future in which all costs and prices would be clearly laid out, allowing people to make informed choices in their lives. They have delivered a world of bizarre, occult financial knowledge, one in which everything from the true cost of a mobile-phone package to the real value of billions of pounds' worth of 'securitised' debt is impossible to gauge.

They promised a greatly expanded middle class of property and share-owning individuals, a New Yeomanry of sturdy, independent citizens. They have delivered the unleashing of havoc on professional and white-collar career structures, smashed up the pension schemes of the middle class and forced their children deep into debt for the privilege of attending university.

But then, none of this ought to be surprising. The New Olympians are unconcerned with – in fact, hostile to – job security (other than their own), social tranquillity, and the traditional middle-class aspiration for both the good life and the quiet life. Our modern day Olympians sit in judgement in their central banks, their skyscraper blocks in the financial districts and in the headquarters of the European Commission, the International Monetary Fund, the World Bank and the World Trade Organisation. In these houses of the holy, they roll their eyes in despair when they hear that the Detroit car worker, the Argentinian shopkeeper or the Cornish fisherman is complaining that their way of life is under threat. Like it or lump it, that's just the way it is and has to be, the New Olympians say.

Thus on February 26 2008, the Treasury's number-two minister, Chief Secretary Yvette Cooper, attended the London annual lunch of the business organisation, the Confederation of British Industry. CBI president Martin Broughton, chairman of British Airways, 'greeted' her:

'Well, if we had met for this lunch in the middle of last year the mood music would doubtless have been a lot different. The renaissance of London would have been a likely topic . . . After all, the City was booming, private equity mega-deals abounded and we had had the good news about Crossrail.

'There would also have been discussion around the tables about whether London had eclipsed New York as a financial centre.'

Alas, some fairly modest tax increases for the wealthiest in the country 'pulled the rug out from the government's decade-long effort to encourage an enterprise culture'. Mr Broughton spoke more in sorrow than anger as he worried over the Treasury's 'loss of composure in recent months'. He did not quite intone to the Chief Secretary the gangster's mantra that she had a nice little place here and that it would be a shame were anything to happen to it, but the message was fairly clear.

At its worst, the arrogance of the New Olympians mimics, albeit in a less lethal form, that of Graham Greene's fictional black marketeer, Harry Lime:

'Look down there,' he went on, pointing through the window at the people moving like black flies at the base of the Wheel. 'Would you really feel any pity if one of those dots stopped moving – for ever? If I said you can have twenty thousand pounds for every dot that stops would you really, old man, tell me to keep my money – without hesitation? Or would you calculate how many dots you could afford to spare? Free of income tax, old man. Free of income tax.'
(The Third Man; Heinemann; 1950)

Britain has been the laboratory mouse for the New Olympian experiment, a fitting metaphor given that its politicians have shown a mouse-like timidity in facing up to the mighty ones of the market economy. Nor have they shown the slightest understanding of the huge risks involved in the Olympians' economic system.

Growth under the Blair and Brown governments has relied excessively on speculation in two forms: that in the City and that by home-owners. Economically, the legacy is a debt-sodden, lopsided and unequal country in which the pay of those at the top rises at ten times the rate of those at the bottom. Instead of taking on the City, the government has turned its attentions to the workforce – both blue-collar and white-collar – which has to be made ready for the global challenge from China and India by being re-skilled and re-educated and by learning how to be 'entrepreneurial'. While this makes for fine speeches, it represents displacement activity on a grand scale. Furthermore, the majority is routinely subjected to ever-more illiberal, intrusive and obnoxious interference from state agencies, whether in terms of visual surveillance and the proposed identity card scheme, or in terms of being instructed to change their 'attitudes' on a range of subjects.

Politically, the legacy is a country where the Labour government caves in to pressure from New Olympians using London as a tax haven but argues that the iron laws of a flexible labour market prevent granting better working conditions to agency workers. While this helps burnish Labour's business-friendly credentials, it alienates those forced to tighten their belts as a result of dearer petrol, higher taxes and nugatory pay increases.

Before taking over from Mr Blair, Mr Brown had joked that there were only two types of chancellors: those who failed and those who got out in time. Six months into his premiership, as the credit crunch bit and the government dithered over whether to take the country's sixth-biggest mortgage lender into public ownership, the joke didn't sound quite so funny.

On July 17, two weeks after Mr Brown ditched the super-casino plan, the American firm Bear Stearns admitted it had serious problems with two of its hedge funds that had been dabbling in securities dependent on the health of the US real estate market. A month later, a similar announcement by BNP Paribas caused the financial markets to have a nervous breakdown from which they have yet to recover.

As the drama unfolded, it became clear that, financially and ecologically, this is a planet living beyond its means. But in the New Olympian era, politicians who responded to demands that they act to safeguard jobs and raise real wages were accused of that most heinous of sins: populism. The Olympians may have been painfully aware that their own creed would be best described as 'un-populism' and that only by insisting on the lack of any alternative would they beat off opposition. Because where exactly was the hard evidence that the sacred tenets of the new faith – free movement of capital, free trade, low taxes, deregulated labour markets – had actually led to an acceleration in the pace of material enrichment to compensate for the additional instability?

In the pages that follow, we will do our best to answer this and other questions. In common with *Fantasy Island*, this book comes with no political baggage. We believe that discontent with the world as it is today spans left and right in Britain, the United States and continental Europe, and that, rightly, there is unease about the sustainability of the prevailing economic model.

And we believe also that the governing ideas served by the Olympian heroes are the gods that failed. Just like the ancient Greek heroes, the New Olympians share human traits even if they aren't all quite human.

The heroes of the Olympian order enjoy enormous wealth, special privileges and cocooned lifestyles. Just like their ancient forebears they can be petty, spiteful, greedy and stupid.

We believe that the days of the New Olympians are drawing to a close, and for the same reason that the days of the Old Olympians drew to a close: people simply stopped believing in them. Far from leading to greater economic stability, speculation has left the global economy more vulnerable to a financial collapse than at any time since 1929. According to the 'sophisticated' models used by market practitioners, a stock-market crash like that in 1929 was likely once in 10,000 years. They said the same about the stock-market crash of 1987, the collapse of the hedge fund Long Term Capital Management in 1998 and the subprime crisis in 2007. Our conclusion is that these models are flawed. Dangerously, and, perhaps, fatally flawed, to the extent that the world is closer to a full-scale financial crisis than at any time since the 1930s. We can envisage a US president within the next few years dusting down a copy of Franklin Roosevelt's inauguration speech in 1933, when he said the 'Practices of the unscrupulous money changers stand indicted in the court of public opinion, rejected by the hearts and minds of men.'

FDR saw it as his job to remove the money changers from the temple, and did his best to tear the temple to the ground. Bit by bit, though, it was rebuilt for the New Olympians to run. In the period before the New Olympian takeover, market capitalism proved remarkably good at providing both peace of mind and material advancement. Living standards rose rapidly, financial crises were rare, banking crises rarer still. The New Olympian regime, by contrast, has offered neither faster growth in living standards (for at least 99 per cent of the population) nor peace of mind. The modern era has been characterised by slower growth in average real incomes, higher levels of debt to maintain living standards, greater job insecurity and financial crises that have become more frequent and more far-reaching as they have edged towards the centre of the global financial system. The only class that has benefited unambiguously from the new world order has been that of the New Olympians.

John Maynard Keynes once said: 'The decadent international but individualistic capitalism in the hands of which we found ourselves after the war is not a success. It is not intelligent. It is not beautiful. It is not just. It is not virtuous. And it doesn't deliver the goods.' The words are as appropriate now as they were between the world wars and we cannot improve on them.

Had the West's politicians had the guts, the second half of 2007 and the first half of 2008 would have been the ideal time to take on the New Olympians. Their business models were broken, their reputations in tatters, their dependency on the state exposed their part in the crisis painfully clearly. We believe this failure of nerve – indeed, of backbone – spells disaster. The rest of this book explains why.

1

Under the Volcano:
1929–1973–20??

Behind us was a dark and dreadful cloud, which, as it
was broken with rapid zigzag flashes, revealed behind it
variously shaped masses of flame: these last were like
sheet lightning, though on a larger scale.
- Pliny the Younger; account of the eruption of
Mount Vesuvius; 79AD

Gatsby believed in the green light, the orgiastic future
that year by year recedes before us. It eluded us then,
but that's no matter – tomorrow we will run faster,
stretch out our arms farther.
- F. Scott Fitgerald; *The Great Gatsby*; 1925

I came to the conclusion that we're perhaps living on the
edge of a volcano. Oil supplies, copper or wheat or
nitrate supplies – inflation – any one of a number of
things could push us over into the lava flow.
- Lee Mackenzie; *The Brothers: A Clean Break*; Sphere
Books, 1976

The ancient Greeks believed their 12 most important gods and
goddesses lived on Mount Olympus. They all had a special

significance. Zeus, the lord of the gods, ruled the sky; he was responsible for thunder and lightning. Poseidon, his brother, was the king of the sea; he could ensure that a traveller returned safely home to port. Aphrodite was the goddess of love, Ares the god of war, Apollo the god of the sun and music.

This book highlights the activities of a new class of super-financier and its helpers in national and international organisations such as central banks, the New Olympians. But while they have names and faces, we believe they themselves are merely a subsidiary 'hero' class that represents the Big Ideas that rule on Mount Olympus, the 'gods', if you like, or the governing spirits.

This chapter opens with 12 such gods and goddesses hovering above and directing modern Western economies. These guiding principles are far from new; indeed the world of the New Olympians, both the gods and their hero-servants – would, barring the personal computer, the mobile phone and blanket smoking bans, have been familiar enough to the characters in an F. Scott Fitzgerald book set in the late 1920s.

But up until a year ago the governing rules of life in the early 21st century went largely unchallenged. Partly this was because those in charge believed that all was for the best in the best of all possible worlds. Partly, it was because there was deemed to be no alternative to the dominant model, however flawed. And partly, perhaps most importantly, it was because nobody was really sure what was happening up there on Mount Olympus. Or, at least, they found it convenient to pretend that they didn't know what was happening. Once Pandora's box flew open, however, that excuse sounded increasingly hollow.

Greek mythology provides plenty of raw material for a book about the failings of modern financial markets. There is the story of King Midas, who found the ability to turn all he touched into gold a curse. The tendency of markets to veer between the wild optimism of booms and the manic depression of busts is akin to the life led by poor Persephone, condemned to live six months of every year in Hades. But

Pandora – a gift from the gods whose beauty belied her baleful influence on the lives of mortals – makes the best metaphor.

Pandora was fascinated, obsessed even, by the box that had been handed to her husband Epimetheus by his brother Prometheus, the titan who according to legend was chained to a rock and had his liver pecked out daily by a vulture for having the temerity to steal fire from the gods. Prometheus had told Epimetheus that on no account was the box to be opened, but Pandora, believing that it might contain precious jewels that would enhance her beauty, was not to be deterred. Eventually, she could contain herself no longer and decided to take a peek in the box. She lifted the lid a fraction, but to her horror found that the box did not contain diamonds and gold but a host of nasty creatures that swarmed over the world bringing all the curses of mankind – plague and old age, disease and dishonesty.

August 9 2007 was the moment the lid came off the modern version of Pandora's box. Few realised it at the time, although there had been a sprinkling of soothsayers warning that the sky was darkening with bad omens. To be sure, the financial markets wobbled, with the Dow Jones industrial average losing almost 400 points in the worst day for Wall Street for four months and the index of London's blue chip shares down by more than 100 points. But reports that the European Central Bank in Frankfurt and the Federal Reserve in Washington had made cheap funds available to banks was confined to the business pages. This was, so editors believed, simply another market wobble. After all, the Dow had closed at an all-time high of above 14,000 only three weeks earlier after the Fed had given reassurance that there would be no contagion effects to the rest of the US economy from the problems in the US subprime mortgage market. On the front page of the *Guardian* the top story concerned a fresh warning about global warming; the back pages were looking forward to the start of the soccer season that coming weekend. In the US, the baseball season was in full swing.

The role of Pandora in August 2007 fell to the giant French bank, BNP Paribas. It announced that it had blocked withdrawals from three investment funds because of what it called the 'complete evaporation' of liquidity. A BNP spokesman said it was a technical issue, which was only partly true. While the link between falling house prices in California and the bottom line of one of France's biggest commercial banks was certainly convoluted, the reason for BNP's action was simple: despite having on its staff some of the country's best mathematical brains, it could not put a price, with any great confidence, on the investments it had made in US asset-backed bonds. Like Pandora, the ECB and the Fed tried desperately to ram the lid back down again. Like Pandora, they failed.

Our list of the 12 gods of the modern Mount Olympus, the ruling ideas served by the overpaid heroes of the City and Wall Street, begins with *globalisation*. The ancient Greeks worshipped Zeus; today's cosmopolitan élite pays homage to a world without borders. From the acceptance that economic power had shifted from the nation state to the global market everything else stems. The sinews of the modern economy are the trade routes that take goods from Shanghai to Los Angeles and capital back in the other direction. Governments that seek to meddle with the global market do so at their peril; the experience of François Mitterand in the early 1980s tends to be cited as the last gasp for Keynesian state intervention. In the modern world, governments are not supposed to tame globalisation but to ready their citizens to compete in a world of cut-throat competition.

There is a wrong way and a right way to do this. The wrong way is to adopt a protectionist approach, putting tariffs on foreign steel or banning a foreign company from buying your ports (as the US has done) or seeking to prevent cheap food from undercutting your farmers (as the French have done). The right way is to invest in education, skills and science in the belief that this will 'brain-up' your population and create a knowledge economy that will find an upmarket niche in a world awash with cut-price goods. This is Gordon Brown's approach.

The twin brother of globalisation is *communication*. While the arrival of the telegraph in the first half of the 19th century marked the start of the revolution in the way information could be transmitted, the development of powerful digital technology has transformed the way the world works. Had a French bank run into difficulties as a result of financing Napoleon's wars in 1807, for example, it would have taken days for the news to arrive in London, and weeks for it to get to New York. Yet when BNP announced that it was having problems with its hedge funds, every dealer in Wall Street and Canary Wharf knew what had happened within seconds. Some argue that the change between the globalisation at the end of the 19th century and that that exists today is that the Gold Standard has been replaced by an information standard. Walter Wriston, the former chairman of Citibank, once noted: 'What it means, very simply, is that bad monetary and fiscal policies anywhere in the world are reflected within minutes on the Reuters screens in the trading rooms of the world. Money only goes where it is wanted and, once you tie the world together with telecommunications and information, the ball game is over. It's a new world, and the fact is, the information standard is more draconian than any gold standard' (quoted in *The Shield of Achilles*; Philip Bobbitt; Allen Lane; 2002).

Nation states, despite the impact of globalisation and communication, retain considerable power. They control the flow of imports into their markets; they have controls on the movement of capital; they run industries that are considered to be strategic; they believe that some sectors of the economy – health and education – should be shielded from the full blast of competition. These are, however, impediments to the smoother running of the global market and thus need to be removed. The World Trade Organisation – a supranational body with punitive powers for governments that transgress its rules – started a new round of talks in November 2001 designed to open up markets in agriculture, manufacturing and services. The International Monetary Fund and the World Bank insist that poor countries receiving financial assistance should abandon state control of their mines, banks and energy companies. In Brussels, the European Commission is dedicated to the removal of the restrictive practices and state subsidies that throw sand under the wheels of the single market. The next three gods are, therefore, *liberalisation*, *privatisation* and *competition*.

The sector of the economy to benefit most from these developments was finance. International banks had always tended to have global reach, they could benefit more than any other sector from more rapid communication, it was in their interests to have barriers on capital removed, they picked up hefty fees for organising privatisations and competition allowed them to wipe out weaker competition. What was not really apparent until the summer of 2007 was not how powerful this sixth god – *financialisation* – had become. In countries like Britain, the expansion of the City of London had been the engine of the economy's growth – the fastest-growing parts of the finance sector expanded at around 7 per cent a year between 1996 and 2006. The increase in size of the financial sector was accompanied by greater power. At one level, this meant that Merrill Lynch, Goldman Sachs and PriceWaterhouseCoopers were able to attract the best brains from the best universities in the annual trawl for promising graduates, with the summer internship between the second and third year replacing what had once been the InterRail tour round Europe. There was an opportunity cost to other sectors of the economy from a state of affairs where the City was able to secure a disproportionate amount of young talent. At a wider level, this mirrored the transfer of income from the 'real' to the financial economy. Furthermore, the opportunity cost of one sector receiving a disproportionate amount of young talent was mirrored by a transfer of income from the 'real' sector of the economy to the financial sector. Manufacturing output stagnated, while incomes for those not working in the City – or in those industries such as financial PR or law firms arranging takeover bids – tended to grow at best only modestly.

Financialisation, it was argued by its proponents, was good for a country like Britain. It allowed the country to specialise in what it was good at, made London the hub of global finance, encouraged innovation and – by allowing the market to decide where capital should go – made the economy more stable. Whether this proves to be true in the long term remains to be seen. In the short term, economic growth did not accelerate, productivity did not surge, there was no miracle cure to the balance of payments and only rare glimpses of trickle down. One commentator summed up the triumph of financialisation as follows: 'Economic growth has been tepid, median wages have stagnated, and income inequality and economic insecurity have both risen. Moreover, there are concerns that the business cycle generated by financialisation may be unstable and end in prolonged stagnation' (Thomas Palley; 'Financialization: What it is and Why it Matters'; November 2007).

As events unfolded in late 2007 and early 2008, this started to look like an accurate assessment. Up until that point, it was easy to argue that the first six gods out of Pandora's box were beneficial to the global economy and at worst neutral. Privatisation in developing countries, for example, was heralded as a way of preventing corrupt ruling cliques from siphoning off profits into Swiss bank accounts. Globalisation was specialisation on a grand scale; the logical conclusion to the sort of division of labour that Adam Smith and David Ricardo had envisaged 200 years ago. The modern world not only means that we can keep in touch by e-mail with our cousins in Cape Town and buy an agreeable Malbec from an Argentinian vineyard in the foothills of the Andes, but also allows our pension fund to buy shares in an Indian software company. On paper, this world of greater choice, freedom and opportunity sounds splendid. It is certainly preferable that modern communication technology allows Mozart's clarinet concerto to be heard on a CD player in any living room rather than being the exclusive preserve of the court of the Austro-Hungarian emperor in Vienna. In reality, however, the world doesn't work this way and that's because the remaining six gods in Pandora's box have such potentially dangerous properties. These are *speculation*, *recklessness*, *greed*, *arrogance*, *oligarchy* and *excess*.

Speculation is not always harmful. Britain's 15 years of uninterrupted economic growth from 1992 onwards was the direct consequence of the then Conservative government being forced to leave the European exchange rate mechanism following an attack on the pound orchestrated by George Soros. Freed from the need to use excessively high interest rates to defend sterling, growth picked up and unemployment came down. Yet the activities of the big banks and the hedge funds in the first half of 2007 had no noble purpose; far from rectifying a glaring public policy error, they exploited a problem in the private sector, the granting of mortgages in the US to those who couldn't really pay them. Financialisation had created an inverted pyramid. Instead of having a broadly based productive economy supporting a financial sector, which had speculation as one of its lucrative but less important activities, a diminished productive sector supported an ever-bigger financial sector which saw speculation as the very reason for its existence.

The risks of speculation are magnified if the speculator behaves recklessly. A millionaire placing a £1,000 bet on red in a well-run casino is speculating, but at (just about) even money could hardly be said to acting imprudently. Not so the jobless punter who mortgages his house to back a hunch that the 50–1 outsider will win the Derby. The history of the past five years is marked by reckless behaviour, not just from the banks and other financial institutions that loaded up on investments backed by American subprime mortgages but from the central banks that were playing with fire when they provided cheap money to maintain the speculative frenzy, the ratings agencies who give securities triple-A ratings because it was a way of securing business from investment houses and the real-estate brokers who kept on selling subprime loans even when it was clear that the US housing boom was long over. Like Pandora, there were plenty of warnings. Like Pandora, the actors in our modern Greek tragedy could not help themselves.

As in all tragedies, the central figure has a fatal character flaw. For Macbeth it is ambition, for Othello jealousy, for Hamlet indecision. The tragedians of 2007 and 2008 displayed not one but two central flaws that help explain their recklessness: greed and arrogance.

It would be naïve to believe that greed could ever be expunged from financial markets; the pursuit of riches is, and always has been, a factor motivating those who buy and sell shares, bonds, currencies and commodities. Nor is it uncommon to find that the brokers and dealers do rather better out of asset-price bubbles than their customers; Fred Schwed wrote a book published in 1940 perceptively titled *Where Are the Customers' Yachts?* (Wiley Investment Classics). Every so often, however, the money lust becomes so pronounced that it crosses the dividing line between cupidity and criminality. In the late 1980s there was an outcry in Britain when salesmen exploited the opportunities provided by financial deregulation to persuade homeowners to take out endowment mortgages rather than repayment loans, and convinced those with inflation-proof public sector pensions to switch into much less attractive portable personal pensions. In both cases, the motivation was the fat commission the salesman could make by closing out a deal and the upfront fees charged by the firms selling the products. Since 2002, a similar wave of mis-selling has been evident in the US real estate market, with tales of pensioners with only a tiny amount outstanding on their loans tricked into remortgaging their homes at ruinous rates of interest by unscrupulous mortgage brokers. The financial equation – from top to bottom in the industry – was skewed towards generating the maximum amount of business, and, because it was more lucrative that way, the riskier the better. The real estate brokers assumed they could not lose; if subprime borrowers failed to keep up their payments the home would be repossessed and sold at a profit in an ever-rising market; those dabbling in mortgage-backed securities believed what their 'rocket-scientist' mathematicians and ratings agencies told them: that they were all gain and no pain. Five months into the crisis, the mood was more contrite. Panellists at a session at the World Economic Forum in Davos on risk management were asked how the big banks of North America and Europe had failed to spot the potential losses from subprime. The one-word answer from a group that included the chairman of Lloyd's of London and the chief risk officer of the insurance company Swiss Re was 'greed'. As one participant put it: 'Those running the big banks didn't have the first idea what their dealers were up to but didn't care because the profits were so high.'

It goes without saying that those responsible for the speculative bubble of early 2007 could not conceive that Bear Stearns would announce problems with its hedge funds in late July or that BNP's problems would give credit markets the equivalent of a stroke a couple of weeks later. That was where the arrogance kicked in. The super-heroes of the New Olympian order were the brightest and the best of their generation. Their activities were making massive profits, a good chunk of which were being paid out in seven-figure bonuses that kept property markets humming in the Cotswolds and the Hamptons. Could it be remotely possible that Citigroup, Merrill Lynch and UBS were guilty of crass stupidity and that their glittering palaces were little more than Potemkin villages? It was unthinkable, and even when cracks did start to appear in the edifice the New Olympian class managed to blame everyone but themselves. On August 10 2007, Countrywide, America's biggest mortgage lender, said in a filing to the Securities and Exchange Commission that it was facing 'unprecedented disruptions' because demand for its home loans had evaporated. According to Countrywide's chief executive officer, Angelo Mozilo, who took home $120 million as a result of the unflagging efforts of his sales force in 2006, the problems were either the fault of the government, which he had blamed less than three months earlier for over-regulating the industry, or borrowers for putting pressure on lenders to offer subprime loans.

This arrogance stemmed from the not-unreasonable belief that big finance was now too big to fail. Mr Mozilo's railings against the iniquities of big government were heard no more after August 2007. Instead they were replaced by a demand, loud and insistent, that the monetary authorities step in with unlimited quantities of financial assistance. Bob Diamond, the American chief executive of Barclays Capital in London, earned £22 million in 2006 and was the sort of person who saw no reason why his money-making activities should be curtailed by red tape. But in August and September 2007, Mr Diamond conducted a vigorous campaign against Mervyn King, the governor of the Bank of England, for failing to provide the same sort of help to banks in the UK as was being provided by the Fed or the ECB. As one commentator noted, this state of affairs was tantamount to the police being forced to provide a getaway car to bank robbers for fear that even greater damage would be caused by not doing so. Mr King was suitably unimpressed, believing that Mr Diamond's outburst was directly linked to concern about the size of his bonus.

The response to the market meltdown helps illustrate the final two principles that govern the modern world. One is that, despite the lip-service paid to democracy, Western societies are effectively run by moneyed oligarchies, who have as little time for their wage slaves as did the ruling élite of ancient Athens. In February 2008, Gordon Brown and his ministers opposed a private member's bill designed to give greater rights in the workplace to agency workers, part-timers who face some of the lowest wages and toughest working conditions of any group. Many agency workers are immigrants, since the New Olympian élite requires an almost endless stream of servants to administer to its needs. Two weeks earlier, and under considerable pressure, Alistair Darling, the chancellor, had announced that he was relaxing his proposals to tax more heavily one group of immigrants – the so-called non-doms (non-domiciled residents) who were mightily wealthy and used London as a tax haven.

To be fair, at least 100 Labour MPs failed to accept the government's view that global competition means that all workers except CEOs and top directors must accept lower real wages and pensions and poorer working conditions. Nor did they find it convincing that globalisation makes all types of labour more abundant, except chief executives. Messrs Brown and Darling, however, seemed to have swallowed the argument that rich people would leave unless taxation was made voluntary at the top end of the scale, although it was hard to see why it was thought that a good way of bringing foreign money into the UK was to let rich foreigners live here without paying taxes so long as they kept most of their money overseas.

It is tempting to say that the final scourge to escape from the modern Pandora's box was weakness, because it was certainly apparent in late 2007 and early 2008 that the apparent strength of the financial markets was illusory. The happy-go-lucky mood evaporated instantly, with the write-down of losses accompanied by some token sackings of executives and followed by more stringent lending for the real victims of the credit crunch – individuals and businesses forced to pay more when they borrowed. In the UK, loans worth 125 per cent of the value of a home disappeared and lenders rediscovered the virtues of thrift when they started to demand that first-time buyers save up for a sizeable deposit before being eligible for a loan. Weakness, though, cannot really be included as a principle of the New Olympians, since nobody willingly seeks to be weak. Rather, our 12th and last principle is excess. It is an axiom of the global order that there is never too much of anything; never too much growth, never too much speculation, never too high a salary, never too many flights, never too many cars, never too much trade. It was for that reason, perhaps, that the financial crisis was accompanied by rising inflation – as demand for oil and food pushed up prices globally – and by almost daily evidence of the impact of global warming. Losses in the financial markets; hardship for pensioners facing dearer heating and food; climate change. There were no prizes for guessing which the New Olympians considered the most pressing issue for policy makers.

Introductions are designed to whet the appetite of readers for what is to come. This is no different, but in truth we find ourselves in the position of the chef in the Michelin-starred restaurant who looks through the larder and wants to try all the ingredients. Choosing some vignettes from the past year has not been easy, so spoiled for choice have we been. Should we, for example, start with the first inkling of the crisis – the two Bear Stearns hedge funds that announced they were having trouble meeting margin calls? After all, these funds were run by a Wall Street hot shot, Ralph Cioffi, and were leveraged 17 times, making them prime examples of the New Olympian paradigm. Or perhaps a tastier offering would be to chart the reputation of Alan Greenspan, which by 2008 was the only thing falling more rapidly than American house prices. There was no longer a great demand in bookstores for Bob Woodward's book *Maestro* about the former Federal Reserve chairman; instead the mood was captured by the subtitle to William Fleckenstein's *Greenspan's Bubbles*, which was *The Age of Ignorance at the Federal Reserve*, a play on the title of Mr Greenspan's own memoir, *The Age of Turbulence*.

Somewhat reluctantly, it has to be said, we narrowed the choice down to three examples that we believe illustrate the themes of this book: the failure of the gods, the impact of this failure on ordinary people and the reality gap between the recognition that something had gone seriously wrong and the willingness to do anything meaningful to put it right.

WOMEN AND CHILDREN LAST: THE CURIOUS AFFAIR OF EGG

As a gleaming and polished vignette of a low, dishonest decade, the 'Egg affair' of January 2008 was hard to equal.

A telephone and internet bank with a giggly name, Egg lost silly amounts of money for its founder, the insurance group Prudential, for the first seven years of its existence until, in 2007, a sillier institution emerged that was willing to pay good money for it – Citigroup, the world's largest bank and, when still known as First National City Bank of New York, one of the pre-eminent names in 20th-century capitalism. Citi paid £546 million for Egg in 2007, a fancy price for a persistent loss-maker. On January 31, as the global credit crunch caused lending of all types to dry up, Citi cancelled the credit cards of 161,000 Egg customers, citing their supposedly poor risk profile.

When it emerged that many of those now cast into financial outer darkness had perfectly good credit records – indeed, some seemed admirable repositories of that vanishing British virtue, thrift – the resulting furore was guaranteed.

Egg never achieved very much in its ten brief years. Yet, strangely, it managed to encapsulate many of the illusions and excrescences of the New Olympian era, starting perhaps with the notion that an insurance company not only could but should seek to branch out into very different areas of financial services, such as banking, and that banks should return the favour.

There was the illusion that the internet had 'changed the rules' and that no way did a new breed of hip young consumers want to have their financial affairs managed by an old-fashioned bank with a buttoned-down branch manager and a tweedy name such as 'National Westminster'. Thus the turn of the century was the era of the branch-less bank with the impeccably twitty name: Egg, Cahoot (part of Abbey National), and Smile (a Co-operative Bank offshoot). More pertinently, given the traditionally more succulent profits available on life assurance and unit trusts compared to straightforward banking activity, or the Prudential's traditional business of general insurance, a telephone and internet bank, it was thought, could provide a new, low-cost, ultra-profitable distribution channel for these products – so much cheaper than the insurance salesmen of yesteryear, now being phased out. Thus profits would be enhanced and a line of responsible, steady but 'too expensive' middle-class employment would be destroyed – vintage Olympian activity. True, this low-cost distribution channel proved to be less profitable than had been envisaged, but not before the height of the dotcom boom of the late 1990s, in the wake of which Egg was given a higher value than British Airways, after its partial share sale in June 2000.

Then there was Egg's role in perhaps the greatest and most damaging fantasy of the New Olympian era: the reckless extension of credit, not least to those ill-equipped to handle it. Egg may not have proved much good at selling mortgages or complex investment products down the computer cable or telephone line, but it certainly shifted credit cards.

At one point, thanks to very keen pricing and a big promotional push, it was one of the biggest three credit card issuers in the country. But, as Katherine Griffiths reported in the *Sunday Telegraph* (February 10 2008):

[It] is generally thought that Egg got the pricing wrong on cards, and on personal loans, from the beginning. Part of the problem was that, as a telephone and internet bank, Egg attracted the customers that bankers call 'rate tarts', who chase the best rates and do not stick with any one provider.

Egg's simplified pricing – with one rate for all rather than the myriad of complex deals offered by rivals – was popular. But it also meant that Egg took on customers with problematic credit histories who, if they had gone elsewhere, would only have been offered a more expensive rate.

Closing in on what may well be one of the most central New Olympian delusions, she added: 'One analyst said that, in contrast to Egg's positioning of its brand as appealing to young professionals, in reality it sucked in a lot of people on low incomes and with poor repayment records.'

Yes, quite. Much of the New Olympian project had been presented as meeting the financial and other needs of a new, affluent and sophisticated consumer, from the 'yuppies' of the 1980s through the 'new men' of the 1990s to the 'metro-sexuals' and 'Alpha females' of the 2000s; in reality, much of it involved the sordid business of selling unaffordable levels of debt to 'people on low incomes and with poor repayment records'. This was a new breed of chronic debtor, a latter-day version of the downtrodden miner who, in the 1947 song 'Sixteen Tons' by country artist Merle Travis, lamented: 'I owe my soul to the company store.' As these lower-income people were to find out in January 2008, they would be dropped like a hot brick at the first sign of trouble and ordered to cut up their plastic cards. But before examining the climax of the Egg affair, it is worth reminding ourselves of the recent 'form' of its new owner, Citigroup. In the 12 months prior to the cancellation of the Egg customers' cards, Citigroup had been one of the most bullish institutions in terms of brushing off any suggestion that the world economy could be heading for trouble. As we shall note in a later chapter, chairman and chief executive Chuck Prince shrugged off fears about global liquidity in July 2007, insisting: '[A]s long as the music is playing, you've got to get up and dance. We're still dancing.'

On November 4 2007, Mr Prince left the dance floor; Citi had announced between $8 billion and $11 billion of potential losses related to subprime mortgages and Mr Prince resigned. As he did so, perhaps he regretted his decision in January 2007 to ditch Citigroup's well-known and friendly 'red umbrella' emblem – in the storms now blowing, a stout brolly was probably just what the bank needed.

Given the scale of Citi's difficulties, any potential

problems at Egg may have appeared to be small beer. Yet Citi's UK operations could have seemed particularly vulnerable to the worldwide credit crisis. Alongside Egg, Citi had a subprime loans business with nearly 50 high street branches, Citi Financial, and a subprime homeloans business called Future Mortgages. At the top end of its British operation, it offered banking services to wealthy international customers. As Ian Kerr, head of Citi's British consumer business, told Katherine Griffiths in the above-mentioned article: 'We've got both ends of the market but not a lot in the middle.'

Olympians usually like it that way; indeed, you could argue that the whole Olympian project, consciously or unconsciously, aims to leave society itself with 'not a lot in the middle'.

Be that as it may, on January 31, Citigroup informed the Stock Exchange that it was writing to 161,000 Egg credit card customers collectively responsible for about £2 billion of spending, to stop using their cards. Citi could not require them immediately to repay all they owed – if anything. But it could stop them from using their cards. As Egg faced a storm of criticism, it responded, on February 8 2008:

It [the decision] was not, as has been suggested, an excuse to exclude some 'unprofitable' customers. In this one-off review we assessed that the credit profiles of these customers had deteriorated from the time they joined Egg until the time Citi acquired Egg in May 2007 and that they presented a higher than acceptable credit risk to the bank.

Not everyone was convinced, to put it mildly. Some believed that the cards had been withdrawn precisely because some of the now-banished Egg customers had never missed a payment, thus were not making Egg any real money, their spending habits being insufficient to generate much by way of the 'merchant fees' paid by shops and other retail outlets to the credit card companies. And some of the ex-Egg customers checked their credit ratings and found nothing amiss. One such was Maya Lucas, a 23-year-old life insurance adviser from Chester. Interviewed by the *Sunday Times* on February 10 2008, she said: 'I don't understand how I can be seen as a credit risk . . . I checked my Experian [a credit reference company] file, which said that I have a very good score.'

But as the same article noted: 'There is no guarantee you will have a good credit score with your bank even if a credit reference file labels you as low risk. This is because lenders have their own rating system which uses 'behavioural' information. It will also weigh information differently from credit reference firms or other banks.'

In other words, they can do as they like and there is no appeal. The credit reference that the customer can access is of little importance compared to the credit reference inside the lending institution that the customer cannot access. This is a not-untypical example of the 'transparency' of which New Olympians are so fond. How many people knew that before the Egg affair?

But while tens of thousands of Egg customers were being shown the door, Mr Prince, the now-departed former head of Citigroup, would probably not be having much difficulty obtaining credit cards or other personal finance facilities. The market's condign punishment for his failures at Citigroup involved a reported payoff of at least £19.5 million. The poor man must have wished he had never been born.

One final aspect of the garish contemporary financial and economic scene fully reflected in the Egg debacle is the fondness for 'securitisation' – selling your IOUs to someone else – of which we shall hear a lot more later in this book. About £2.2 billion of Egg's credit card 'assets' (i.e. money owed by borrowers) was in a vehicle called Pillar Trust, set up in 2002.

To sum up, Egg was launched as an unstuffy new type of financial institution that would use modern technology to deliver sophisticated products to a demanding new breed of affluent and aspirational customers. Having failed to acquire these sorts of customers in the volumes needed to produce the expected bumper profits, it was sold to an institution that had a rather better understanding of many of the sort of customers that it *had* managed to attract: subprime borrowers. Citigroup also appeared to understand that when a bank makes a lot of stupid mistakes, costing billions of pounds, and trouble is looming, those least able to hit back must be the first to suffer, that the top people are fully entitled to scramble over the women and children into the lifeboats.

No, Egg never achieved very much in its ten brief years. But by its action on January 31 2008, it managed to encapsulate so very much of what is so very wrong with the world the New Olympians have tried to create.

WINTER LIGHTNING: 96 HOURS THAT SHOOK MOUNT OLYMPUS

The Egg affair took our fancy as an episode from the early part of 2008 that seemed to sum up the economic and financial events of the time. But in truth, we were spoiled for choice. By the spring of the year, it was obvious that the global financial crisis was not mending itself; on the contrary, there were plenty of signs that it was getting worse.

There was, for instance, the week ending Saturday January 26, the week when all the signs were that the New Olympians' scam was finally coming apart. On Monday January 21, Chancellor Alistair Darling said he had given up on hopes of persuading a private sector buyer to assume the £24 billion that stricken bank Northern Rock owed to the Bank of England, which had pumped in the money to keep the Rock in business. The Rock had been brought to its knees by drinking deep of the cup of commercial liberalisation and financial engineering. Mr Darling proposed that taxpayers should gulp down a big draught of the same medicine.

He announced plans to turn the £24 billion into bonds

that would be sold on the open market, with a government guarantee. Whoever ended up owning the Rock would have to put aside a portion of the future income from customers' mortgage payments to pay the dividends on the bonds. Put in lay person's terms, this is how the bond scheme worked.

Someone owes you money and cannot pay you back; you take that person's IOU and sell it to a third party, thus getting your money back. But the only reason the third party will touch this IOU with a bargepole is that you have guaranteed it – in effect, you have underwritten someone else's debt to you.

Thus did the sort of financial engineering in which the Olympians specialise come full circle; having put one of the UK's largest mortgage lenders deeply in debt to the public purse, it was now being employed by ministers, it was hoped, to package up that debt and sell it to someone else. But any hopes that this would expedite a sale of Northern Rock to the private sector were cruelly disappointed within a very short period of time – on February 17 2008, Mr Darling announced that the bank was to be nationalised.

On the day after Mr Darling's bond scheme was announced, Tuesday January 22, America's central bank, the Federal Reserve Board, stunned financial markets with the sudden announcement that the US official rate of interest was to be cut by 0.75 percentage points to 3.5 per cent. This was the biggest single cut in 23 years. It was also the first time the Fed had cut the rate other than on its scheduled meeting date since a between-meeting cut in September 2001 after the terrorist attacks on New York and Washington. The move by Fed chairman Ben Bernanke and his colleagues reeked of panic and was reminiscent of nothing so much as a drug pusher desperately hoping that one more fix will get his groggy customers back on their feet. The Fed statement seemed anything but reassuring:

[We] took this action in view of a weakening of the economic outlook and increasing downside risks to growth. While strains in short-term

funding markets have eased somewhat, broader financial market condi-
tions have continued to deteriorate and credit has tightened further for
some businesses and households. Moreover, incoming information indicates
a deepening of the housing contraction as well as some softening in labour
markets . . . Appreciable downside risks to growth remain. The Committee
will continue to assess the effects of financial and other developments on
economic prospects and will act in a timely manner as needed to address
those risks.

It did that all right, with another cut, this one of 0.5
percentage points to 3 per cent, on January 30. The communiqué read:

Financial markets remain under considerable stress, and credit has tightened
further for some businesses and households. Moreover, recent information indi-
cates a deepening of the housing contraction as well as some softening in
labour markets.

But guess what? '[Downside] risks to growth remain . . .
[We] will continue to assess the effects of financial and other
developments on economic prospects and will act in a timely
manner as needed to address those risks.'

This all sounded very much like bureaucrat-speak for:
'Help!'

Since the share price falls on October 1987, the response of
the Fed to any threat to asset prices had been to pump the
system full of cheap money via a cut in interest rates. There
seemed not a glimmer of understanding at the Fed that the
crisis of 2007–2008 was the working out of 20 years of this
policy, not the result of insufficient application of it.

After a day's respite, the week's third bombshell went off
on January 24. French bank Société Générale, one of the
country's most respected financial institutions, announced it
had faced a €4.9 billion (£3.7 billion) hole in its accounts and
it had needed an emergency cash injection from shareholders
of €5.5 billion (£4.1 billion). Blame was immediately ascribed
to a 'rogue trader' of the type familiar from the 1990s (Nick

Leeson, the British trader who broke Barings Bank in 1995, was probably the best known).

The name in the frame was that of Jerome Kerviel, a 31-year-old Paris-based trader working on the bank's European equities derivatives desk. According to the January 25 edition of the *Financial Times:* 'He was already being portrayed by the governor of the Banque de France yesterday as a "genius of fraud."'

It certainly seemed to be the case that Mr Kerviel had made very large, and very unauthorised, bets on European stock markets and had managed to keep them from the attention of those above him at SocGen, but SocGen has said that direct financial gain did not seem to be his motive.

Furthermore, the very expression 'rogue trading' in contexts such as these suggests some deeply deviant activity far removed from the usually straight-laced world of financial services. In fact, taking bets – speculation, in other words – is what traders are paid to do by the investment banks, commodities houses or other type of institution for which they work.

It would be going too far to suggest that Mr Kerviel was as much a scapegoat for the system's failings as were those thrifty people among the 161,000 Egg customers who had their credit cards withdrawn. But the desperation of all concerned to blame a 'rogue trader' in such circumstances suggests a great deal about the New Olympians' secret fears. The rogue trader can offer a comforting explanation for sudden lurches into financial instability. His behaviour can be described as wicked, or simply inexplicable. He is the financial equivalent of the 'bad apple' police officer found taking bribes or framing suspects. His 'rogue' status means he can be safely labelled as bad, sad or mad but never as simply someone who went a little too far in pursuing a type of market activity that is utterly routine, indeed is essential to the New Olympian order. That would give rise to the thought that the rogue trader is merely a product of a rogue financial system, and that would never do.

For Société Générale, there was one crumb of comfort.

Elsewhere in the above-mentioned *Financial Times* report it was noted that: 'The fraud also overshadowed SocGen's announcement yesterday of a €2 billion [£1.5 billion] hit from the US mortgage crisis, in addition to the €375 million [£282 million] of write-downs taken in the third quarter.'

Every cloud, it seems, still has a silver lining.

U-TURN, THEY TURN: THE GENTLE ART OF CLIMBING DOWN

But while Olympus shook, the heroes of business and finance could take comfort from the fact that some people were still trying to make them happy. Britain's Treasury ministers, for instance, who spent the early months of 2008 back-tracking on what had been, in truth, modest proposals to extract some additional tax from them.

On February 12 came Mr Darling's retreat on the issue of taxing non-domiciled residents, or non-doms – wealthy individuals who, while living in the UK, claimed their residence to be elsewhere and paid tax only on income shown to have been earned in Britain. The 120,000 odd non-doms were, in other words, true Olympians.

In his Pre-Budget Report on October 9 2007, the Chancellor had proposed a tougher regime for those 20,000-odd non-doms who had been in Britain for seven years or more, a regime that included the payment of an annual £30,000 flat tax to the Exchequer. The backlash from the assembled bankers, shipowners and other tycoons was predictable, as their political and media apologists lauded their contribution to economic growth and employment and warned of disaster should these philanthropists take themselves elsewhere.

Writing on February 24 2008, Vince Cable MP, Liberal Democrat Treasury spokesman, noted the bizarre nature of the campaign being waged:

We hear stories that a high proportion of non-doms will flee . . . It is also claimed that public discussion of non-dom taxation is dangerous because it might frighten these fragile creatures away.

This is effective propaganda. We are in the absurd position that some taxpayers on modest incomes have started to feel sorry for the wealthy tax avoiders. ('Liechtenstein on Thames'; the Mail on Sunday)

Mr Darling duly backtracked. The charge would stay, but into the waste-bin went earlier suggestions of making non-doms report on the source of their earnings abroad. Furthermore, there was a pledge that works of art on loan to British galleries would not attract tax and a categorical statement that the tax changes would not be retrospective.

Not that this was the end of Mr Darling's problems. Talks with the American authorities on allowing US non-doms to offset the £30,000 charge against the American tax bill seemed to be alive and well on February 12; by the end of the week, they were in a state of near-collapse. The US would not accept that the charge was a 'tax' within the meaning of the British-American so-called double taxation treaty, because it was both optional (non-doms could opt to pay ordinary British tax if that proved more advantageous) and unrelated to income. The 10,000 non-doms thought to be Americans – about half the total likely to be immediately affected by the new regime – thus faced a double tax bill, and could well take themselves to another jurisdiction, precisely the result the Treasury had sought to avoid.

Even the climbdowns, it seemed, could not be perfectly choreographed. In parallel with this was the backtracking on a second 'tough' measure which, as with the non-dom proposal, had first been flagged in the October 2007 Pre-Budget Report. In order to encourage 'enterprise' – since the Tory years of the mid-1980s, a reference to any government-approved business activity – Gordon Brown as chancellor had introduced a special 10 per cent rate of Capital Gains Tax (CGT) on business assets held for four years or more. This measure had been meant to stimulate people to start their own, generally small, enterprises, but had left the door wide open for so-called private equity partners (extremely wealthy investors) to transform their income into a capital gain, hold it for four years and end up paying a rate of tax not only lower than the 40 per cent top rate they would normally expect but even lower than the 20 per cent basic rate of income tax. This led to a position admitted by at least one New Olympian to involve private equity tycoons paying tax at a lower rate than their cleaners.

Mr Darling scrapped the 10 per cent rate. He scrapped all the other rates, including the top 40 per cent CGT rate, and instigated a flat 18 per cent rate on everything. The package could be faulted on a number of grounds, not least that those selling second homes would now see the profit on such sales taxed at 18 per cent – less than half the previous 40 per cent rate. But it could be defended on the ground of simplification. And it was so defended, until the climbdown, announced on January 24. With certain provisos, the first £1 million of capital gains from the sale of a trading business would be tax exempt – this 'entrepreneurs' relief' would apply across any individual's lifetime and could be used in the sales of one or more businesses. Simplification went out the window. An obvious by-product of this would be the need for HM Revenue & Customs to track each individual across their lifetime, to make sure they had not claimed the £1 million relief more than once. This was not impossible – such lifetime records had been kept with regard to Capital Transfer Tax, the forerunner to Inheritance Tax, between 1974 and 1986. But in the wake of HMRC's loss of two discs containing the details of 25 million child benefit claimants – announced by Mr Darling to MPs on November 20 2007 – there were doubts, to say the least, as to the Revenue's competence in managing such lifetime records.

The doubters need not have worried. On February 3 2008, it emerged that HMRC intended to keep no such records (which would at least ensure the records could not go missing) and would be trusting almost entirely to the honesty of the

people concerned. That this would allow unscrupulous operators to claim the £1 million exemption more than once did
not seem to trouble the Revenue.

It may be thought that the non-dom and CGT U-turns
merely showed the British government scrabbling round trying
to 'make nice' to the rich and powerful. But the curious case
of the 'phantom' civil service job cuts, which also surfaced in
the opening months of 2008, suggested that it went deeper
than this, and that the authorities were doing their best to
conduct themselves by what they thought were the standards
and principles of the New Olympians.

In his Spending Review for the next three years,
announced on July 12 2004, Gordon Brown unveiled a plan
to axe 84,150 civil service jobs by April 2008. About 13,000
of the people affected would be offered new posts on the
'front line' (a macho expression suggestive of military
combat but actually referring to other civil service tasks),
leaving a real reduction of about 70,600, according to the
independent public finance think tank, the Institute for Fiscal
Studies. The cuts always seemed a little strange, given that
the chancellor had, almost up until the announcement of
the efficiency drive, characterised the notion of widespread
waste in the public sector as a baseless Tory slur on hard-
working servants of the common good. Now it was a central
feature of his management of the state machine. Fans of
the chancellor suggested he was merely ensuring that, in
line with the New Labour mantra of the time, 'resources
go hand in hand with reform'. Critics suggested he was
trying to avoid accusations of going from boom to bust by
having boom and bust at the same time, in the public sector
at least.

A third explanation would be simply that Mr Brown and
his colleagues really had bought the New Olympian spiel
in which the 'costs' of a large business ought forever to be
'taken out' with 'layers of management' always being
'stripped away'. But, in early 2008, it emerged that, like
many a dieter who has set himself over-ambitious reduction

targets, the Treasury was taking a creative view of the results.

On January 30 the IFS published research showing the Treasury had exaggerated the success of the job reduction scheme. It said ministers were using a little-known get-out in the programme to claim they had cut considerably more posts than had actually been eliminated. It seemed that a 'new burdens' clause stated that were the civil service workload to expand as a result of unforeseen factors, 'departments can make a case to have these additional posts excluded from progress against their efficiency programme'. The IFS called on the government to come clean about how many jobs are covered by this clause. But the Treasury refused, claiming the 'top line' figure of supposed job cuts is the important one.

'We are left with job cuts that the government has not explained,' said Paul Johnson of the IFS. 'It seems pointless to have a target and not say how you reached it.' The IFS said: 'It is not at all clear that across government the exclusion is legitimate. If a target to reduce posts makes sense, it is hard to see why one would accept increases as a result of new burdens.'

Old Labourites and those sceptical in general about the New Olympians' long-standing mania to 'strip out costs' (other than their own, of course) may find something to cheer in the 'new burdens' clause, which looks at first blush rather like the sort of refreshingly cynical device that may have been dreamed up by grandees from Labour's moderate wing at a time such as the mid-1970s when the party was under critical pressure from international bankers and ideologues, all baying for public spending cuts. This is the sort of stroke that could have been pulled by Denis Healey or Anthony Crosland – pretend to be slashing away at the state sector while doing rather less than the sound and fury suggests. Of course, the 2004–2008 efficiency drive did not arise from a period of economic crisis, a fact that would undermine in part this take on events. But even so, it could be seen as a smart way of gaining the trust of the City by pretending to adopt its values while making few real sacrifices.

If that were to be the case, the City ought to feel rather foolish. It is all vaguely reminiscent of a long-ago episode of *Inspector Morse* (ITV; 1987–2000). Entitled *The Day of the Devil*, and first screened on January 13 1993, it opens with a deranged killer going missing from a supposedly secure facility, having – it turns out – stowed away in the boot of a car driven by the liberal-minded psychiatrist who has been treating him and whose commuting habits he has apparently memorised. Informing the bewildered and rather drippy psychiatrist that she unwittingly drove the killer to freedom, a scathing Morse tells her: 'You weren't studying *him*, doctor. He was studying *you.*'

Could this be the key to New Labour's relationship with the New Olympians, that of sweet-talking the heroes of finance and banking into buying government bonds, keeping sterling and interest rates steady and generating the City-related tax revenues that have helped to pay for large increases in public spending during the past 11 years or more? Perhaps ministers do indeed assure themselves in private that the New Olympians are simply rather pampered beasts of burden and that, contrary to appearances, the ministers have outsmarted the giants of finance. But in light of the back-tracking on non-doms and CGT, not to mention the huge financial support for Northern Rock, that seems a highly unlikely, although comforting, notion. After all, on all three occasions, the beasts have flatly refused even a modest increase to their burden and have proved adept at orches-trating their case and forcing either a retreat, in the tax cases, or a further commitment of public money. That is not so much the behaviour of dumb oxen as that of the wisest serpents. Thus it would seem safest to assume that the politicians' relationship with the New Olympians really is as servile as it appears, and that New Labour's failure to hit its public sector job reduction targets was not for want of trying.

Funnily enough, that was very much the case in the

above-mentioned television drama. It turned out Inspector Morse had got it wrong, that the 'drippy' psychiatrist had orchestrated the whole thing and that the 'escape' was part of her long-planned revenge on the prisoner concerned for a long-ago crime.

THE PRIDE AND THE FALL: HUBRIS EXPLAINED

The Greeks gave us the word hubris, which means insolent pride towards the gods. Many might argue that Alan Greenspan was guilty of just such presumption when he said in his self-serving memoirs: 'I would tell audiences that we were facing not a bubble but a froth – lots of small local bubbles that never grew to a scale that could threaten the health of the overall economy' (*The Age of Turbulence;* Allen Lane; 2007).

Traditionally, hubris was followed by nemesis – retribution and downfall – and, in the early months of 2008, there was plenty of evidence to suggest that the age-old pattern was repeating itself. House prices were falling, consumer confidence was collapsing, borrowing conditions were being toughened and inflation was rising. Banks in the West were increasingly looking to sovereign wealth funds – state-owned companies from oil-rich or export-heavy countries – for injections of capital to compensate for the write-downs on their bad loans. Peloton Partners, a London-based hedge fund, put the £1bn in assets of their flagship fund up for sale only a month after it had been named best new fixed-income fund. The deputy governor of the Bank of England, Rachel Lomax, said the world was facing its biggest ever peacetime liquidity crisis. Cassandras tend to be lonely figures, but by the spring it was as if the battlements of Troy were heaving with prophets of doom jostling to make themselves heard.

Big financial crises tend to go through a number of distinct phases. The first phase is the *wild boom* – the period when there is plenty of easy money to be made and the mood is euphoric. This was the world in early 2007, as private equity firms went on the prowl for takeover victims and the financial markets boomed. The second phase is marked by *denial*: a refusal to accept that the manic behaviour is having malign consequences and needs to end. After a brief period of denial in the spring and early summer of 2007, the crisis entered its third phase: *panic*. At this point, the walls of the temple start to buckle and there is a rush for the exit. In most cases, panic is followed by recovery. Not every period of financial turmoil is followed by recession, and precious few recessions lead to slumps. Some do, however, with 1929 the most obvious example. On these rare occasions, the fourth phase of the crisis is capitulation as it becomes clear that the crisis is far, far worse than previously appreciated and that the conventional policy response is not adequate to deal with it. This book explains why this, indeed, is shaping up to be the 'Big One'. We trace the origins of the crisis, how it unfolded and what its implications may be. The final chapter looks at what could be done to cut the New Olympians down to size and make the world a saner, safer place.

These, then, are the inhabitants of our 21st-century Mount Olympus, the 'gods' – each of which embodies one of the big ideas of modern-day economics and finance, and their pampered servants, the 'heroes', the investment bankers and central bankers, the hedge fund managers and private equity buccaneers. As with the characters of ancient mythology, both the gods and the heroes share their privileged existence with titans and exotic monsters: incorporated companies, offshore investment vehicles, exotic financial instruments and the like. From time to time, the gods, heroes and titans and monsters have lived together in tropical tax-haven islands, as well as in legal fictions such as the Eurodollar market.

The heroes are, as in the ancient world, mortals who have achieved near-divine status through their allegiance to the gods and through their sporadic (and hard to verify) claims to have tamed the various titans and monsters.

But the gods, the heroes and the titans/monsters, fascinating or frightening as they may be, can be banished, if we have the courage. It is to be hoped that we have, and ending on a hopeful note is, we believe, fitting, since hope was the last thing to emerge from Pandora's box.

2

Northern Rock:

Just like a rolling stone

Q: How many fingers do you have?
A: Ten.
Q: Count them.
A: One, two, three, four, five . . .
Q: And the other hand makes ten, nine, eight, seven, six?
A: Yes.
Q: Five and six make?
A: Eleven.
   – Children's playground riddle; Sussex; c. 1970

As a cashier I was particularly inept because I could
never get the tills to balance
   – Adam Applegarth; chief executive of Northern Rock;
   quoted in the *Independent on Sunday*; September 16 2007

The failure of Northern Rock, while primarily a failure
of its directors, was also a failure of its regulator. The
FSA appears to have systematically failed in its duty and
this failure contributed significantly to the difficulties and
risks to the public purse that have followed.
   – John McFall MP; chairman of the Treasury Select
   Committee; January 26 2008

For New Labour, it was bitterest wormwood and gall, not merely a nationalisation, but the nationalisation of a bank.

In the circumstances, Chancellor Alistair Darling's performance on February 17 2008 appeared far less fraught than it could have done. Dressed in a dark suit, white shirt and shiny purple tie, Mr Darling held a televised press conference on that crisp Sunday afternoon in late winter to announce the taking into public ownership of Northern Rock, a bank that had been kept open for nearly six months solely by British government support.

For Mr Darling and his colleagues, 'nationalisation' was New Labour's biggest no-no. As the BBC's business editor Robert Peston noted on the day in question: 'It's a momentous moment. Nationalisation has become a dirty word associated with industrial failures of the past.

'Financial services, by contrast, have been considered the great British success story – so for such a seemingly growing bank to end up being nationalised is a big moment for the City and a big moment for the government.'

It had not always been that way, of course. The post-war Labour government nationalised a swathe of concerns, from the railways and the mines to the Bank of England. As recently as the mid-1970s, Labour in power had created three big, almost totemic, state-owned manufacturers: British Leyland, British Shipbuilding and British Aerospace. In contrast to Mr Darling, Labour ministers 30 years ago were proud of what they had done and did not feel the need to assure one and all that public ownership would be a temporary phenomenon.

But in 2008, as Mr Peston noted, it was all very different. The Northern Rock crisis was where Labour's past collided with the sort of shiny, free-market future it envisaged for Britain, where the gleaming new machinery of liberalised financial services demanded the oily rag of 'old-fashioned' state support, where ministers wriggled and writhed to avoid doing the one thing that would once have been second nature to the Labour movement – nationalisation.

So what was Northern Rock, and what went wrong?

'OH, WHAT HAPPENED TO YOU?': THE RISE AND FALL OF THE HOUSE THAT ADAM BUILT

It started as a medium-sized regional building society and became a flashy, stop-at-nothing bank. Its rapid growth saw it become the biggest private sector employer in its hometown and was seen as the triumph of the service sector driven renaissance of a economy that for two centuries had been synonymous with the rise and fall of British manufacturing. It came from a region that had a history of producing business chiefs who, like Icarus, were tempted to fly a little too close to the sun. It was seen as an example of Britain's transformation into a knowledge economy right up to the point when it was clear the people running it were not quite so smart after all. It took high risks. It was greedy and arrogant. Northern Rock was the perfect totem for the economy under Labour, with its rise and fall neatly book-ended by Tony Blair's premiership. Created as a building society in 1965 from two Victorian lending institutions, it converted to a bank in October 1997, five months after Labour came to power, and by the time Blair announced in May 2007 that he was resigning as prime minister it was for a short period offering more new mortgages than any other lender. In short, the financial crisis that engulfed Gordon Brown's fledgling government in the autumn of 1997 had its origins in a region synonymous with Labour machine politics and in the sector of the economy – housing – that was emblematic of the borrow-and-spend country Britain had become over the previous decade.

Just as there had been fears that the economy was growing too dependent on speculation to keep it moving, so there were concerns that Northern Rock was too dependent on one form of financing – borrowing from the City's money markets. In both cases, the warnings were ignored. The aggressive marketing of Britain as an offshore financial sector with a light-touch regulatory regime meant those running Northern

Rock were allowed to run the bank not just with a highly risky Plan A but without the back-up of a Plan B. Likewise, the collapse of Northern Rock exposed the weakness of the government's much-vaunted system for overseeing the financial sector; dividing responsibility between the Treasury, the Bank of England and the Financial Services Authority looked good on paper, but failed in its first real test. As one of the main participants put it: 'The system worked well in peacetime. This turned out to be a different kind of war.'

That was some admission; a military parallel would be the chief of staff of the French army saying in June 1940: 'The Maginot Line was fine up until the moment Hitler decided to attack through the Ardennes' (interview with the authors).

Finally, the crisis exposed both the superficial nature of the alleged transformation of the economy in the decade after 1997 and the intellectual bankruptcy of New Labour as it floundered around for months looking for a third-way solution to the future of the bank. For years, Britain had been sustained by three engines of growth: the housing market, the City of London and the public sector. By 2008, all three had stalled and the money-go-round was fast slowing down.

Likewise, ministers flunked the first real financial crisis they had had to face. There were only two real options for Northern Rock: to let the bank go into administration or to nationalise it. The first meant job losses, 6,000 of them in a part of the world where the political map was dominated by Labour red; the second ran the risks that the government would be accused of turning the clock back to the 'bad old days of the 1970s'. So instead of the clean free-market solution or a state-ownership solution akin to that devised (by a Conservative government) for Rolls-Royce when it collapsed in 1971, the Treasury called in the New Olympians to help sort out a problem caused by the New Olympians. The investment bank Goldman Sachs presented a number of options. One was that a private company should take over Northern Rock, with the Treasury standing behind the new owners with a £55 billion government guarantee. The government strained every sinew to make the public-private partnership work – anything to avoid the stigma of nationalisation.

Put another way, for six months Labour flunked making the only realistic decision, to nationalise, while they tried to come up with an Olympian escape plan. In the end, even New Labour shied away from handing a fat taxpayer-funded cheque to Sir Richard Branson so that he could have the profit while the state took the risk.

Goldmans, interestingly, had told Mr Darling from the moment it was consulted that nationalisation was the best bet.

Not that it would have seemed that way to Treasury ministers when the crisis first broke. On the evening of September 13 2007, Britain had been ruled by six monarchs, seen 25 different prime ministers come and go at 10 Downing Street, fought two world wars, lost an empire and seen five serious sterling crises since the last run on a major high street bank. The 15th anniversary of the last of these financial humiliations, the expulsion of sterling from the European Exchange Rate Mechanism, was by coincidence only three days away. Labour ministers were convinced that their stranglehold on power was, in no small measure, due to the admiration of the City of London and Wall Street for the prudent economic and fiscal policies pursued in the decade since Tony Blair had first come to power.

All that changed when the BBC news reported that the Bank of England had offered to act as the lender of last resort to Northern Rock. At Threadneedle Street, as at the Treasury and the Financial Services Authority, there was irritation that the announcement planned for the following morning had leaked, but it was strongly believed that the authority of the central bank would act as a confidence-building measure, as it had many times in the past. Within minutes, this proved to be a serious misjudgement as investors in Northern Rock watching the broadcast tried to log on to the troubled bank's website so that they could remove their savings. The system duly crashed, preventing Northern Rock from winning the dubious accolade of being the first bank to have suffered a virtual run on its assets. Not that it mattered much, since the next morning Northern Rock's customers turned up in person at the bank's branches to get their money and, as the queues lengthened, used another piece of modern technology to tell their friends and relatives to come along before the cash ran out. Far from helping to solve the problems of Northern Rock, the revelation that the Bank of England was using its lender of last resort facility prompted scenes not seen since Overend and Gurney went bust in the summer of 1866.

There were striking similarities between the two bank runs. Founded by Quakers in 1800, Overend and Gurney had become the biggest commercial bank in Britain by the 1860s and had become so by sticking at what it was good at – discounting bills of exchange for merchants. This was a steady, profitable business that required sound judgement and a degree of caution, since the bank had to assess whether traders bringing in goods from the far reaches of the empire would be good for their debts. In its way, Overend and Gurney was like a traditional building society, specialising in a lucrative, if slightly dull, line of business and doing it well. In the 1860s, however, a new breed of managers took over at Overend and Gurney, for whom discounting bills was far less exciting than involving the bank in the railway mania of the mid-Victorian period. Overend and Gurney invested heavily in these long-term projects but relied on short-term deposits to pay for them, and in 1866 it faced a severe cash flow problem that led to the public queuing outside its prestigious offices in Lombard Street, a stone's throw from the Bank of England.

In important respects, however, Overend and Gurney was a crisis unlike that of Northern Rock. The Bank of England tried to come to the rescue of Northern Rock; in 1866 it was prepared to watch 200 companies fail – some of them banks – rather than provide financial help to a bank that it felt had acted imprudently. This was not just a blatant display of patrician distaste for the *arrivistes* who had ruined Overend and Gurney (although that may have had something to do with it); it was also that the financial sector in the 1860s was the servant of the real economy rather than its master. For perhaps the only time in its history, Britain's economic centre of gravity was in the regions outside of London and the South, in the coal fields, cotton mills and shipyards of Scotland, Wales and the North. The final difference was that Overend and Gurney went to the wall more than half a century before the arrival of television; its demise was not beamed around the world on 24-hour satellite TV. The rest of this chapter will be divided into three parts – the build-up to the crisis; the events of August and early September leading up to the run on Northern Rock; and the subsequent attempts to find a buyer for the stricken lender.

Adam Applegarth was a big man in the North East. Born in Sunderland, he went to Durham University before joining Northern Rock in 1983. Unlike many of his generation, he didn't migrate south when the North East suffered grievously from two deep wounds – the recession of 1980–1981 that cut the UK's manufacturing capacity by a fifth and the 1984–1985 miners' strike – but rose through the ranks of the building society. Mr Applegarth, who had never worked for another company, became the youngest chief executive of a FTSE 100 company in 1999, two years after a windfall payment of £2,355 persuaded Northern Rock's customers that they could accept the idea of becoming a public limited company quoted on the stock exchange.

Mr Applegarth was proud of his roots and proud of his company. He wanted the Northern Rock to vie with the country's biggest lenders – the Halifax, the Abbey and the Nationwide – as a provider of mortgages. If the Halifax could do it from West Yorkshire, there was no reason why a bank with the right sort of strategy could not do the same from Gosforth, three miles north of Newcastle city centre. As it expanded rapidly, Northern Rock came to be as much a symbol of brash Geordie self-confidence as the young men who insisted on exposing their ample torsos in all weathers at Newcastle United games. Indeed, the replica football shirts

discarded by the supporters were emblazoned with the name
of the bank, the club's main sponsors, and the rapid growth of
the Rock became as much a symbol of the North East's
renaissance as the bars, restaurants, hotels and galleries that
flourished in the shadow of the Tyne Bridge. Only the
churlish would point out that the regeneration was only
superficial and that a couple of miles in either direction –
west towards Scotswood or east towards Wallsend – the scars
of de-industrialisation were deep.

Mr Applegarth, whose first love was cricket, not football,
and who still played to decent league standard in the North
East, also sponsored Durham in the county championship,
and a professional golf tournament. Northern Rock was not
really in the same league as the élite New Olympian organisations – the investment banks of Canary Wharf and Wall
Street – but it had ambitions, even down to the charitable
foundation that gave money to a host of good causes in the
North East. Nor was this simply affectation. While salting
away their stratospheric salaries, those running Barclays
Capital, Merrill Lynch and UBS liked to give the impression
that they were giving something back to the community; they
sponsored exhibitions; they put money into sport; they raised
a bit of money for good causes. Northern Rock was slightly
different, though; its foundation was more than a PR exercise,
channelling 5 per cent of pre-tax profits to charity in 2006,
making it the third most generous company in the FTSE 100
(Northern Rock annual report, 2006). The company's annual
report liked to trumpet the bank's links with sport, claiming,
for example, that its sponsorship of Newcastle United 'has
significantly raised our profile in both the UK and Europe'.
In retrospect the pun used to accompany the picture of a
dynamic soccer star – 'alive and kicking' – was a touch unfortunate, but unlike the faceless City behemoths in the steel and
glass towers of Canary Wharf, the Rock was genuinely popular
in its own community. The local evening newspaper – the
Newcastle Chronicle – was in the vanguard of the campaign to
prevent the authorities in London from shutting it down.

While Mr Applegarth lived a luxury lifestyle in his mansion in Matfen, a village in the Northumberland countryside ten miles north-west of Newcastle, he was still considered a real Geordie at heart, showing those down south a thing or two.

With Mr Applegarth at its head, Northern Rock saw no reason to make a secret of what it was up to. The bank lacked the branch network of its rivals: a handicap that before the financial deregulation of the 1980s and 1990s would have hindered its expansion plans. Up until the late 1960s, British banks held 25 per cent of their assets in liquid form so that they could be sold easily in the event of trouble. Usually, this meant they had large stocks of government bonds, where assets could be sold instantly and without the identity of the distressed bank becoming immediately apparent. Ever since, there has been a steady decline in holdings of liquid assets and a switch from government bonds to holdings dominated by residential mortgages. As one commentator noted (Charles Goodhart; *Prospect;* February 2008), mortgages get high ratings from credit agencies but are less easy to sell quickly. 'So the scale and quality of bank liquid assets has been declining.'

Two other trends also disturbed what had once been the placid waters of the home loan business. Mortgage lenders had traditionally relied heavily – and in the case of many of the smaller building societies, exclusively – on their retail savings to finance their lending business, but by the time Mr Applegarth took over at Northern Rock it was commonplace for lenders to borrow in the world's money markets. In addition, from the turn of the millennium, lenders also developed a taste for securitisation, which, as described in an earlier chapter, involved bundling up parcels of mortgages and selling them for a lump sum. As the Bank of England noted in its post-mortem examination, Northern Rock was eager to take advantage of both these new developments in banking and had its own offshore securitisation arm, known as Granite, based in the tax haven of Jersey. Granite was not to be part of the nationalisation, because, according to the chancellor, its bonds were the property of third parties (such as other

banks) and legal action would have ensued. There remains
some doubt as to whether Granite contains better than average
Rock mortgages or merely an averagely mixed bag.

*At the time of conversion it was a retail-funded lender, but from the second
half of 1999 it embarked on a growth strategy which was increasingly
dependent on securitisation and other secured borrowing in a range of
currencies and targeting investors in both UK and foreign capital markets.
(Bank of England Financial Stability Review, October 2007)*

Year after year of 20 per cent growth saw Northern Rock
expand its share of the UK mortgage market rapidly; it more
than trebled under Mr Applegarth from 6 per cent to 19 per
cent, but at a cost. Mortgage lenders make their profits from
the spread between the rate at which they borrow and the
rate at which they lend, and Northern Rock saw its spreads
compressed to levels that were lower than those of its rivals.
This did not affect its profits, because the business was
expanding so fast; nor, despite the fact that in 2002 it started
to offer mortgages worth 120 per cent of a home's market
value, did it have the 'trailer trash' problem of US subprime
lenders.

That is not to say that the problems of August and
September 2007 arrived out of a clear blue sky, which was the
impression Mr Applegarth and his fellow directors sought to
give when the crisis broke. In 2004, Northern Rock's profits
suffered when the Bank of England raised interest rates. The
bank pledged that in future half its loans would be matched
by retail deposits, a promise that was quietly reneged on once
interest rates came down again. By the time it ran into trouble,
80 per cent of Northern Rock's funding came from the wholesale money markets.

Quite clearly, this was a potential weakness, although there
was no recognition of this in the bank's annual report for 2006
– a document now rich in bathos if not comic potential.
Shareholders would have been reassured by Mr Applegarth's
boast that Northern Rock was 'focused on delivering our

strategic targets' and would 'continue to build on the foundations we have in place'. Any of a nervous disposition worried by the fact that what had been a provincial building society less than a decade earlier was now heavily involved in off-shore tax havens and the unpredictable world of derivatives were treated to a six-page explanation of the bank's strategy for managing risk. 'Northern Rock,' the report noted, 'aims to maintain high and profitable growth whilst retaining a low risk profile.'

What the allegedly risk-averse Mr Applegarth and his team failed to take into account was that Northern Rock lacked adequate alternative sources of funding if, for any reason, there was no appetite in the markets for its securitisation issues. This was a threat not unlike that to Achilles after his mother made all of his body immortal bar the ankle by which she held him as she dipped him in the River Styx; small but potentially deadly. In both cases the danger was ignored until it was too late.

Mervyn King, the governor of the Bank of England, noted after the crisis broke that Northern Rock had neglected to take the same sort of precautions as Countrywide, the biggest US mortgage lender and an institution that was heavily exposed to subprime loans. Countrywide had taken out insurance so that it could call on extensive lines of credit should it get into trouble; Northern Rock could call on only £1.5 billion at a time when its loan book was worth more than £100 billion.

But at the start of 2007, Mr Applegarth had reason to be confident. To be sure, the Bank of England had started to ratchet up interest rates after becoming concerned about mounting inflationary pressure in the British economy, and this raised the question of whether the seemingly insatiable appetite for consumer debt would at some point be sated. But with house prices rising quickly, this seemed a remote prospect and in January 2007 Northern Rock announced that profits were up 27 per cent to a record £627 million. It was already Britain's fifth-biggest mortgage lender and had ambitions to become the third biggest before too long. In the heady market conditions of early 2007 there were months when it was making more loans than the Halifax, even though its branch network had shrunk from 128 at the time of conversion from building society to bank to 76. One warning of trouble ahead was the Northern Rock share price, which had been under pressure from the very beginning of 2007 amid concerns in the City that the bank's earnings would suffer if it could not expand at its planned rapid pace. It later emerged that Mr Applegarth, who had a taste for the expensive things in life, had sold shares at their £12 peak in January to purchase sports cars, and the share price had already fallen markedly before Northern Rock announced at the end of June that its profits would be at the bottom end of the 15–25 per cent it had previously forecast.

This, according to *The Economist*, was the moment alarm bells should have begun to ring at the FSA. 'A falling share price, an explosive increase in market share and a profit warning: three reasons, one might think, for a newish banking supervisor to start sweating about one of its charges. Yet the FSA remained cool. Indeed, it chilled out even more on June 29th, giving Northern Rock a stamp of approval that allowed the mortgage lender, under new international banking rules, to set aside less capital against its loans. Northern Rock promptly announced an increased dividend (even though it expected profits to fall). At around the same time, bizarrely, the FSA was urging the lender to toughen its "stress tests"'(October 20 2007).

AN OMINOUS SORT OF TICK: TIME RUNS OUT FOR NORTHERN ROCK

One of the great fallacies of modern financial markets is that nothing ever happens in August. True, this is the month when those running the show (or, to be more accurate, allegedly in control of the hurtling express) leave their deputies in control while they head for the beach, but in recent times August has seen the Iraqi invasion of Kuwait in 1990, the launch of the speculative attack on sterling in 1992 and the Russian debt default of 1998. Northern Rock's fall from grace fitted the pattern; it took just over five weeks for a funding crisis to become a full-scale bank run. For all but the final four days, the customers of the bank were, as a senior government source put it, 'blissfully ignorant' of what was happening (interview with the authors).

Both the Bank of England and the FSA knew that there was a risk of a problem. In December 2006, the tripartite authorities – the Bank, the Treasury and the FSA – had conducted a 'war game' to simulate a crisis at one of Britain's high street banks. The mock-up came up with one striking conclusion: the UK's compensation scheme for depositors was inadequate. In the event that a bank failed, depositors would get only the first £2000 of their savings back in full, and then 90 per cent of the next £31,500. This, it was agreed, created an incentive for customers to get their money out of a troubled bank as quickly as possible. The Treasury, which has responsibility for the scheme, started work on an improved scheme, but saw no reason to make it a priority.

In the days before financial liberalisation, it was said that financiers sailing too close to the wind would have an audience at the Bank of England at which the governor would raise an eyebrow which was sufficient to bring an immediate halt to the risky behaviour. Between the war game in December 2006 and August 2007 both the Bank and the FSA metaphorically raised an eyebrow but to little effect. In the spring of 2007, the Bank used its half-yearly Financial Stability Review to note: 'Over the period since the July 2006 report, an increase in risk-taking at the same time as a possible fall in the quality of risk assessment have potentially increased the vulnerability of the financial system as a whole.'

The FSA voiced similar warnings. At a meeting in July to announce his appointment, the new chief executive, Hector

Sants, said 'sudden and abrupt' changes in normally liquid capital markets were being ignored by some banks.

When it came to action against specific banks, the FSA was less aggressive. Under the terms of the new system of financial regulation brought in by Gordon Brown in 1997 there was no doubt that Mr Sants was the man directly responsible for Northern Rock, but the FSA had picked up the mood music from the government: the City is our friend. Ministers sought to contrast the easy-going atmosphere of London with the stifling regulations that burdened the financial sector in New York, particularly after Congress passed the Sarbanes-Oxley Act to clean up corporate governance in the US following the Enron and Worldcom frauds.

Mr Brown had decided in 1997 that the price the Bank had to pay for being given the power to set interest rates was to lose its responsibility for regulating Britain's banks; henceforth it would have a role in safeguarding the stability of the entire financial system but would cede day-to-day scrutiny of financial institutions. Bank insiders (in interviews with the authors) admit that this was a painful process (indeed, the former governor, Lord George, contemplated resignation after being taken by surprise by the decision) but Mr King – an academic economist – had no wish to be diverted from his core business of running monetary policy in order to call errant commercial bankers into his office for a dressing down. The FSA regulated the individual institutions, but it was the sort of regulation the New Olympians preferred: discreet and permissive.

So while the Bank had misgivings about the cavalier attitude to risk being displayed by banks – not just in the UK but in the US and Europe as well – and may have had an inkling that Northern Rock, with its dependence on the City for the bulk of its funding, was one of those sailing close to the wind, it was not formally involved until the crisis had broken. Sir John Gieve, the deputy governor of the Bank of England with responsibility for financial stability, told the Treasury Select Committee on September 20 2007: 'I was concerned in a general way about the growth of wholesale lending. Did I know the details of Northern Rock's position before this blew up? No I did not.'

The FSA, on the other hand, knew what was happening at Northern Rock, but far from telling Mr Applegarth to act more prudently, the City watchdog appeared to endorse his strategy. In May, Northern Rock succeeded in securitising a package of mortgages worth £5.75 billion. By then more than two-thirds of its £110 billion mortgage lending had been financed by short-term loans or securitisations – bond issues – mostly through Granite, which owned 70 per cent of its mortgage book by the time the bank hit trouble. The bank's profits, which grew 14 per cent in the first half of 2007 to £274 million, were almost entirely generated by mortgage lending.

When Northern Rock alerted investors to a decline in profit growth in June, it said rising interest rates in the US and the UK would deter homebuyers from taking out mortgages, while the higher cost of borrowing would also cut into margins. Investors began to take flight and Northern Rock's share price fell, yet the FSA signed off the bank's request to cut its capital base, allowed under the new international banking regulations. The FSA said it warned that a review of its borrowings was needed but was brushed aside. The watchdog has admitted it was toothless and with hindsight should have insisted. 'Northern Rock didn't foresee anything going wrong with its model,' said one FSA source (interview with the authors). 'It wasn't in their mindset.' But nor, apparently, was it in the FSA's mindset either. It knew that Mr Applegarth had a securitisation planned for mid-September but didn't envisage that the global markets would freeze up in the interim, leaving Northern Rock with no alternative source of cash. 'We didn't see it but we were asking them to stress test.'

The FSA admitted subsequently that 'lessons have to be learned' (interview with the authors). One source said the fundamental question the watchdog had to ask was whether the company was making good judgements. 'At Northern Rock they didn't and we didn't push them to think through the limits to the bank's business and whether it was compatible with the risks.'

In these circumstances of at best benign neglect, it was little wonder that Northern Rock carried on regardless. According to Derek Wanless, the former NatWest banker who headed Northern Rock's risk committee, June and July passed without a thought of an impending credit crunch (*Guardian*, November 14 2007), while even as his customers were about to besiege their local branch on the first day of the bank run in September, Mr Applegarth was unabashed.

Interviewed by Ed Stourton on the BBC's *Today* programme, he was asked whether it had been wise to increase the size of the bank's mortgage book by 50 per cent in a short period of time. Mr Applegarth responded: 'We've been growing strongly for a number of years. Once we realised . . . The world changed on one day, the ninth of August. When we realised what was happening on the ninth of August we slowed down our lending. You'll actually see that from the ninth of August onwards we've been deliberately running much slower lending volumes.'

By that time, however, it was too late, because on the previous day the French bank Banque Paribas acted as the catalyst for the seizing up of the world's credit markets when it announced big losses on the US subprime mortgage market. Mr King responded by telling his staff not to get involved with individual banks. 'Don't tread on the toes of the FSA,' he said. In addition, he started to review banks' liquidity positions, although he was aware that the move had come too late. In retrospect, he said, one of his big regrets was that he had not been provided with a daily update on the health of the UK's 30 biggest banks.

Mr Applegarth, the chief executive of one of those banks, knew immediately that unless the crisis proved temporary Northern Rock would have serious funding problems and on

August 10 discussed the matter with the bank's chairman Matt Ridley. In one of the delicious coincidences that punctuate the rise and fall of the New Olympians, Mr Ridley – the nephew of the former Conservative cabinet minister Nicholas Ridley – had battled tirelessly against the dead hand of the state in his former job as a crusading free-market journalist. On August 13 he told the FSA about Northern Rock's impending cash flow problem, and the following day the Bank of England was for the first time formally told that a high street bank was in trouble.

The Bank's public account of what happened next suggests that the imminent collapse of Northern Rock was little more than a minor irritant. 'On August 14, the authorities discussed the potential problems that would be faced by Northern Rock were it to be unable to tap the securitisation and covered bond markets and face difficulties in securing new money market funding or rolling over existing market borrowing.'

The sober official prose belied the Bank's real level of concern. A week earlier, the governor, Mervyn King, had used a press conference to launch his institution's quarterly assessment of the economy to confess that he didn't yet know how serious the recent tremors in the financial markets would prove to be.

In the past few weeks there have been falls in equity prices and credit spreads have widened, especially on riskier debt. We don't know whether these tremors in financial markets signal a more disruptive movement to come, or constitute a gradual release of pressure on spreads that had built up over some time. So it's impossible at this stage to judge how large and how persistent this tightening of credit conditions is likely to be. (Opening remarks to a Bank of England Inflation Report press conference; August 8 2007)

On August 14, Mr King had his answer. To its horror, the Bank found that Northern Rock was less a bank than one of the fancy new vehicles that had been created to trade in mortgage-backed securities. 'By August 9 2007 it was basically a "gigantic SIV". It had gigantic maturity mismatch. It had assets it couldn't sell and it couldn't borrow against them because other banks were hoarding liquidity' (interview with the authors).

At both the FSA and the Bank, there was now the unmistakeable clang of stable doors being slammed. Northern Rock was subjected to an intensive monitoring of its means of financing itself and plans began to be drawn up for Bank of England support. Every aspect of this proposal – its merits, the mechanics and its legality – were explored. Every aspect bar one: what might happen in the event of a run on Northern Rock by its depositors.

Mr King and his team at the Bank were convinced that Northern Rock had a long-term future. It had, after all, a mortgage book worth well in excess of £100 billion, which could be sold or borrowed against. In the short term, though, it was effectively bust and, with the help of the Bank and the FSA, the board of Northern Rock put the company up for sale.

From the governor downwards, there was sympathy at the Bank of England for the middle managers at Northern Rock who had tried to ensure that lending – even when the mortgage was for 125 per cent of the value of the home being bought – was responsible. A far more critical view was taken of Mr Applegarth and the other directors of the bank, for their inability to think through the limitations of their business model. In its rush to join the ranks of the big four high street lenders in the UK – HSBC, Lloyds TSB, Barclays and HBOS – Northern Rock failed to recognise that its rivals could diversify when times got rough in one aspect of their business. Mr Applegarth and his team had no such luxury. As one Bank official put it: 'Suddenly anybody who knew anything about Northern Rock could see that it had lots of liquid liabilities and lots of illiquid assets.'

It was at this point – as the phoney peace of the past six months was shattered – that the government's regulatory regime for the City was tested for the first time under battle conditions. While regulators in the US and Brussels were clear that it was important to prevent a collapse in confidence in wholesale money markets, even if it meant bailing out reckless banks, in Britain the response was confused by disagreements inside the tripartite group. Despite denials of any conflicts, the Bank cared less about propping up banks (and their profits) than the FSA did. The Bank was concerned only with a risk of widespread financial instability.

As a result, Mr King refused to lend small sums to Northern Rock in early August, despite pleading from the FSA that lending at commercial rates could save the bank and could be done in a covert exercise shielded from the stock market. Mr King argued that only large sums could save the bank and was unwilling to lend at anything other than a penal rate.

Mr Sants told the central bank behind the scenes that Mr King's concerns were undermining attempts to rescue a bank that was about to go bust. The Treasury, reluctant to undermine the governor, backed him against the FSA. Two banks approached the governor in September to prevent him lending at a commercial rate to banks in trouble; their message, that reckless lending and a refusal to heed warnings of an impending credit crunch should be punished rather than rewarded, chimed with the views of the governor.

Mr King was bolstered and felt vindicated in sticking to his argument that lending at a discount to resolve short-term issues created a 'moral hazard'. Without extra funds from the Bank, the only other option for Northern Rock was a buyer and talks began with Lloyds TSB. Unsurprisingly, given both the state of the financial markets and the parlous condition of Northern Rock, Lloyds TSB tried to strike a hard bargain, pressing for the Bank of England to provide loans of up to £30 billion over two years to Northern Rock. In retrospect, the Lloyds TSB offer looks quite generous.

Again there was disagreement. The FSA, believing Northern Rock was bust, needed a benefactor and one with the solid reputation only a high street clearing bank could provide. It recommended talks. Mr King objected, arguing that it was not the Bank's job to support takeovers. If the government wanted to use money in this way, it would need to make the facility open to all comers, and that might involve sums of £300 billion, enough to prompt fears that the entire British banking system was at risk. The Treasury again backed the governor and by September 10 the idea of a takeover for Northern Rock was dead in the water.

The discussions with Lloyds TSB had taken place in secret, but speculation about the financial health of Northern Rock – and two other lenders heavily exposed to the world's traumatised financial markets, the Alliance & Leicester and the Bradford & Bingley – was growing. One perceptive piece written just before the weekend of the bank run noted that there were only two banks in Europe, one Danish and one Italian, that had a higher ratio of loans to deposits than Northern Rock (*Business*, September 15 2007).

With all other options closed off, Northern Rock had no choice but to turn to the Bank of England for help. Under the government's tripartite system of regulating the financial markets, both the Bank of England and the FSA were required to make separate assessments of how serious the situation was before seeking the approval of Mr Darling for emergency help. Both decided that the Northern Rock's enfeebled state and the risk of contagion to the rest of the system warranted emergency assistance from Threadneedle Street. The FSA also judged that Northern Rock was solvent, exceeded its minimum regulatory capital requirements and had a good-quality loan book. Mr Darling, who had a reputation for being the Cabinet's safe pair of hands but who had been grappling with an intensifying financial crisis from his first few weeks at the Treasury, rubber-stamped the request.

The Bank of England 'court', made up of the great and the good of the City, convened on the evening of Thursday 13 to hear the shocking truth that a bank was going bust and needed rescue. On September 14 a profits warning from the Northern Rock coincided with a statement by the tripartite authorities that the Bank of England stood ready with its lender of last resort facilities to help not just the Newcastle-based bank but any other institution that might run into trouble during the global market turbulence. It was all too late, though, because by then the queues had formed outside every Northern Rock branch in the country.

Despite the TV pictures, the authorities waited to see if the panic would subside once Northern Rock customers knew that the bank now had a cast-iron guarantee that would keep it trading. Saturday, however, saw even longer queues. On Sunday morning – which by unhappy coincidence was the 15th anniversary of Black Wednesday, when sterling was ejected from Europe's Exchange Rate Mechanism – the chancellor, Alistair Darling, met Callum McCarthy, chairman of the FSA and Mr King at the Treasury. It was agreed the next step would have to be a blanket commitment to safeguard all deposits in Northern Rock. Again, however, the decision was taken to delay an announcement.

Treasury insiders say this was for two reasons. First, it was felt that if Mr Darling said something on Sunday night or on the Radio 4 *Today* programme on Monday morning it might make matters worse. Second, and somewhat implausibly given the abortive discussions of the previous few weeks, there was still hope that a bid from Lloyds TSB could be arranged. Unsurprisingly, that hope proved forlorn. The queues formed once more outside branches and by Monday afternoon, with shares falling in Alliance & Leicester and Bradford & Bingley, it was clear that there could be no further delay.

Mr Darling used a press conference with the US Treasury secretary, Henry Paulson, to announce that deposits in Northern Rock, and any other bank that might experience similar difficulties, would be guaranteed. The run was over. But if September 17 proved to be the high-water mark of the affair, it quickly became apparent that the crisis for the bank, and for the tripartite system of regulation – the Bank of England, the FSA and the Treasury – was far from over.

LAST EXIT FROM TYNESIDE: HOW THE ROCK BECAME A MILLSTONE ROUND THE GOVERNMENT'S NECK

It has become something of a cliché to describe Alistair Darling as a man with a reverse Midas touch, an uncanny ability to turn gold into dross. This was far from clear, however, in the immediate aftermath of his September 17 guarantee. Not only did the run on the bank come to an end, but the political fallout from the affair seemed to be limited, to say the least.

[I]t is his [Mr Brown's] good fortune to be seen as the ideal antidote to the froth and shallowness of the past ten years. David Cameron, having presented himself as the 'heir to Blair', is in more urgent need of a new image than Mr Brown. The Prime Minister has in his gift the decision of whether to press home his advantage by calling an election for next month . . . Events, including the attempted terrorist bombings late in June, the foot and mouth outbreak and the crisis over Northern Rock, have occupied the news agenda. His handling of them has gone down well. (Sunday Times; *leader article; September 23 2007)*

What went wrong? Some may put a finger on Mr Darling's October 9 decision, which seemed strange to say the least, to extend the guarantee to all *new* retail deposits at the bank, making Northern Rock far and away the safest home for anyone's spare cash. Others may blame the apparent months of dithering by Mr Darling and his boss, Gordon Brown, among the various options: nationalisation, receivership or a sale to one of several suitors. What was certain was that by the early spring of 2008, Mr Darling's predicament resembled that of a character in a silent comedy film from the

early days of cinema, walking blamelessly along one moment
and the next becoming hopelessly entangled in a revolving
door, or a sticky patch of road surfacing or a bramble bush.
As it became clear that even an instant sale to the most
accommodating of purchasers was likely still to leave the
British government with exposure to Northern Rock for
several years, Mr Darling would have been less than human
had he not felt profoundly that here were three syllables,
three vowels and nine consonants he never wished to hear
again.

To veterans of bank rescues, the complexities of finding a
solution to the Rock's problems must have been puzzling.
When the Slater Walker finance and business group, a slow-
burn victim of the 1974 crash, was nationalised by the Bank
of England in 1977, one large phoenix rose from the ashes in
fairly short order, the fund management group Britannia
Arrow. When Johnson Matthey Bankers (JMB), offshoot of the
eponymous speciality metals group, suffered the same fate in
1984, the Bank of England simply took over the bullion bank,
fulfilled its obligations in the London gold market and, in 1986,
was ready to sell it to the Australian bank, Westpac.

Both Slater Walker and JMB were complex institutions.
Northern Rock was supposed to be a straightforward mortgage lender. Yet sorting out the Rock seemed, at times, to
pose almost insuperable problems.

This must have been due, in large part, to the sheer number
of players involved – numbers that had actually swelled since
the bank's crisis began. In classical economic theory, a troubled institution sees shareholders and others behave like the
proverbial rats abandoning a sinking ship. But in the New
Olympian playground of London, with its obliging civil
service and ever-open law courts, the Rock's problems were
an open invitation to financial vultures of various types. Nor
was there any doubt that the government itself would be a
target for lawsuits from any disgruntled party with deep
enough pockets to hire Britain's famously well-remunerated
legal eagles.

Perhaps prudently, the government armed itself with the services of top City solicitors Slaughter & May and the finest financial advice courtesy of the investment bank Goldman Sachs.

Arrayed against ministers were would-be buyers and shareholders. The largest single stake in the Rock, 11 per cent, was held by a hedge fund, SRM Global, whose Monaco base was in sharp contrast to the Rock's North-Eastern abode. In second place, with 8.8 per cent, was the UK-based hedge fund manager RAB Capital. In third place, with 4.8 per cent, was Legal & General Investment Management.

Among the would-be buyers, Sir Richard Branson's Virgin group held an on-again, off-again position as favourite. Sir Brian Pitman, the heavyweight former Lloyds TSB chairman, who headed the Virgin consortium bidding for the beleaguered mortgage lender, is no ordinary banker. However, the above-mentioned two largest shareholders were thought to be hostile to the Virgin plan, which would merge the Rock with the Virgin Money subsidiary, and preferred the likely returns on an alternative plan being put forward by the Rock's own management, led by non-executive director Paul Thompson.

By the end of February, Sir Richard's was certainly the only half-credible outside offer for the bank. Earlier bidders, such as the private equity group Olivant, had backed away. Olivant pulled out on February 4, blaming inflexible terms laid down by the government. This was yet one more blow to Mr Darling, leaving just the management bid and that of Sir Richard as the only realistic sale prospects.

Earlier, US private equity firm JC Flowers withdrew from any bidding for the Rock, stating that it could not make the returns on equity it expected under the terms laid down by the government.

Come the crunch weekend of February 16 and 17, following which the Treasury was expected to indicate whether the future lay with Virgin, the management team, nationalisation or receivership, the air was thick with threats of legal action.

In particular, SRM Global and RAB Capital were thought to be contemplating going to court should Mr Darling favour the Virgin option, given that this proposal involved significant dilution of the stakes of existing shareholders. Receivership, also, was an option expected to trigger a blizzard of litigation against the government and a source close to the management said it had not ruled out going to court should the Treasury try to impose a deal.

In a final twist, there were suggestions that Northern Rock shareholders would be well advised to vote down any Virgin deal, even if it were the only offer on the table, because this would force the government to nationalise the bank, and legal advice suggested this would have to be at the bank's book value of £4 a share, at a time when the actual shares were trading at just below £1.

In other words, pretty much any of the possible outcomes looked likely to lead to lawsuits against the British authorities and possibly against other parties as well.

Ultimately, neither the Virgin offer nor that of the Rock's management came to anything, leaving nationalisation as the only realistic option on the table.

But while London's lawyers may have been forgiven for salivating with ill-disguised greed at this prospective legal bunfight, Goldman Sachs had cooked up an ingenious scheme to waft away the £24 billion total amount lent to the Rock by the Bank of England. Under the plan, whose status under the nationalisation proposals has yet to be clarified, the whole £24 billion would be converted into government-backed bonds and sold, as and when market conditions were propitious, to private investors. As these bonds were dribbled out on to the open market, they would eventually transfer the whole burden of the loan on to private individuals or companies attracted by the 'gilt-edged' guarantee. Whoever took over Northern Rock would set aside a portion of the income from mortage payments and use it to pay dividends on the bonds.

It seemed elegant enough and doubts surfaced only on a

second reading. Doubts such as the fact that the bonds would, initially at least, sit on the government's own books, thus the proposal's starting point was that the British government (represented by the Treasury) would promise solemnly to pay £24 billion to the British government (represented by the Bank of England). True, private investors may come along and allow the Treasury to recoup some or all of that money, but that was for later.

Another dubious aspect of the plan was that even assuming the private investors took the whole bond issue off the government's hands, the government guarantee would remain in place, possibly for as long as five years. Provided the housing and employment market was buoyant, and people with steady wages were able to service their mortgages, and provided the value of their properties remained steady at least and, preferably, went upwards, that guarantee would be unlikely to be called in.

But were the housing market to slide badly at any time during those five years, the guarantees could well be called in. Vince Cable MP, Treasury spokesman for the Liberal Democrat Party, was scathing in the House of Commons on January 21 2008, alleging that the taxpayer was 'being taken for a very big ride'. The Treasury plan would leave the private sector bidder with the 'opportunity . . . to make an absolute killing', he said. 'In order to save face [Gordon] Brown has decided that losses of Northern Rock should be nationalised, but that profits should be privatised.'

The Office for National Statistics promptly ruled that the whole £100 billion worth of potential government exposure to the Rock ought to be dumped on to the public accounts. This was made up of the £24 billion of loans from the Bank of England, which had filled the gap left by the refusal of the money markets to renew the Rock's short-term IOUs, plus government guarantees covering about £54 billion of retail deposits and about £30 billion of wholesale deposits and derivatives transactions.

This immediately put the Treasury in breach of the rule

invented by Gordon Brown during his time as chancellor that stated that public debt must remain below 40 per cent of gross domestic product (GDP) at all times. But Treasury sources pointed out a little-noticed get-out clause in Chancellor Brown's 'code for fiscal stability', which states that the chancellor may temporarily depart from the rules, provided that he specifies the reasons. Furthermore, he has to state what are the new rules that will apply during the suspension of the old rules, although it is not clear whether the new rules, too, can be suspended, should the chancellor wish.

All this delicious nonsense was highly diverting, as were press disclosures on January 20 2008 that the European Commission's price for allowing the Bank of England loans, the government guarantees and any other state aid, would be that Northern Rock would need to be made deliberately less competitive in the future. It emerged that European Union competition rules demanded that the competitive advantage enjoyed in the present by the receipt of state aid, had to be 'given back' in the future to its competitors. In other words the firm would have to be hobbled in some way in its future activities.

According to one Brussels competition lawyer, interviewed by the authors, this could take the form of pulling out of a major area of business, of closing branches or subsidiaries, of a reduction in the size of the business or of ceasing to offer some products.

But, he added, the hamstringing of the business must not affect its viability – that would bar the rescue plan from gaining EU approval, because future viability is a precondition of such a rescue. On the other hand, nor could the activities being disposed of or withdrawn from be loss-making or otherwise easy-to-lose activities – the pain had to be real. Thus as the March 17 2008 deadline approached, by which time the EU authorities would need to see the British proposal, the Treasury would have been beavering away at ideas for making a stricken bank less competitive but still viable, a bizarre occupation for the bright men and women toiling on the chancellor's behalf.

And indeed, as Mr Darling made clear on the afternoon of February 17 2008, this deadline had weighed heavily in the balance in terms of persuading ministers to favour nationalisation over either of the private sector options or that of receivership.

'In order to provide certainty for all interested parties and meet state-aid rules, a solution has to be found by March 17,' he said. 'It is not possible, nor would it be desirable to go beyond that time.'

As for the details of the proposed nationalisation, Mr Darling's statement contained what seemed one gem of self-denial. He declared that: 'Northern Rock will continue operating as a bank on a commercial basis.' That was an intriguing notion, given that the bank was operating at all only on the basis of massive state support.

But it contained also what seemed a bracing dose of realism about the real implications of the much sought after and allegedly desirable 'private sector solution':

Both proposals [the board's and Virgin's] involve a degree of risk for taxpayers and very significant implicit subsidy from the Treasury, involving a payment below the market rate to the Government for continuation of its guarantee arrangements and for the financing we would be putting in place . . . By contrast, under public ownership the Government will secure the entire proceeds from the future sale of the business in return for bearing the risks in this period of market uncertainty.

At long last, it seemed, the almost superstitious terror of nationalisation and the equally irrational determination to achiever a 'private sector solution' had been dispelled by the realisation that a key component of the New Olympian economic system is that private sector solutions routinely require large amounts of public money.

Aside from the fate of the bank itself, the fallout from Northern Rock produced no end of suggestions for tightening the supervision of banks and generally ensuring that such a collapse 'can never happen again'. There was, rightly, a focus on the role of the Financial Services Authority, and the right-ness or otherwise of Gordon Brown's decision in 1997 to take banking supervision away from the Bank of England and hand it to the FSA. With Mr Brown now prime minister, there was little chance of such reflection inside the government. On the contrary, Mr Darling made it clear the FSA ought to take more of a lead role in future crises, which suggested that protecting the Brown legacy may be more important than reforming a creaking system of financial regulation.

Not that the Treasury Select Committee did any better. Its report on the Northern Rock affair, published on January 25, suggested creating a new, powerful deputy governor post at the Bank of England responsible for financial stability and using new powers to rescue troubled banks. A more certain recipe for bureaucratic turf wars, both within the Bank and between the Bank and the FSA, would be hard to imagine.

The problem is the FSA itself, a lumbering monster created by the cross-fertilisation of New Labour's twin loves: for large, bureaucratic 'strategic' units on the one hand and for the financial services industry on the other. The FSA has always seen itself as some sort of service company, and was launched in the late 1990s as a 'world class' regulator, which suggested that from the start it saw those whom it regulates as customers to be satisfied rather than as the sources of potential instability or even fraud. It would make a lot more sense to put 'prudential' institutions – banks, fund managers and big insurers – back under the super-vision of a much-expanded new wing of the Bank of England and pack off those whose activities do not have any systemic impact (small mortgage and insurance brokers, credit unions, friendly societies) to the section of the Office of Fair Trading that already deals with pawnbrokers and the like.

A second modest suggestion would be to restrict greatly

the proportion of funding that mortgage lenders can raise on the wholesale money markets. Such funding ought to smooth the gaps that occur between an institution's deposits and loans; it ought never to become the mainstay of funding.

We have more to say about reforming banking and finance in our final chapter. For now, we would just make one last point: what is so terrible about having one government-owned bank among so many commercial banks? Would it be the end of the world were Northern Rock to stay indefinitely in the public sector?

Such a bank did exist once. It was called National Giro (later National Girobank), it operated through the Post Office network and it was launched in 1968. It was sold in 1989 as part of the privatisation programme. The buyer, ironically, was Alliance & Leicester – ironic because Alliance & Leicester was one of a handful of institutions who, in the backwash from Northern Rock, were feared – groundlessly, as it turned out – to face the possibility of similar problems.

By the spring of 2008, it was clear there were wider implications of the affair. The first was for Northern Rock itself, which under its new Darling-appointed chairman Ron Sandler was going to shrink in size. Unions feared that half the 6,000 workforce might be culled. The idea was to return it to the sort of size it had been before Mr Applegarth's pell-mell expansion, that is a lender with around a sixth of the market. Under the European Union state-aid rules mentioned above, there was little choice and, in any event, the Rock's high street rivals were alive to the possibility that the newly nationalised lender might cost them business if Mr Sandler were allowed to pursue an aggressive business model.

The second implication was that in the wake of the crisis, lenders started to become much choosier about whom they lent money to and at what price; the 125 per cent mortgages that had been emblematic of Britain's borrowing binge were withdrawn from the market and the Nationwide said first-time buyers would have to save up for a bigger deposit.

This suggests a third implication, that Northern Rock could not be seen as a one-off but was emblematic of the state of the debt-laden UK economy, to which we turn in detail later in this book.

But first, we need to retrace the road to the Rock, to the disintegration of a once-solid savings institution, back to its starting point. Perhaps surprisingly, the intellectual journey to credit-crunched Tyneside in 2007–2008 began 60 years earlier – on a mountain, in Switzerland.

3

Let's Go Round Again:
The free-marketeers' Sixty Years' War

For the first 80 years of this century, the left has been in the ascendant. Those who argued for rationalism and planning in human affairs put their faith in the power of the state. Socialism enjoyed the support of most intellectuals. Now, under the patronage of Margaret Thatcher and Ronald Reagan, the liberal revival is enjoying some success.

> – David Graham and Peter Clarke; *The New Enlightenment;* Macmillan/Channel Four; 1986

'The Empire may have disintegrated and the UK may now be a third-rate power, but the City of London has staged a comeback which would be the envy of any child movie star reaching maturity.'

> – Professor Ira Scott, speaking in 1969, quoted by Margaret Reid in *The Secondary Banking Crisis 1973–5;* Macmillan; 1982

'I'm a 19th Century liberal,' says Miss Callendar. 'You can't be,' says Howard, 'this is the 20th Century, near the end of it. There are no resources.' 'I know,' says Miss Callendar, 'that's why I am one.'

> – Malcolm Bradbury; *The History Man;* Martin Secker & Warburg; 1975

This particular journey began on All Fool's Day 1947 when the conspirators gathered in a Swiss hotel overlooking Lac Leman. These were not conspirators with murder in their hearts, let alone blood on their hands, but with ideas in their heads and this was an awesome collection of brain power. Freidrich von Hayek, Ludvig von Mises, Karl Popper and a youthful Milton Friedman were among the 38 participants meeting at the Hotel du Parc on Mont Pèlerin to chart the fightback for classical liberalism against what was seen as the tyranny of the collective.

It ended, as we saw in the first chapter, in the autumn of 2007, with Bob Diamond, the chief executive of Barclays Bank, orchestrating a campaign in the City of London to demand that Mervyn King, governor of the Bank of England, capitulate to demands from London's financial élite for cheap money to rescue them from the consequences of their own stupidity. Whether Hayek et al. would have been on the side of Mr Diamond and his cronies is doubtful. The Mont Pèlerin society was formed to roll back the power of the state, and was hostile to any notion of feather-bedding. Logically – and Messrs Hayek and Popper were thinkers who prided themselves on their capacity for logic – they would have been as opposed to handouts to investment banks as they would have been to the Common Agricultural Policy or to giving blank cheques to ailing manufacturing firms. Mr King himself contrasted the dependency culture among investment banks with the hard-nosed view of the modern world taken by British manufacturers. Industry, the governor noted in the aftermath of the run on Northern Rock, knew that it was pointless and even self-defeating to plead for cuts in interest rates to bring down the value of the pound. The result would simply be higher inflation, which would negate the beneficial impact of cheaper exports. Industry, perhaps, through bitter experience, knew that life was tough; manufacturers expected to have to work hard to make a profit and they knew that some among their number would go to the wall. Investment banks, by contrast, saw no reason why any of their charmed circle should suffer a fall in profitability let alone go out of business.

Such is the law of unintended consequences. The free-market

fight-back against the post-war consensus culminated in the rich and powerful sucking deep and long on the teat of the state; it swept away a form of subsidy that sought to defend the jobs and living standards of ordinary people with another form of subsidy that put money in the hands of those with seven-figure bonuses. The evolution of the global economy in the six decades from a series of spring seminars in a Swiss canton to the fall-out from mortgage defaults in Las Vegas trailer parks was not smooth or linear. It took years, many years in fact, for the Mont Pèlerin conspirators to see their plans come to fruition. So how did it happen? How did the world of 1947 – when the financial interest was caged so that ordinary folk could be guaranteed work and income security – turn into a world where the only freedom that mattered was that of Goldman Sachs and JP Morgan to continue making money?

What do we mean by 'ordinary folk'? Pretty much everybody apart from the very rich. Paul Krugman in his recent book, *The Conscience of a Liberal* (Norton; 2007), argues that the New Deal helped create a middle-class America. We would claim that the same applies to Britain with regard to the welfare state policies pursued after 1945. Between the 1929 crash and the late 1950s, the purchasing power of the median family in the US doubled, while the real incomes of those in the top 0.1 per cent of earners had halved. At least four factors lay behind what Professor Krugman calls the Great Compression: stronger trade unions, sharply progressive taxation, controls on the free movement of capital and managed trade. A fifth factor, immigration controls, also contributed to rising real incomes of blue-collar workers.

FROM RIOT TO MARKET RENAISSANCE: THE LEGACY OF THE YEAR OF LIVING DANGEROUSLY

At first free market ideas were confined to some well-funded think tanks and the fringes of academic economics. The attempt to revive eighteenth-century liberalism had limited appeal at a time when the New Deal, the Welfare State and other versions of the mixed economy were delivering unprecedented prosperity. That began to change in the year that became a hinge between the social democratic settlement and the bastardised form of the free market that we now find ourselves with.

Although it may appear curious to some, that year was 1968, the year students took to the streets of Paris, of demonstrations against the war in Vietnam, of riots in the Watts ghetto of Los Angeles. It was the year theatre censorship was abolished in London, it was the year Lindsay Anderson made the film *If* about a group of schoolboys mounting an insurrection at their public school; it was the year the first abortion clinic opened in Britain; it was the year rock's aristocracy – The Beatles, The Rolling Stones, Bob Dylan – ditched psychedelia and made plain unadorned albums that returned them to their roots. But for all that and more, it was the moment, a bit like El Alamein in 1942, when the tide turned.

Nineteen sixty-eight was a pivotal year, but not in the sense that is sometimes suggested today. Even at the time there were those supposedly in the vanguard of the revolution who sensed that the impact of the counter-culture would be transitory and superficial. Interviewed by Robin Blackburn and Tariq Ali for the underground magazine *Red Mole* in January 1971, John Lennon summed things up like this: 'Of course, there are a lot of people walking around with long hair now and some trendy middle-class kids in pretty clothes. But nothing changed except that we all dressed up a bit, leaving the same bastards running everything.'

To which we would merely add that the trendy middle-class kids in pretty clothes have now cut their hair, wear sober suits and make speeches in praise of free markets and welfare reform (for the poor and middle classes, if not the rich).

At one level, of course, 1968 was a logical conclusion to the anti-colonial spirit of the post-war era; the difference only that the protests were directed at the new hegemony in the

Western hemisphere, the United States, for its war in Vietnam, rather against the empire on which the sun now only very intermittently rose. There are those in their fifties in Britain who still look back fondly on the days when they swarmed outside the American embassy in Grosvenor Square – something that the fight against global terrorism has long since made impossible.

Yet at another level, the 1968 protestors were the solvent that started the process of dissolving the post-war settlement. This was not so much that the violence in Detroit, Paris and London engendered a conservative backlash – although it did – but that the protestors themselves willingly allied themselves, in a rather bizarre echo of the 1939 Ribbentrop-Molotov Pact, with the sleepers of the new right in an attack on the post-war order. While there was certainly one wing of the protest movement that took to the streets in pursuit of the traditional working-class demands for higher wages and a shorter week, the other wing, the middle-class student wing, was inimical to the bourgeois Keynesian state, with its top-down control and emphasis on material well-being. This sense of distaste at the trappings of Western democracy was fully manifested in the 1970s with the flowering of violent revolutionary groups such as the Baader-Meinhof gang in Germany and the Red Brigades in Italy. Once captured by the 'Nazi pig state', however, they would wax lyrical about habeas corpus and police brutality, suddenly able, at that point, to tell the difference between a justice system run by the Federal Republic of Germany or the Italian state and one run by the Gestapo. Nor, to be frank, was the cultural underpinning of 1968 built on sturdy foundations. By the early 1970s, when they were all safely tax exiles in the south of France, the idea of The Rolling Stones singing 'Street Fighting Man' seemed rather absurd, although it has to be admitted that 'Street Fighting Accountant' doesn't have quite the same ring about it.

As Peter Doggett noted in a recent book, on the same day in December 1969 that police arrested some members of

Charles Manson's 'family' in California, Mick Jagger was in London with the Stones' business adviser, Prince Rupert Lowenstein, discussing ways of minimising certain tax liabilities (*There's a Riot Going On: Revolutionaries, Rock Stars and the Rise and Fall of 1960s Counter-Culture;* Canongate; 2007).

Nineteen sixty-eight saw severe and growing strains on the post-war settlement of both Lord Keynes and Lord Beveridge (and their transatlantic equivalents), mixing economic management and social welfare, not least because a second generation was coming into adult life that had known nothing but the state-guaranteed prosperity of the time and was not minded to be grateful for it. This predisposition to take abundance for granted was epitomised by the behaviour of Lyndon Johnson's administration in America, which tried simultaneously to fight a war in south-east Asia, to increase greatly welfare spending at home and to keep a lid on taxes. In some ways, President Johnson and his lieutenants were grand-scale versions of the self-centred Benjamin Braddock character played by Dustin Hoffman in the film of the previous year, *The Graduate.* Both 'Braddock' and Johnson seemed to take for granted America's near-limitless capacity to generate wealth.

In the inevitable international financial dislocation that followed Johnson's unsustainable economic, military and social policies, the renascent freebooting financial speculators sniffed their first openings. Hitherto thought of as disreputable figures confined to entrepots such as Tangier or Macao, outside the Bretton Woods system, they were coming on to the centre stage as important players in the 'Eurodollar' and other financial markets. The suspension of US gold payments in 1968 to all overseas dollar holders other than national governments was a harbinger of what was to come, with the Tet offensive by the North Vietnamese leading to the first concerted pressure on the American currency in the post-war era.

Sterling had been devalued the previous autumn and the 1968 weakening of the dollar's link to gold presaged the devaluation of the US currency in August 1971. The Bretton Woods system was coming apart.

Few periods in recent history have aroused as much passion and dispute as 1968. Almost before it ended, its legacy was being fought over by radicals, liberals, conservatives and people from just about every viewpoint. Through the eyes of Malcolm Bradbury's fictional left-wing lecturer Howard Kirk it was 'the radical year . . . Everything seemed wide open; individual expectations coincided with historical drive' (*The History Man*; Secker & Warburg; 1975). Kirk's hopes went unfulfilled, however, as did those of many real-life '68-ers: '[B]y the end of 1968 that dream was in a ragged state. The cries of rage had all been in vain; the new age was conclusively stillborn. Nixon was in the White House and the [Vietnam] war went on' (David Downing; *Future Rock;* Panther Books; 1976). What is more, after being in power for only eight of the past 36 years (and even then with the un-ideological Dwight Eisenhower as president) the Republicans had, in Richard Nixon, a perhaps unlikely harbinger of a period of Republican domination of the White House that has seen only two Democrats – Jimmy Carter and Bill Clinton – as chief executive and commander. And these were Democrats with a noticeable conservative bent, hailing as they did from states in the Deep South. The old Democrat alliance of the industrial north and the patrician east went down to defeat under candidates Walter Mondale (1984), Michael Dukakis (1988) and John Kerry (2004).

It was a far cry from the days when most Republicans had felt tied in to the post-war settlement. Writing to his brother Edgar in 1954, Eisenhower said: 'Should any political party attempt to abolish social security, unemployment insurance and eliminate labor laws and farm programs you would not hear of that party again in our political history. There is a tiny splinter group, of course, that believes you can do those things. Among them are H.L.Hunt (you possibly know his background), a few other Texas oil millionaires, and an occasional politician or business man from other areas. Their number is negligible and they are stupid.'

In the half-decade from 1968 to 1973, the post-war system lost its moorings. The economic squalls associated with rising public spending in the United States became the hurricane inflation winds of a fivefold increase in oil prices. After years of rapid economic growth, the Keynesian model listed in the doldrums of unemployment. And below decks, there was talk of mutiny. From the late 1950s there had been creeping attempts to circumvent the strict controls on the movement of capital, with the US authorities choosing not to control the rise of the Eurodollar market, which found its home in the City of London. Despite its name, the market had nothing much to do with Europe and simply described any pool of American dollars held outside the US and available for loans and investments unregulated by the US authorities.

Through the Eurodollar market, despite increased domestic capital controls, US banks were largely enabled to continue their foreign lending from their overseas bases, and US multi-national corporations enabled to meet their borrowing and investment needs throughout the period. (Robert Brenner; 'The Economics of Global Turbulence'; New Left Review 229, May/June 1998; p 117)

As such, there were reasons, perhaps almost hidden at the time, for the new right to be quietly cheerful as the students prised the cobblestones from the boulevards of the Latin Quarter to hurl at the police and as the Russian tanks rumbled into Prague later in the summer to crush Alexander Dubček's attempt at liberal communism. They may even have quoted Winston Churchill, who, on the occasion of the 8th Army's victory over the Afrika Korps, explained the battle's significance thus: 'Now, this is not the end,' said the then prime minister. 'It is not even the beginning of the end. But it is, perhaps, the end of the beginning.' As we shall now see, the 'beginning of the end' for the post-war order was not to be long delayed.

THE BETTER TOMORROW: FROM WELFARE STATE TO MARKET STATE

As an opening to a new premiership, it was not auspicious. The Opposition had just won, against almost all the predictions of the opinion polls.

There was a large crowd in Smith Square, outside Conservative Central Office, through which Mr [Edward] Heath had to thrust his way without police protection. One disappointed citizen stubbed out a lighted cigarette on his neck, burning him painfully. (Douglas Hurd; An End to Promises; Collins; 1979*)*

To this day, Mr Heath – he was knighted long after leaving office – is seen as someone who was burned again and again by the pressure of outside events. The surprise winner of the June 1970 general election, he has gone into the history books as having entered office on a near-Thatcherite radical programme of creating 'a new economic order, deliberately based on the disciplines of a market economy' (Harold Wilson, *Final Term*, Weidenfeld and Nicolson, 1979). Mr Heath had promised a 'quiet revolution' (Hurd; *ibid*) and his 1970 manifesto had been entitled *A Better Tomorrow*. In the conventional reading of the unhappy and crisis-torn government of 1970–74, early attempts by the Heath government at forcing British industry into the cold shower of market 'discipline' ran into two insuperable, and linked, obstacles: the strength of organised labour (relatively short-lived although it was to prove to be) and the amalgam of crises that were to kill off what the French called the *trente glorieuses* – the 30 golden years from the mid-1940s to the mid-1970s.

And there seemed to be something in this. Between taking office and the end of 1971, the Tories, backed by their own laws to control trade union activity, had attempted to break the back of pay inflation with a pay policy, applied only to the public sector, called 'N minus one', under which each settlement had to be lower than the last one. Defeats at the hands of local authority workers in 1970 were balanced by better results against power station workers at the turn of the year and the Union of Post Office Workers in 1971. Meanwhile, the government insisted loss-making companies would be allowed to fail, that there would be no state rescues for 'lame ducks'.

This second pillar of the policy was to collapse much more quickly than the confrontation with the unions. In February 1971, the government faced not so much a lame duck as a lame pterodactyl, the now bankrupt engineering group Rolls-Royce. Best known for its luxury cars, the company's strategic value related to aero-engines, and its collapse threatened to leave a number of airlines and air forces in the lurch. Mr Heath's immediate decision to nationalise the company contrasted sharply with Gordon Brown's dithering over Northern Rock, and was subsequently vindicated, as Rolls-Royce is today one of Britain's few manufacturers of international stature.

The subsequent Rolls-Royce bail-out killed off the lame-ducks policy, and one year after the company's insolvency the government agreed to a rescue package for Upper Clyde Shipbuilders (UCS), scene of a world-famous 'work-in' to beat off the threat of closure. But by this time, the Tories' reasonably hot streak in terms of industrial action had gone cold, courtesy of the 1971–1972 miners' strike.

The shipbuilders' less probable allies included John Lennon and Yoko Ono, who delivered flowers to the work-in with a card attached declaring: 'Oppression is bad for you.' But they were merely at the far edge of a long platform of middle-class support for the strikers of the Heath era.

In the early 1970s, playwright Arnold Wesker spent time as a guest of the *Sunday Times*. In one editorial meeting, the paper discusses its attitude to pay disputes in society. Wesker muses:

It has always seemed manifest lunacy to me that workers are expected to be happy, civilised, fulfilled and unfearful of the future, doing the work they do for the wages they receive.

(Journey into Journalism; *Writers and Readers Publishing Cooperative;* 1977)

Bernard Levin, not usually counted a friend of union activists, wrote thus on a pay dispute on the railways:

Has he [Edward Heath] any idea what a man earning £20 a week feels when he sees speculators about to make untold millions by befouling Piccadilly Circus and Covent Garden and indeed any other bits of any other city that they can get their hands on? (The Times, May 30 1972)

Christopher Booker, another writer not always in sympathy with the unions, concentrated on Mr Heath's personality in the crisis that engulfed his government:

Amid the greatest collapse in share prices and property values since 1929, the 'second' miners' strike, the 'Three Day Week' and all the rest, the Heath government in March 1974 finally fell (Heath himself being simply not psychologically equipped, with his wooden, unvisionary stubbornness, to do anything other than make the situation worse). (The Seventies: Allen Lane; 1980)

Referring to a time when the fall of Edward Heath was still in the future, Paul Foot – in some ways the epitome of upper middle-class radicalism – put it this way.

So it was that the miners' strike of 1972 transformed British industrial relations . . . All this led to an unparalleled blossoming of democracy. Political discussion and debate, for so long confined to parliamentary chambers, suddenly became part of the daily lives of many thousands of workers. Anyone even remotely involved in those nine dramatic weeks can testify to that. (The Vote; Viking; 2005)

But what Mr Foot called 'the industrial and democratic volcano of 1972' was a peak, never to be scaled again, in the alliance between organised labour and liberal-minded middle-class intellectuals. As noted above by Mr Booker, a second miners' strike, two years later, helped tip Mr Heath's Conservatives out of office, but only just – the Tories won more votes than had the incoming, minority Labour government.

Mr Heath's attempts to bring greater control and order to trade union affairs and hence to industrial relations had not emerged from a clear blue sky in the summer of 1970. Organised labour had not featured as an election issue in 1966, and, as we shall see later, it was routine at this time for schoolchildren to be taught that the growth of the unions was a type of social progress. But by the late 1960s, under the twin pressures of higher inflation and the rise of a new, more militant breed of shop steward, the number of days lost to strikes started to rise, and the Labour government decided to act. A Royal Commission under Lord Donovan had been set up as early as 1965 to look at the modernisation of the unions, and when it reported in June 1968 it recommended a number of largely voluntary reforms to industrial relations.

Barbara Castle, then secretary of state for Employment and Productivity, decided to go much further; in January 1969, her draft White Paper *In Place of Strife* proposed compulsory registration of trade unions, with strike ballots and cooling-off periods in certain circumstances.

The proposals were defeated by internal Labour Party opposition, as Mr Heath's legal framework was destroyed by the turmoil of the mid-1970s. But for organised labour, the clock was ticking, despite a general feeling that, having seen off Mrs Castle and Mr Heath, the unions were invincible.

Away from political and industrial battles, cultural changes augured poorly for the future of the 20-year intellectual fascination with the 'authenticity' of British working-class life, expressed in innumerable 'kitchen sink' plays and television dramas, in popular music and art photography.

On television, the quintessential 'gritty' northern series, *Z Cars* (BBC TV 1962–1978) was well past its creative peak, most of its senior actors having been despatched south to solve crime in the more middle-class pastures of *Softly, Softly* (1966–1976), a successful spin-off. The two main characters in *The Likely Lads* (BBC TV 1964–1966) returned in *Whatever Happened to the Likely Lads?* (1973–1974), a rhetor-

ical question as what had 'happened' was that one had joined
the middle class and the other remained resolutely upwardly
immobile.

Popular music, along with professional sport, had been a
traditional escape route from the back streets, and, indeed, a
number of major rock acts spent the early 1970s ruminating
on the humble backgrounds of the modern British star, some
more convincingly than others. In many cases, these rumin-
ations had an elegiac quality. Alan Price, formerly of
Newcastle band The Animals, went further than most,
reprising one of the legendary moments of Labour history,
the Jarrow March of unemployed workers to London in
October 1936 ('Jarrow Song'; 1974). David Bowie's alter ego
Ziggy Stardust confined himself to recalling that an old mate
had joined the Army to escape poverty and to name-checking
post-war Labour health minister Aneurin Bevan. Elton John's
rock-star narrator in 'Goodbye Yellow Brick Road' hinted,
improbably, at a farming background ('I'm going back to my
plough'). Interestingly, the era's indisputably working-class
band, Slade, produced a string of best-selling records
containing almost no references to blue-collar British life, the
narratives, such as they were, being set in a sketchy middle
America in which raunchy women drank whisky and obeyed
the injunction: 'Girls grab the boys.'

On screen, the disengagement between the intellectuals and
the working class was illustrated by the gulf between two
depictions of two youths at tough comprehensive schools. *Kes*,
released in 1969, was based on a novel of the previous year
by Barry Hines entitled *A Kestrel for a Knave* (Michael Joseph).
In what was widely recognised to be an evocative and moving
film, the main character, Billy, nurses an injured kestrel back
to health.

Eight years later, in April 1977, BBC's Play for Today transmitted *Gotcha!*, written by Barrie Keefe and featuring a no-hope
16-year-old school leaver who, on the spur of the moment, at
the end of his last term, takes two teachers hostage. The youth
is never named, underlining the fact that none of his 'teachers'

can remember who he is. The play ends with the youth being overpowered by one of the male teachers, who then beats him up.

Mr Keefe, presumably, hoped the audience would sympathise with a youth facing what was then the resurgent spectre of unemployment and deplore the violence to which he was treated. In the atmosphere of 1977, he may well, had there been a reliable method of measurement, have been disappointed.

Because the fact was that Mr Heath had not failed, but succeeded: in both the 'market economy' and the need to 'discipline'; the trade unions were firmly on the agenda – neither, as we mentioned, had been an issue at all during his first general election as leader, that of 1966. True, he had failed *to remain as prime minister*. But that was of no great interest to anyone other than himself. And this failure was far from pre-ordained – indeed, he fell probably because of confusion as to his choice of weapons, rather than choice of battlefield:

[Mr Heath] was . . . trying to go in contradictory directions. On the one hand he was trying to take the unions on board into a tripartite management of the domestic economy; on the other he was attacking them with his industrial relations legislation; on the one hand seeking an investment boom in Britain via cheap credit; on the other unwittingly allowing the introduction of a system which explicitly promised increases in interest rates [a forerunner of the current system of Bank of England independence] to 'control' the supply of credit. (Robin Ramsay; Prawn Cocktail Party; Vision; *1998)*

Mr Heath may well have been confused as to the compatibility of European social-market democracy on German lines and the unfettered capital markets the City demanded. But his most enduring domestic legacies (this is not the place to consider the effects of his successful attempt to take Britain into what was then the European Community) were, first, the beginning of the process whereby the City would be freed from the post-war controls that it found so irksome and, second, the embedding of the trade unions as a 'problem' in much of the public mind.

The 'freeing' of the City centred on a mendaciously entitled package of changes entitled Competition & Credit Control (CCC), under which banks would be allowed to wriggle free of much of the regime under which they had been supervised. The official interest rate (Bank Rate) would cease to be what it had been since the 1940s – effectively an instruction issued by the Bank of England – and became instead the 'market driven' Minimum Lending Rate. City bankers, through the package proposed by the Bank of England, were being given back control of borrowing costs.

Furthermore, inter-bank borrowing would no longer use as security certain assets (chiefly government securities) held by the borrowing bank. Instead, these banks would simply pledge their own paper as security – a change that was to have profound implications more than three decades later in the Northern Rock debacle. Lending limits were lifted.

Here is the authentic voice of the British banker struggling to throw off the restrictions of government and begin seriously milking the British economy. (Ramsay; ibid)

Adopted as government policy in September 1971, CCC had nothing much to do with either control or competition, but a lot to do with credit. Even Tory grandee Edward du Cann, himself a merchant banker, was alarmed when attending a meeting of backbench MPs at which the package was discussed:

I looked round the room and wondered how many of the MPs present fully comprehended . . . [the package]. I doubt whether more than half a dozen had the least idea. (Edward du Cann; Two Lives; Images Publishing; 1995)

He added: 'It was generally supposed that all that was occurring was the replacement of one system of control by another: it was certainly not appreciated, perhaps not even by the banking sector generally, that the competition part of the package meant virtually unbridled liberalism, leading to new and unforeseen risk.'

Put another way:

It was simply the old order being re-imposed on the British economy. This was the climax of all those attempts since the post-war era to get rid of government controls. Under the new system the banks could lend what they liked and, when it was decided that there was too much credit in the system, they would put the interest rates up. What a truly wonderful racket! (Ramsay; ibid)

One might have thought the financial market cataclysm of 1973–1974, much of it directly resulting from the inflationary and destabilising effects of the 'reforms', would have buried CCC. Far from it. A theme of this book is that all setbacks for the financial interest are treated as temporary and all advances are treated as permanent, an approach summed up admirably by this wonderful, fictional conversation:

Sir Desmond Glazebrook: 'Surely a decision's a decision?'
Sir Humphrey Appleby: 'Only if it's the decision you want. If not it's just a temporary setback.' (From Yes, Minister; BBC TV; episode 'The Quality of Life'; first broadcast March 30 1981)

Thus the head of the Labour government that took office in March 1974 wrote later:

It is only fair to say that . . . some of the main features of CCC still operate in the City, and are working. (Wilson; ibid)

Indeed, the 1974–1979 Labour government gave a (probably unintended) further forward shove to the unshackling of the City in 1976, when the Restrictive Practices Act was extended to cover the supply of services as well as goods. Shortly afterwards, Labour referred the rulebook of the London Stock Exchange to the Office of Fair Trading. Two aspects of the exchange's operations were likely to be of particular concern: the system of 'minimum commission', under which small shareholders were effectively subsidised on their share deals by large ones, and firms were prevented from full-blooded competition, and 'single capacity', under which brokers, market makers and merchant bankers had all to be separate from each other.

This reference led directly to the Big Bang reforms of 1986; at that time, it seemed ironic that a Labour government had been responsible for the huge enrichment of City partners now free to sell up their stakes to the new breed of investment banks. It seems, perhaps, less ironic now, after ten years of Labour's obeisance to the financial sector.

Mr Heath's financial legacy rolled on after his departure: through the abolition of exchange controls in 1979, privatisation (which he started in a small way in the early 1970s, selling the Thomas Cook travel agent and a clutch of bizarrely government-owned pubs in the Carlisle area) and perhaps above all from the phenomenon of the 2000s described in sepulchral tones by younger financial journalists as 'private equity', a grand-sounding phrase for the sort of asset-stripping that flourished during the Heath years.

As for the second strand of the Heath legacy – mounting hostility to organised labour – it is worth recalling that, until the early 1970s, the rise of the trade unions had been regarded as an indicator of social progress:

[T]he Trades Union Congress, an organisation which has been called the 'Parliament of the Workers', has met almost every year and has now come to be recognised as the spokesman for workers of this country. Today it is a much-respected organisation and is consulted by governments on all matters concerning working people. (The Hamlyn Children's Encyclopedia; Hamlyn; 1971)

By the end of the 1970s, it was very different. Many, perhaps most, of the million-plus workers involved in the so-called winter of discontent in 1978–1979 were much worse off than the miners and others who had enjoyed such a large measure of public sympathy in the earlier part of the decade. But you would not have known it from the coverage, this from broadcasting organisations which have traditionally, because of the legal obligations of balance, been fairer to the unions than the press:

[In an interview with the regional secretary of the health-service union CoHSE] What if somebody did die, would we be able to sue CoHSE? – BBC Radio Birmingham; February 5 1979

Well-cherished the weekend that lies ahead because on Monday we're due for more industrial action. One and a half million public service workers will be staging a day of action, a euphemism for a one-day strike. – BBC Radio 4 Today programme; January 19 1979

[In an interview with a union representative, these three questions were asked] How do you justify putting lives at risk?; If somebody dies will it be on your conscience?; Is . . . more money worth a life? – BBC2 News; January 19 1979

[Questioning a union official] One understands the basis of your claim, but isn't the strike by ambulancemen potentially one of the most disastrous things that could happen to society? – BBC1 Nationwide, January 16 1979
(All taken from A Cause for Concern; *Trades Union Congress publication; 1979)*

Press comment, by and large, was, of course, very much more hostile still. Mr Heath had succeeded; the trade unions were now an 'issue', perhaps one of the top three or four issues in the public mind. And his own reputation, in relation to his struggle with the trade unions, tended to rise as the decade progressed. His former political secretary Douglas Hurd was in no doubt Mr Heath had been a man ahead of his time. In 1977, he compared the work of the Heath administration with that of a fictional government in 1931, insisting on rearmament. Even had it lost office, turfed out by an appeasement-minded electorate, and its new warplanes been scrapped by a pacifistic Labour government, said Mr Hurd: 'By 1939 the British people might have looked back with regret.'

By apparently comparing 1970s trade unionism with 1930s fascism, Douglas Hurd (later to hold a number of senior Cabinet positions) showed the extent of even moderate Conservative opposition to organised labour. It marked also the distance travelled by centre-right politicians since the post-war decades in which their support for the social and economic settlement could be taken for granted. It is to the ferocity of the attack on this settlement that we now turn.

TARGET FOR TONIGHT: THE MIXED ECONOMY

Whether or not the inaugural meeting of the Mont Pèlerin society had been a deliberate attempt to ape the meeting in a New Hampshire hotel three years earlier that had pieced together the architecture for the post-war international order and given it its name, Bretton Woods, the collection of economists and political theorists who met for nine days in Switzerland in the spring of 1947 had an entirely different vision of the post-war world. What's more they knew they were in it for the long haul.

The West, less than two years after the Red Army had unfurled the hammer and sickle over Berlin's Brandenburg Gate, could hardly have been less promising for those who believed in the power of market forces to provide the best possible combination of prosperity and freedom. The retreat from liberalism prompted by the economic slump of the 1930s had been hastened by the need to harness the power of the state to defeat Hitler. Seeking a theme for the 1945 general election, Winston Churchill had borrowed from Dr Hayek's seminal 1944 work, *The Road to Serfdom*, to claim that a vote for Clement Attlee's Labour Party would result in the arrival in Britain of the Gestapo, if not immediately, then at some point in the future once the initial good intentions of those dedicated to planning the economy hardened into a form of totalitarianism. Churchill's attack flopped. Attlee, a cricket-loving First World War major and former social worker, was not the sort of person the average British voter could imagine armed with a rubber truncheon in a torture chamber. Furthermore, he cleverly exploited paranoia about all things Germanic by using an election broadcast to emphasise the 'von' between the Friedrich and the Hayek. More to the point, perhaps, the tide of collectivism was at its height. Not only was there enormous respect for the part communist Russia had played in the defeat of Hitler, but there was a sense that it had only been by pulling together that Britain had survived in the dark days from the summer of 1940 to the arrival of the United States in the war in December 1941. There was a demand that the same meticulous planning that had charac-terised the war economy should be used to confront the problems of peacetime, and in particular the five giants iden-tified in the 1942 Beveridge report – Want, Ignorance, Squalor, Disease and Idleness.

The luminaries of the Mont Pèlerin society knew what they were up against. Dr Hayek drew comparisons with the under-cover struggle waged by resistance fighters in the war, urging his friends to 'raise and train an army of freedom fighters' (from Dr Hayek's paper on *The Prospect of Freedom* quoted in Richard Cockett; *Thinking the Unthinkable;* Fontana Press; 1995; page 104). He added: 'If we do not flinch at this task, if we do not throw up our hands in the face of overwhelming public opinion but work to shape and guide that opinion, our cause is by no means hopeless. But it is late in the day and we have not too much time to spare.'

Dr Hayek was right about that. Faith in Wall Street and Big Finance generally had been shattered by the Great Depression, so much so that President Roosevelt was able to launch the sort of populist attack in his inauguration speech that today would be found only in the pages of *Socialist Worker*. Yet with unemployment at 25 per cent, and industrial production down by 50 per cent in three years, FDR had the public on his side when he said of those who had enjoyed the fruits of the Gilded Age: 'True they have tried, but their efforts have been cast in the pattern of an outworn tradition . . . They have no vision, and when there is no vision the people perish. The money changers have fled from their high seats in the temple of our civilization. We may now restore that temple to the ancient truths. The measure of the restoration lies in the extent to which we apply social values more noble than mere monetary profit.'

As Howard Wachtel wrote in his book *Street of Dreams* (Pluto Press; 2003, p. 182):

These were words Wall Street had never before heard from Pennsylvania Avenue, but their defences were down, having been shattered by a financial and economic reality and decades-long public debate. Now the representatives of a popular politics on Main Street had the upper hand, and the Street found itself in an unfamiliarly defensive position.

Roosevelt kept up the pressure. Speaking to Adolph Berle, a professor at Columbia University and a former member of FDR's original brains trust, after Professor Berle accepted an offer to join the New York Stock Exchange's advisory board, the president said: 'The fundamental trouble with this whole stock exchange crowd is their complete lack of elementary education. I do not mean lack of college diplomas, etc., but just inability to understand the country or public or their obligations to their fellow men. Perhaps you can help them acquire a kindergarten knowledge of these subjects. More power to you' (quoted in *Wall Street*, by Steve Fraser; Faber and Faber; 2005; p. 391).

It was Roosevelt who referred to the new era's stock-market seers and fantasists as object lessons in how the country had departed from the basics of Ben Franklin republicanism. It was Roosevelt who decried Samuel Insull's pyramid of watered stock, its arbitrary write-up of assets, its milking of subsidies and vast overcharging of customers. It was the president who confirmed a long-held populist suspicion that fewer than three dozen private banking houses and stock-selling adjuncts in the commercial banks, 'have directed the flow of capital within the country and outside it, pledging that the government would become the effective counterweight to this financial oligarchy'.

Roosevelt backed his words with action – the Glass-Steagal Act of 1933 had offered protection for ordinary depositors by banning commercial banks from acting like investment banks and by establishing an insurance fund, the Federal Deposit Insurance Corporation. In 1934, the Securities and Exchange Act legislated for transparency in the financial markets, creating the Securities and Exchange Commission to police Wall Street. Wachtel says the essence of the new legislation was that *caveat vendor* replaced *caveat emptor*.

The third pillar of the new post-crash system involved the installation of a populist banker from Utah, Marriner Eccles, as chairman of the Federal Reserve Board. He reformed the central bank by putting control of interest rates under an open market committee, thus removing it from the hands of Wall Street's so-called money-centre banks, those with a large market presence and a major role in providing funds for corporations and governments.

The regulatory regime established during the 1930s prevailed until its undoing in the deregulatory movement of the 1980s. In that half century the American economy grew faster than in any other comparable period in its history. It was also the only such half-century without a single or even minor financial crisis on Wall Street, which had become used to one every ten years or so from its origins in 1792 to the 1930s. (Wachtel; page 187)

Roosevelt's scathing remarks had an echo in Britain, where John Maynard Keynes said: 'Speculators may do no harm as bubbles on a steady stream of enterprise. But the position is serious when enterprise becomes the bubble on a whirlpool of speculation' (*The General Theory of Employment, Interest and Money*; 1936). A decade earlier, when Winston Churchill had been persuaded against his better judgement to return Britain to the Gold Standard, the future prime minister wrote in a February 1925 memo to Treasury Permanent Secretary Otto Niemeyer that he 'would rather see finance less proud and industry more content'.

Yet, despite all this, Professor Hayek's faith was rewarded. Unlike the left after the setbacks of the 1970s, the believers in classical free-market liberalism did not throw in the towel. Even though the Great Depression was a far more serious economic crisis than that triggered by the energy cartel, the Organisation of Petroleum Exporting Countries (Opec) in the autumn of 1973, Dr Hayek and his friends never doubted that they would eventually be proved right. As such, they ignored the nationalisation of the coal mines in Britain that took place three months before Mont Pèlerin; they were undeterred when the National Health Service introduced socialised medicine little more than a year later; they saw the 'we're all in it together' spirit of the classic Ealing comedy film *Passport to Pimlico* as a challenge, something to be shaped and guided, as Dr Hayek put it, rather than something that implied surrender. As far as the Mont Pèlerin conspirators were concerned, the post-war settlement was the equivalent of the *Titanic*, seemingly unsinkable but inevitably heading for disaster. As we shall see later in this chapter, the post-war consensus hit the iceberg in 1968 and, although the band played on for a few more years, it slipped beneath the waves five years later.

So what was it about the post-war settlement that the classical liberals loathed so much? As we have seen, it was, in truth, a somewhat bloodless and technical construct whose shorthand name – the 'mixed economy' – captured admirably its blend of welfare, state economic management and private enterprise. It was a very far cry indeed from the totalitarian state feared by Hayek et al., which was hardly surprising since the two men who did more to bury classical liberalism – John Maynard Keynes and Franklin Delano Roosevelt – were both from the patrician class in their respective countries. Neither Lord Keynes nor President Roosevelt was remotely interested in creating a workers' state to mirror that in the Soviet Union; they saw themselves as practical men seeking to cope with the world as it was rather than as how it should be if the economic textbooks were right. No more than Dr Hayek did Lord Keynes want private enterprise to be abandoned in favour of state socialism, but neither economist thought that a wholly market economy was possible. Responding to *The Road to Serfdom*, Keynes said: 'You agree that the line has to be drawn somewhere, and that the logical extreme is not possible. But you give us no guidance whatever as to where to draw it . . . but as soon as you admit that the extreme is not possible, and that a line has to be drawn, you are, on your own argument, done for since you are trying to persuade us that as soon as one moves an inch in the planned direction you are necessarily launched on the slippery path which will lead you in due course over the precipice.'

SEQUEL: THE MARKET COMEBACK, FROM ARTHUR HALLEY TO THE ABBEY NATIONAL

Credit where it is due, the financiers, the offshore capitalists, the investment bankers and the speculators fought back from an extraordinarily unfavourable position immediately after the war to perhaps *the* key position in the world economy. It is hard to recall now just how despised were the financial traders and traffickers of the early post-war period, both in political discourse (Harold Wilson's famous 'gnomes of Zurich') and in fiction (at least two Ian Fleming villains, Hugo Drax and Auric Goldfinger, are, among other things, metals speculators). They were the shadowy, wealthier and often expatriate counterparts of the 'coupon clippers' and the 'dividend drawers', the faded rentier class living in Eastbourne or Cheltenham and doomed to extinction in the new Britain of the post-war world. Even the relatively respectable merchant banks were treated with suspicion and widely thought to have a rather limited future. Until the late 1960s, the activities of the financial interest were severely curtailed by instruments such as exchange control, high and selective levels of taxation, strict banking regulation and official surveillance. Emerging from the intellectual and economic chaos of 40 years ago, those representing that interest are now perhaps the most important figures on the economic stage. Their opinions are sought on financial and political issues, their 'confidence' must be maintained at all costs by those, such as central bankers, charged with economic management and their 'contribution' to the public good is routinely praised by politicians, even when that contribution amounts to little more than asset stripping. National laws and international treaties entrench their position. They argue that their dominance is the 'natural' order of things, and that political or social action can only 'distort' this natural order.

Until the 1970s, they confronted a system that combined strict official control over finance and industry, tight supervision of banking and the active management of the economy in the interests of the many, coupled with a hands-off approach to people's personal lifestyles and attitudes, whether of the traditional variety or, as the 1950s and 1960s progressed, the freewheeling sort. This formula has since been turned on its head – a remarkable achievement. But then, the financial interest and its intellectual companions were not just determined but were as wise as serpents. They treated every reverse as temporary and every advance as permanent. In the first category, not including the sweeping measures of the 1945 Labour government, were the defeat in the highest levels of government of the Operation Robot proposals to float the pound in 1952, the import surcharge of the post-1964 Labour government, the nationalisation of aerospace and shipbuilding in the 1970s and, at the same time, the imposition of 'corset' arrangements on British banks. In the second category were the above-mentioned Heath liberalisation of the City, the 1979 abolition of exchange control, the granting of operational independence to the Bank of England's Monetary Policy Committee and the entire post-1979 privatisation programme.

Despite the energy crisis and rampant inflation in the 1970s, victory for the free-marketeers was very far from assured. Well into the early 1970s, fashionable Western political leaders (such as they were) remained on the centre-left: Olaf Palme, Willy Brandt, Shirley Williams. Centre-right leaders (Richard Nixon, Edward Heath) were forced into centre-leftist economic management once initial attempts to restore old-fashioned 'market discipline' had failed. Indeed, the first two or three years of Margaret Thatcher's first government had all the hall-marks of a period of high inflation, high unemployment and confrontation with the trade unions that had marked the first two years of Heath in office. As the crisis of the mid-1970s deepened, the smart money would probably have been staked on a further shift to the left in the Western democracies as the cheap energy and cheap money that had, from a left-ist perspective, papered over the cracks in the post-war system started rapidly to evaporate.

In 1976, the French commentator Jean-François Revel (a committed socialist with a sceptical view of his fellow leftists) wrote scathingly: 'Yes, you [other socialists] loftily claim to possess the only remedy, to offer the only possible choice. Every day we read titles of this sort: "Socialism: The Only Solution to the World Crisis." You talk as if you had in your hands a completely constructed society, a fully proven solution with an obviously favourable balance sheet' (*The Totalitarian Temptation;* English edition, Secker & Warburg; 1977).

Thus the battle for untrammelled financial markets was long and bitter. It was engaged on every front, from the populist (such as privatisation and the liberalisation of credit markets) to the diplomatic (getting governments to sign away in treaty agreements their rights to aspects of economic management) to the social (deriding opponents as hopelessly old-fashioned and harbouring disreputable prejudices) to the engagement of state forces in head-on confrontations with organised labour (such as the 1981 air-traffic controllers' strike in America and the 1984–1985 miners' strike in Britain).

Gusting behind these developments, helping them move along, were the warm zephyrs from the fallout from 1968. If Messrs Hayek, Friedman and company would have been a little long in the tooth convincingly to pose as 1960s 'faces', this was less of a problem for someone who was a major influence on the man who was to become perhaps the single most important figure in the fantastical bubble economy of the early 21st century, Federal Reserve Board chairman Alan Greenspan.

Ayn Rand was a Russian-born and Soviet-educated thinker who took advantage of a visa to visit American relations in 1925 to leave the Soviet Union for good. Fiercely intelligent, strikingly attractive and utterly outspoken, she founded the movement that she called Objectivism and which would probably now be recognisable as right-wing or free-market libertarianism. While not exactly a first-division 1960s celebrity, she was well known and had a large number of followers, particularly in North America – the 1970s hard-rock band Rush among them.

She called capitalism 'the unknown ideal', she dismissed as 'slavery' the taxing of one person in order to make welfare payments to another (i.e. the routine operation of Western systems of social benefits) and believed the unfortunate ought to rely entirely on charity. Miss Rand, flatly opposed to any kind of regulation of monopolies, described big business as 'America's persecuted minority', was scathing about the student rebellion of the 1960s and employed the word 'altruist' as a term of abuse.

An unlikely hipster? Not so fast. She opposed conscription ('the draft') as another form of slavery, was a fierce opponent of the war in Vietnam, despised the politics of consensus and – perhaps inevitably – loathed with a vengeance the Democratic Party leader and US president, Lyndon Johnson, someone whose policies encompassed pretty much all that she saw wrong with the world (all taken from *Capitalism: The Unknown Ideal*; Signet; 1967).

With views such as these that chimed exactly with those of the student rebels and the 'underground', Miss Rand was a whole lot funkier than Dr Hayek; she even teased dark-suited Mr Greenspan by calling him 'the Undertaker' (Alan Greenspan; *The Age of Turbulence*; Penguin; 2007).

This sort of thinking took a little while to drift across the Atlantic, but drift it did. In 1975, British author Terry Arthur produced an extremely funny book billed as 'a plain man's guide to British politics' with the cheeky but not entirely inaccurate title (then or now) *95 per cent is Crap*. Trawling through the political statements of the recent past (which included two general elections in the course of 1974), Arthur skewered again and again the dishonest formulations and double-speak of British politicians, ably assisted by excellent cartoons from 'Cummings'. Only on a careful second reading would one realise the skewering comes from one direction only – that of the free-market perspective – with Tory politicians being attacked on the same grounds as Labour and Liberal ones. It may take a careful third reading to spot that the publisher is Libertarian Books, of Bedford.

Linked to this sort of hip and unstuffy free-market thinking was a new type of populism that sought to make the cause of financial deregulation the cause of the ordinary people. It is hard to pinpoint the start of this movement or its originators. Suffice to say that, by the end of the 1970s, deregulation was seen as a vote winner on both sides of the Atlantic. Intriguingly, it was to be sold with a leftist slant in both Britain and the US.

In America, the airline deregulation bill that passed in 1978 was sponsored by Senator Edward Kennedy. President Jimmy Carter was to oversee the deregulation of a number of other industries, including rail and truck transport, communications and finance. Regulation had traditionally been seen as a way to protect the public. Increasingly, it was being portrayed as a conspiracy against the public.

The hero of Arthur Hailey's 1975 novel *The Moneychangers* (Michael Joseph) is a liberal banker called Alex Vandervoort, whose long-standing girlfriend is a feminist lawyer. Hailey has Vandervoort interviewed by the *New York Times*, where Vandervoort blends social liberalism with a call for bank deregulation:

Vandervoort: What ought to happen is that laws should stop protecting banks and protect people instead.

Question: By protecting people you mean letting those with savings enjoy the maximum interest rate and other services which any bank will give?

Vandervoort: Yes, I do.

There is more in the same vein.

A real-life Vandervoort was a British businessman called Clive Thornton. As chief general manager of the Abbey National Building Society, he broke away in 1983 from the system whereby the Building Societies Association met monthly to fix mortgage rates. From now on, the Abbey would do its own thing. Within a few years, the old system had fallen apart and mortgage rates had become completely deregulated.

But in contrast to Sir Freddie Laker, who had battled the big airlines in the late 1970s to bring fares down on transatlantic routes, Mr Thornton never came across as the typical hard-boiled Tory entrepreneur. Indeed, in the years immediately following Abbey's 1983 move, he became associated with leftish projects such as reviving the fortunes of the Labour-supporting paper, the *Daily Mirror*, and with launching a radical new title, *News on Sunday*.

In the euphoria that followed the collapse of the old fixed system of interest rates, and with it the 'queue' under which would-be mortgage borrowers had first to build up a track record of savings, few seemed to notice that the net effect of deregulation, over time, would be to raise the cost of home loans. Indeed, six years after the Abbey went its own way on interest rates, it became the first building society to turn itself into a bank, with members becoming holders of shares that could be sold for a windfall profit.

This, in turn, was part of a wider populist movement to 'widen' share ownership, usually through the sale at below-market prices to the public of shares in former nationalised industries. It seemed everybody was on board the people's privatisation express other than out-of-touch characters such as the Earl of Stockton (formerly Harold Macmillan), who warned against 'selling the family silver', or the Law Lords, who effectively asked in 1986 how the government could sell something (the Trustee Savings Bank) that it did not actually own.

Of course, the various elements of the market revival – populist, diplomatic, social and so on – did not operate in isolation. For example, the Single European Act, which became operative in 1992 and severely restricted the ability of European governments to carry out effective economic intervention, was advertised through the British authorities' populist campaign 'Europe is open for business'. In turn, the post-1992 European Commission required nationalised industries to be run on commercial lines, adding to the impetus for privatisations, some of which involved attempts at mass share ownership. Social contempt for old-fashioned unionised 'male' jobs and workforce 'inflexibility' could be fostered by (rarely repeated) bonus payments from companies in return for employees adapting to new technology and by staff share schemes.

By the late 1980s, novelist David Lodge could enivisage a trendy English lecturer writing to his similarly employed girl-friend informing her of a career switch – to merchant banking. Part of his rationale speaks volumes about the change in attitudes:

You and I, Robyn, grew up in a period when the state was smart: state schools, state universities, state-subsidised arts, state welfare, state medi-cine – these were things progressive, energetic people believed in. It isn't like that any more. (Nice Work; Secker & Warburg, 1988)

THE NOT SO GREAT DEFENDER (OR WHERE WAS THE LEFT?)

As noted earlier, if 1968 was the year in which the financial interest began to test the notion of shrugging off the super-structure of the post-war settlement, it was also the year in which the middle-class leftist intelligentsia began, tentatively, to do the same thing. The one-time home of the likes of George Orwell started to give up on the Western working class as ever likely to abandon material advancement and turn instead to cultural improvement (the goal of the inside left) or start a revolution (the goal of the outside left). In no apparent need of their self-appointed saviours, the 'workers' ceased to be the great ally and became instead the enemy – as, by happy coincidence, they were becoming to the new, aggressive breed of financiers and super-rich.

Some middle-class leftists drifted away from political engagement of any kind and into well-heeled employment; their allegiance became a sort of fashion accessory, some-thing the sharp-eyed spotted fairly quickly. In his column of television criticism in the *Observer* on October 8 1978, Clive James had great fun:

The Italian Marxist composer Luigi Nono (BBC 2) proclaims the necessity for contemporary music to intervene in something called the sonic reality of our time. Apparently it should do this by being as tuneless as possible. There were shots of Nono's apartments to indicate that he is even better off than the usual run of Italian Marxist composers. (From The Crystal Bucket; *Jonathan Cape; 1981)*

The failure of the working class to live up to middle-class leftists' hopes had been disguised for decades by, first, the struggle against fascism in Europe and then by various campaigns, including anti-colonialism and the struggle for civil rights. All were noble causes and all were largely victor-ious by the end of the 1960s. But rather than return to the once all-important struggle of the workers (whose demands for Ford Cortinas and spin driers were so distressing) they invented 'new proletariats' that they could control, either external (as in campaigns for entities less likely to answer back such as children's rights and animal 'rights') or internal (members of the middle-class left themselves, albeit wearing various different badges: gays, women, disabled people, 'trans-gender' and so on).

For the New Olympians, this displacement activity by the left was highly convenient, since it coincided with the end of the Golden Age of post-war social democracy in the early 1970s. Progressive parties lost their nerve, gradually distancing themselves from economic reform in favour of identity politics and social engineering combined with a broad acceptance that the message of the financial Olympians was not only right, but may not go far enough.

The left's new distaste for working-class affluence led it into strange company. Let us ponder what, in practice, was the difference between this statement:

Late industrial society has increased rather than reduced the need for parasitical and alienated functions . . . Advertising, public relations, indoctrination, planned obsolescence are no longer unproductive overhead costs but rather elements of basic production costs . . . a rising standard of living is the almost unavoidable by-product of the politically manipulated industrial society . . . there is no reason to insist on self-determination if the administered life is the comfortable and even the 'good' life.

And this one:

[W]hat is nowadays meant by prosperity . . . [is] that the working classes will have more of everything they like: fish fingers, over-cooked meats, transistor wirelesses to take out of doors with them, caravans and motor cruisers to fasten behind their cars.

In terms of the utter contempt for the materialist aspirations of working people there is little to choose between the first author, much-travelled radical professor Herbert Marcuse (*One Dimensional Man*; Routledge and Kegan Paul; 1964), and the second, the often-splenetic conservative journalist Auberon Waugh (*Another Voice*; Firethorn Press; 1986).

Nick Cohen has written of: '[T]he nagging feeling that not all the bourgeois reformers' efforts to improve the lot of the masses had gone as planned', adding of 'the failure of the masses to pass muster in Bohemia' (*What's Left: How liberals lost their way;* Fourth Estate; 2007).

While some leftist commentators proclaimed the death of the working class, others 'accepted that the working class lived on, but were obsessed by identity politics' (Cohen; *ibid*).

Concludes Cohen: 'From the theorists in the universities to the pundits in Canary Wharf [home of many British national newspapers], the intellectuals weren't interested in the working class and the working class wasn't interested in the intellectuals.

'You could not have found a more lethal way to kill left-wing politics if you had tried.'

And as the middle-class left snubbed the working class, the compliment was returned. The economic and social turmoil at the end of the 1960s saw the beginning of a decades-long trend in which blue-collar voters not only felt free to abandon centre-left parties, but also to leap-frog contemptuously over traditional centre-right politicians into the arms of right-wingers with both a much harder policy edge and an ability to assure working people that their background and culture was nothing about which to be ashamed. While apologising in advance to any of those who take offence at being grouped with some of the others, we would list among these new-right 'working-class heroes' George Wallace and Ronald Reagan in the United States, Ian Paisley in Northern Ireland, Margaret Thatcher and Norman Tebbit in Great Britain and John Howard and Pauline Hanson in Australia. We stress, it is simply the hard policy edge and the affirming stance towards blue-collar attitudes and lifestyles that links these and other figures – we are not suggesting, for example, that John Howard is 'the same as' the segregationist George Wallace. By the mid 1970s, with the fall of Edward Heath in Britain and Gerald Ford in the States, it was becoming clear that moderate conservatives could not expect to be the beneficiaries of the crisis in post-war social democracy.

But then, the middle-class left may have been past caring. It is interesting to note that Cohen mentions in passing, and in a different context, a remarkable play by Trevor Griffiths, first staged at the National Theatre in London against a real-life background of crisis in December 1973. *The Party* is set during the upheavals in Paris in 1968; a group of metropol-itan London leftists have gathered to discuss what the rioting is all about. They are joined by the genuine article, a trad-itional revolutionary socialist called John Tagg.

Having heard his hosts' analysis of the situation, heavy on identity politics, Tagg lets fly:

You say: The working class has been assimilated, corrupted, demoralised. You point to his car and his house and his pension scheme and his respectability, and you write him off . . . then you start backing the field: blacks, students, homosexuals, terrorist groupings, Mao, Che Guevara, anybody, just so long as they represent some repressed minority still capable of anger and the need for self-assertion. (Pause) Well. Which workers have you spoken with recently? And for how long? How do you know they're not as frustrated as you are?' (Faber and Faber; 1974)

'Tagg' was right, but he had missed the point. Not only had the middle-class left found substitutes (including its own members) for the working class, but it was in the process of turning this newly invented 'proletariat' into a source of lucra-tive career opportunities mainly, although not exclusively, in the public sector. A new type of public servant would be created, one concerned not with providing any actual service (nursing, for example, or teaching), but with changing people's 'attitudes' and 'lifestyles'.

According to the centre-right think tank Reform, there were

4,945,000 people in the public sector in 1998; this had risen to 5,454,000 by 2003. Reform added:

Not all of the increase in public sector employment is accounted for by 'front-line workers' such as doctors, nurses, teachers and police officers . . . [We] have shown that between 1997 and 2003, the number of doctors, nurses, teachers and police officers in the UK increased by 131,000. Assuming the same rate of increase in the numbers of each profession, between 2003 and 2006, the increase would be of the order of 70,000.

Alternatively, assuming teachers, doctors, nurses and police officers remain the same proportion of public sector employment, the increase would be around 100,000.

The think tank then compared these figures to the 84,150 civil service jobs scheduled to be cut between 2004 and 2008. '[For] every one "head office" civil service job cut, another four new public sector employees will be recruited, of which just one will be a doctor, teacher, nurse or police officer.'

Reform noted that Conservative front-bench MP Oliver Letwin had calculated that, even when midwives and prison officers were added to the recruitment of these four groups of professions, 'only 45 per cent of the growth in public sector employment would be composed of "front-line staff"' (*Costing Britain – falling productivity in the public sector*; Graeme Leach; Reform; 2004).

The others will include those recruited to fill the so-called joke jobs: the outreach co-ordinators and healthy living strategists, the breast-feeding advisers and the tobacco control officers.

Most desirable of all, from the perspective of the post-1968 middle-class left, was a job in the burgeoning equality (or 'equalities', to use the modish word) industry. Given that they themselves (wearing the various badges of approved 'victim groups') had become a dominant chunk of the new 'pro-letariat', nothing could be more convenient than that they should staff the bureaucracies set up to 'tackle' (a suitably vague bureaucratic word) the injustices from which they suffered. In some cases, these bureaucracies were established inside large private companies in order to keep the management on the right side of an expanding volume of laws and 'guidelines' aimed at addressing the various grievances of these victim groups.

The growth of this new class of functionaries has caused a huge shift in the balance of power on the left. Nearly 25 years after the 1984–1985 miners' strike, the outcome of that dispute looks increasingly like the best possible news for the white-collar public sector masses, whatever they might have thought at the time.

Defeat for the pitmen cleared the way for the 'downsizing' and ultimately the sale of coal, steel, electricity, water, car and aircraft manufacturing and the railways. With these entities now largely off the government's books, cash was available for the steady expansion of state sector positions not only of dubious utility, to put it mildly, but often actively involved in social engineering projects aimed squarely at members of the traditional working class, whether assaults on their diet or lack of exercise or attempts to change their 'attitudes' (or 'thoughts', to put it less coyly). In July 2007, a lawyer reported a bookshop in St Albans for selling *Tintin in the Congo*, first published in 1931 and full of offensive depictions of African people. As Hertfordshire police confirmed they were treating it as a 'racial incident', David Sexton was bemused in the London *Evening Standard*:

What protests does the utterly dreadful state of the Congo itself occasion? None. But finding an anachronistic Tintin book on sale in St Albans – now that's completely intolerable. (July 13 2007)

In an eerie parallel with the liberation of financial speculators from post-war controls, the middle-class left was now free of working people. It was self-sufficient, supplying from its own ranks both the new downtrodden masses and the personnel who would end their misery (not too quickly, however, lest all those jobs disappear). These New

Functionaries were a sort of mirror image of the New Olympians, united in two things: an ability to talk in terms unintelligible to the ordinary person and a disdain for those self-same people. True, the former group enjoyed very much smaller pay packets than those of the latter group; on the other hand, there were very many more Functionaries than Olympians.

In the process, of course, any notion of greater income equality for ordinary working people took a back seat.

Thus at the 2007 Conservative Party conference, Barclays Bank sponsored an event entitled Absolutely Equal. Given that the £1 million pay packet of Barclays' chief executive John Varley was something like 40 times the national average, one might have guessed that this absolute equality had nothing to do with money or wealth and everything to do with middle-class 'identity issues'. One would have been right.

TO CAP IT ALL: THE OLYMPIANS RATTLE THE BEGGING BOWL

Does any of the following sound familiar? World markets are in turmoil, pulled down by a sinking dollar. In Britain, the crisis is particularly acute in the case of one institution and there are clamours for government help. After insisting that no help will be forthcoming, the authorities give way and the Bank of England is sent into the breach. As events unfold, interest rates are cut on both sides of the Atlantic as a determined effort gets under way to reflate shares.

That was October 1987, during the stock-market crash that had followed the Great Storm of the night of October 16. Unknown at the time, it became the model for everything that has followed. Then, it was shares rather than bank deposits that were falling and the troubled institution was not Northern Rock but the energy group British Petroleum, whose open market share price had dropped below the 'bargain' level at which the final government stake was to be sold to the public.

This meant banks in London and Wall Street, which had under-written the 'surefire' share offer believing that the fees involved would be money for nothing, faced huge losses. These exemplars of free enterprise insisted the government get them off the hook, which it did, arranging for the Bank to put a floor under the share price.

In retrospect, everyone was remarkably polite about the BP debacle. The then chancellor Nigel Lawson, a self-styled 'Tory radical', was required to spend little time explaining why subsidies for the recently defeated coal-miners or the shrinking British car industry were pointless and wasteful, while subsidies (albeit of a stand-by nature) for investment banks were rational and fruitful. This question was especially piquant in light of the fact that these banks were being asked to do only what they had contracted to do as underwriters.

But in what was to become the soothing muzak of all such bail-outs, the public was told that 'market stability' and the 'smooth functioning of the system' were the key issues, along with the 'restoration of confidence'. This was not a subsidy to any particular institution or group of institutions. Perish the thought.

Twenty years later, in the Northern Rock debacle, not a dot, not a comma is different. All that has changed, over the years, is that everyone involved has become rather more blatant.

In September 1998, the Federal Reserve Board, America's central bank, made little secret of the fact that it had arranged a bail-out for the Long Term Capital Management hedge fund, which despite (or perhaps because of) being staffed by incredibly brainy New Olympians had taken up sufficient bad market positions to cause an international financial crisis were it allowed to go bust. No nonsense there about not helping a specific institution. But at least that bail-out involved the funds of other major US banks, rather than of US taxpayers.

Nine years on from that episode, and the summer storms of 2007 saw bankers and financiers in Britain and America demanding either public money or lower interest rates – or both – with all the nonchalance of young women in the Swinging London of the 1960s insisting their fuddy-duddy general practitioners put them on the pill. Indeed, the language used by one anonymous City bigwig to the *Daily Telegraph* on September 4 – suggesting the Bank of England harboured a 'Victorian' reluctance to provide support – was eerily reminiscent of the sort of accusation aimed by the 'love generation' at its 'square' elders.

But this was mild stuff compared to the outburst on August 20 2007 from US stock-market guru Jim Cramer on the business channel CNBC. Like a desperate junkie begging for one more 'hit', Mr Cramer demanded the Federal Reserve Board bail out Wall Street. This is just part of his rant:

And Bill Poole [president of the Federal Reserve Bank of St Louis]? [He] has no idea what it's like out there! My people have been in this game for 25 years. And they are losing their jobs and these firms are going to go out of business, and he's nuts! They're nuts! They know nothing! We have Armageddon. In the fixed income markets, we have Armageddon.

Irish commentator Gene Kerrigan was merciless: 'This was the genuine voice of big capital. Whining, hysterical, demanding that the state grabs its chestnuts out of the fire . . . Isn't high finance great gas altogether!' ('Chestnuts roasting on melting markets'; *Sunday Independent;* September 2 2007)

Avinash Persaud, founder and chairman of London advisory group Intelligence Capital, was a little more measured in remarks on January 3 2008:

It is interesting that while by day bankers justify the egregious compensation packages they pay colleagues on the basis that they are forced to do so by the cold ruthlessness of the marketplace they inhabit, by night, when things go wrong, they are bailed out by easy money from local central banks, regulatory forebearance and fresh capital from government investment agencies. Bankers would appear to take a market view of rewards but a public welfare view on risks.

In extremis, or even in cases of mild discomfort, bankers, brokers, investment managers and speculators forget their free-market principles in the blink of an eye. Many would have cheered support for journalist Ambrose Evans-Pritchard, who commented:

US Treasury Secretary Hank Paulson can be forgiven for pushing through a rescue plan last week that amounts to a flagrant abuse of contract law and capitalist principles ... Would free marketeers rather see the whole edifice of capitalism burned to the ground to make their point?

He concluded: 'The strategic failure of a whole generation of economists, bankers and policymakers has been so enormous that it may now take a strong draught of socialism to save the western democracies' (*Daily Telegraph;* December 10 2007).

Philip Larkin once wrote of hippy-ish youths whose 'Oriental contempt for "the bread"' was matched only by their voracious appetite for it (*Required Writing;* Faber and Faber; 1983). Much the same attitude would seem to link high finance and public subsidies, as seen in the Bear Stearns bail-out.

The New Olympians' failure to meet their basic boast – that they needed no public money because their operations mirrored the 'natural' workings of the market – may appear to be the fundamental flaw in the system. In fact, it is the symptom of all the other failings. They have to borrow money from the public purse because their system does not work.

Debt is the key to the new economic order. Because British industry has been largely wiped out by New Olympian economic policies, we need to borrow from countries such as China to buy their goods. The United States is in a similar position, but on a larger scale. This debt is then bundled up in different ways by financial institutions to produce a profit. The institutions themselves, as we saw with Northern Rock, are heavy borrowers, and their debt, in turn, can be traded on the open market.

It is the central belief of New Olympians that any asset –

a mortgage, a loan, a title deed – can be made more valu-able by cutting it into different-shaped pieces and trading it to different institutions. This was the thinking behind 'collateralised debt obligations' and remains the thinking behind complex derivatives that supposedly make two and two equal five. They had every reason to believe this of course. All these fancy-sounding financial products meant they could maximise their profits from the Anglo-American debt binge of the last decade.

Not for nothing were the early New Olympians children of the 1960s. In their dreamy way, they and their successors are rebelling against 'The Man' – i.e. the conventional banker or financier, the member of parliament or finance minister. They believe reserve requirements, loan ratios, mark-to-market rules and all the rest are just obstacles to a financial nirvana. They want to take advantage of the beautiful new world of internationalism and technology. What is so wrong with that?

Apart from the fact that they have brought our economy to the brink of collapse, nothing whatsoever.

4

Sunday, Monday, Happy Days:

The Goldilocks economy

All is for the best in the best of possible worlds.
  – Voltaire; *Candide;* 1759

My idea was that as the world absorbed information technology and learned to put it to work, we had entered what
would prove to be a protracted period of lower inflation,
lower interest rates, increased productivity and full employment. 'I've been looking at business cycles since the late
1940s,' I said. 'There has been nothing like this.'
  – Alan Greenspan; *The Age of Turbulence;* Penguin;
  2007

There's a lake of gin we can both jump in, and the
handouts grow on bushes In the new-mown hay we can
sleep all day, and the bars all have free lunches
  – Harry McClintock; 'Big Rock Candy Mountain'; first
  recorded 1928

Right up to the moment she was awoken, Goldilocks had been
sleeping peacefully. Deep in the forest, miles from home and
totally lost, Goldilocks had been having the sweetest of dreams.
It was of unlimited quantities of the most delicious porridge

she had ever tasted, sweet and toothsome and – crucially – neither too hot nor too cold. In her dream, Goldilocks saw herself living in this little cottage with flowers round the door for ever.

Then the three bears arrived back home.

Strange though it may seem, the hard-nosed men and women managing (sic) the world's financial markets are devout believers in fairy stories. Just like Zeus and Hera, the New Olympians like nothing better than to hear tales of their derring-do. Pressures of work may mean that they have to sub-contract the job of reading bedtime stories to their own children to an army of nannies and au pairs, but this has not made them any less susceptible to a charming tale in which everybody lives happily ever after (albeit with some living just a bit more happily than others).

For the past 15 years, the idea of the Goldilocks economy has been the prevailing metaphor for the fairy-tale enthusiasts of the global economy. After the inflationary decade of the 1970s and the bust-boom decade of the 1980s, there would be porridge on offer in ever-increasing quantities and at ever-lower prices. The global economy would be neither too hot nor too cold but just right, and the reason it would be perfect was that the New Olympians were in control, not just of policy-making at a national level (important though that was), but at supra-national and sub-national level as well. The key New Olympian organisations were independent central banks, international bodies such as the International Monetary Fund, the World Bank, the European Commission, the World Trade Organisation, and the International Court of Justice. On the face of it, these were disparate bodies with different spheres of influence and different constituencies; in practice they were linked by two threads: all wielded extraordinary power and all could do so while paying lip-service to the democratically elected governments that they were supposed to serve. If they listened to anyone, the New Olympian policy makers paid heed to their brothers-in arms – the men and women running international banks and multinational companies. And at home, the lack of patience, even contempt, for democracy meant the growth of the new quangocracy; bodies of public sector 'heroes' who could be relied on to put New Olympian thinking into practice at a local level. Providing the link between the two was a burgeoning army of management consultants, steeped in the same ideology of labour market flexibility, privatisation, cuts in taxation and the paring back of welfare states.

THE MAGIC MOUNTAIN: DRESSING DOWN IN DAVOS

The key date in the New Olympian calendar was the week in late January when, fittingly enough, the entire tribe gathered in conclave in the Swiss ski resort of Davos, 5,000 feet up in the Alps and just down the valley from the fictional lair of Blofeld in the Ian Fleming novel *On Her Majesty's Secret Service* (Jonathan Cape; 1963). For many years, anti-globalisation protestors tried but failed to do what 007 managed in the book, to breach the defences thrown around the annual meeting of the World Economic Forum. Here it was that the New Olympians were encouraged to bring their trophy wives, to replace the business suit with a Lacoste polo shirt and chinos, and to solve the problems of a globalised world. High up above the clouds, Bill Gates would get the chance to chew the fat with the governor of the European Central Bank, Jean-Claude Trichet; Pascal Lamy, the director general of the World Trade Organisation would gather a cabal of trade ministers to press for action in the Doha Round of trade liberalisation, each year warning that those of a protectionist bent were 'drinking in the last chance saloon' or some similar cliché. A smattering of trade unionists and officials from the less 'extreme' development-based non-governmental organisations were meant to give Davos a patina of accessibility and openness; in truth, long gone were the days when mere mortals were given some say in the way things should be managed.

Coming up with the formula for the Goldilocks economy had been painstaking work; the New Olympians were in no mood to allow electorates to mess around with the ingredients, let alone the self-appointed guardians of civil society.

It is fair to say, at this point, that there were those who from an early stage were concerned about the safety of Goldilocks as she tripped happily through the forest. We count ourselves among their number. The warnings, needless to say, were ignored, not least because it seemed – for a while – that the New Olympians did indeed have the Midas touch.

The origins of the Goldilocks economy go back several decades, to the late 1970s and the early 1980s. We have already described how our heroes had planned their return to Mount Olympus after the humiliations heaped on them in the 1930s and 1940s; when the post-war Keynesian order collapsed after the oil shocks of 1973 and 1979, there was an opportunity to try out all the potions that the wizards of high finance had been brewing up in secret. All the separate cadres that made up the New Olympian class played their part in bringing about the new order.

Central bankers were the first into the fray. Germany, Switzerland and the Netherlands had been the countries least-badly affected by the inflationary surge of the 1970s, and these countries' central banks were not run by meddling politicians with an eye on the next election. Instead they were managed by fiercely independent technocrats trustworthy enough to look beyond the need to boost growth in the short term in order to win votes. For central banks, the timing was perfect. By the time they became viewed as the only check on the inflationary impulses of democratically elected politicians, the price shocks of the 1970s were actually already abating, making the job of achieving price stability very much easier. Looking back from early 2008, a clear pattern emerges of an inflationary earthquake in 1973–1974 followed by a series of after-shocks of ever-diminishing force. In the United Kingdom, inflation peaked at 27 per cent in 1975, falling to 20 per cent in 1980, 11 per cent in 1990 and just 3 per cent in early 2007. This should come as little surprise, since low inflation has been the norm for capitalism ever since the dawn of the industrial age 250 years ago. True, there have been pulses of inflation, but these have tended to be confined to wartime, when monetary prudence is less important than defence of the realm. The Napoleonic War was a period when inflationary pressures were strong; the First World War was another. But in the 99 years between the Battle of Waterloo and the assassination of Archduke Franz Ferdinand at Sarajevo, prices fell. For the baby boomers born in the 15 years after the Second World War, high inflation may have appeared to be the norm; in the context of the economic history of the past 250 years, the peacetime explosion of the cost of living in the 1970s was very much the exception.

Central banks, unsurprisingly perhaps, credit themselves with bringing about this change. Those involved in pay talks or in setting prices in company boardrooms no longer believe, as they did in the bad old days of the 1960s and 1970s, that soft-hearted politicians will pump money into the economy every time there is the merest threat that growth will slow and that unemployment might rise. Central banks use technical phrases such as 'managing inflation expectations' but what they really mean is that the huddled masses are petrified that a recessionary thunderbolt will come thudding down from Mount Olympus if they get too uppity. The governor of the Bank of England, Mervyn King, believes that the pound's traumatic expulsion from the Exchange Rate Mechanism on Black Wednesday in September 1992 was a turning point for monetary policy in Britain, since it resulted in the government setting a clear target for inflation that policy makers were expected to meet. For the previous 15 years, the Treasury and the Bank had targeted the level of public borrowing, various measures of the money supply and, finally, pegged the pound to the German mark, in an attempt to find a way of keeping inflation low. After Black Wednesday they gave up on the idea of finding a proxy for inflation and simply targeted inflation itself. Full independence for the Bank to set interest rates –

the first big initiative of Tony Blair's government in May 1997 – strengthened the anti-inflation regime, according to Mr King, and has helped ensure that in the years since the annual increase in the cost of living in the UK has run at only a tenth of the levels seen at its peak in the 1970s. Under the terms of the Bank's mandate, the governor is required to write a letter to the chancellor of the exchequer should inflation deviate by more than a percentage point from its 2 per cent target; only one such epistle has so far had to be penned.

The idea that independent central banks deserve the credit for putting Western economies back on the straight and narrow after the inflationary excesses of the late Keynesian era does not convince everybody. Brian Henry, a UK economist of many years experience, wrote a paper at the end of 2007 in which he argued that as far as the Bank of England was concerned it happened to be in the right place at the right time. It has been able to get the kudos for something that was happening anyway. Henry argues that the trade-off between unemployment and inflation was improving of its own accord after the blows to the economy of the 1970s and early 1980s but that it took policy makers time to work out what had happened. 'The major movements in unemployment and inflation heralded by some as due to the regime of inflation targeting and central bank independence can instead be accounted for by a mixture of external shocks and a slow process of recognition of the effects of these by the authorities' (Brian Henry; *Monetary Policy, Unemployment and Inflation; Evidence from the UK;* National Institute for Economic and Social Research; January 2008).

Another British economist, Paul Ormerod, agrees, saying that the hallmark of industrial capitalism has been intense competition and it has been the pressure of the marketplace that has prevented prices from rising too fast (conversations with one of the authors). What differentiated the golden era of post-war prosperity from both earlier and later epochs of capitalism was the array of curbs on market forces – tariffs, nationalised industries, strong trade unions, full employment policies and the absence from the global capitalist economy of the world's two most populous nations – China and India. Changes wrought over the past quarter of a century – tamed trade unions, privatisation, the breaking down of trade barriers, the emergence of price stability as the ultimate economic policy goal and the widening of the global economy to include new low-cost sources of production – have meant that the world of 2008 is more akin to that of 1908 than 1958.

Of all these factors, the most crucial for the creation of the Goldilocks economy has been the spread of the market around the world. China's post-Mao embrace of capitalism, the collapse of the Soviet Union in 1991 and the decision by India in the same year to abandon its autarkic economic strategy have vastly increased the potential to supply goods and services at low cost. Between them China and India account for almost half the world's population, and the sudden increase in the global supply of labour has had a profound impact on prices in the West.

If the notion that hard-nosed central bankers will take no risks with inflation has been insufficient to 'discipline' Western workforces, the prospect of jobs disappearing to Shanghai and Bangalore has normally done the trick. Trade unions that might once have responded to calls for pay restraint with industrial militancy have had to think twice about striking for better terms and conditions. That is not to say a more emollient approach has worked any better, particularly for those trade unions with members working in traditional manufacturing. The difference in labour and social costs between employing someone in a textile mill in China, Vietnam or Bangladesh and employing the same person in Yorkshire or North Carolina has meant that production has shifted eastwards. Every country in the West has seen the share of its working population employed in manufacturing fall over the past quarter of a century, although some have seen sharper falls than others. In America, for example, the rise of sunrise industries such as computers and biotechnology together with the impact of military spending on the defence industry has meant that the size of the industrial workforce remained unchanged. In the UK, by contrast, it halved.

TAKING THE WAITING OUT OF WANTING: FINANCE IS SET FREE

The final ingredient for the Goldilocks economy has been financial deregulation, because it was the demolition of the controls on free movement of capital imposed in the 1930s and 1940s that allowed the trade surpluses amassed by the newly industrialising countries of the Pacific Rim to be recycled into the West. Central banks, despite their role as guarantors of low inflation, were strong supporters of these changes, although normally taking a back-seat role while politicians and banks made the case for reform. The politicians, egged on by the Mont Pèlerin crowd, saw controls on capital as an intolerable curb on liberty and symbolic of the post-war welfarist culture they despised so much. For the commercial bankers, it was a question of the bottom line. While hardly on their uppers during the 1950s and 1960s, they saw the ability to extend more credit and to move capital around the world at will as leading to higher profits. This, of course, was not the way change was dressed up for public consumption. When it came to the intellectual argument, the case centred on the efficiency of markets. Putting impediments in the way of free movement of finance – exchange controls, quantitative limits on credit growth, mortgage rationing – meant capital was being misallocated. Removing restrictions would mean that capital would go to where it could be most efficiently used. There was some truth in this argument, since the financial system that existed, certainly in the UK, at the end of the 1970s was riddled with restrictive commercial practices and discouraged innovation.

A simpler explanation of the need for change was made to consumers: removing capital controls would make credit easier and cheaper to obtain. Queueing for mortgages was unpopular, conjuring up images of rationing during the Second World War and the austerity era that followed it. A more liberal approach to credit also chimed with the post-1960s mood of personal freedom, although it did sit oddly with the Victorian values of thrift and self-restraint that Mrs Thatcher also promulgated. There was a ready-made demand for higher borrowing, since one of the more popular measures of Thatcher's first term had been selling council homes to tenants at discount prices. Financial deregulation – it could be argued – was the logical next step to this process, providing those on low incomes or living on relatively tight budgets to get their foot on the housing ladder. The argument that financial deregulation was really a giant leap forward for democracy is still regularly deployed. Extending mortgages to those without regular incomes or savings in the United States was not about a bunch of financial sharks preying on the weak and vulnerable. Instead, it was an attempt to spread home ownership to those at the bottom of the pile; to Afro-Americans, native Americans, Latinos, poor whites. This was not about banks picking up fat commissions for all sorts of live-now, pay-later loans to people who really could not afford them; it was proof that the American dream was alive and well.

Perhaps unsurprisingly, Alan Greenspan was keen to promote this version of events in his memoirs:

Since 1994, the proportion of American householders who became home-owners had accelerated. By 2006, nearly 69 per cent of households owned their own home, up from 64 per cent in 1994 and 44 per cent in 1940. The gains were especially dramatic among Hispanics and blacks, as increasing affluence as well as government encouragement of subprime mortgage programs enabled many members of minority groups to become first-time home buyers. This expansion of ownership gave more people a stake in the future and boded well for the cohesion of the nation, I thought. (The Age of Turbulence; Penguin; 2007)

Faced with this combination of political will, financial sector muscle and consumer demand, resistance to reform was easily defeated and change was swift. Within a decade of Mrs Thatcher's abolition of foreign exchange controls – again, sold to the public as allowing them to take more currency out of the country on their foreign holidays rather than as the green light for the City and Wall Street to move capital around the world unhindered – there were no more mortgage queues, building societies no longer had to rely on savings from individual depositors and foreign banks and investment houses controlled much of the City of London. Many building societies ceased to be owned by their customers, changing themselves into publicly quoted banks where managers ceased to be figures of chilly probity and instead became salesman for debt. Whereas an invitation to visit the bank manager at the end of the 1970s was the grown-up version of a summons to the headmaster's study, a decade later the job of the bank manager was to entice, encourage and cajole customers into taking out loans. The new mood was aptly summed up by a billboard advertisement for the Halifax, Britain's biggest mortgage lender and one of the building societies that had demutualised. Under a photograph of the Taj Mahal, the bank made it clear that it was now perfectly acceptable to take out an unsecured loan for a holiday. The slogan was: 'Take your girlfriend out for a curry'.

This was the heyday of American credit management guru Abe WalkingBear Sanchez, a big draw at corporate conferences. His message to companies was simple: 'Is all bad debt bad? No.' For firms with a high level of fixed costs, whether people or machinery, he argued, it makes sense to sign up riskier borrowers because even with their naturally higher rate of default, those that do pay will have generated juicier profits from unused capacity in the firm. 'Learn how to control bad debt, not run scared of it.'

This assumes that the level of default among the new, riskier customers can be predicted and managed – history suggests this is far from always being the case. To be fair, Mr Sanchez made clear in his presentations the need for active management of debts, but his overall message was that old notions of business credit were old hat: 'Many companies still operate their credit departments as they did in the 1950s. Times have moved on . . . Credit should be no exception. It is no longer a privilege. It is a way of securing profitable sales that would otherwise be lost.' (All taken from Mr Sanchez's contribution to the report 'Corporate Wizardry; turning credit into cash', published by credit insurer Atradius, February 2004.)

There were some, of course, who questioned the wisdom of these changes, particularly since the borrowing free-for-all that inevitably followed financial deregulation led to the excesses of the late 1980s, when a colossal boom in house prices was only ended with punitive increases in interest rates that led to record numbers of homes being repossessed. Having allowed the beast out of the cage, policy makers could no longer fall back on the controls they had once used to regulate credit; they had only the blunt instrument of interest rates. Writing in the late 1990s (*Debt and Delusion;* Allen Lane; The Penguin Press; 1999), Peter Warburton said:

The negative aspects (of deregulation) include the commitment of extra financial capital to lending activities (which presumes a rapid expansion in personal and corporate borrowing), and the likelihood that bank and non-bank diversification into unfamiliar business areas will bring an increased incidence of failure. While central banks cannot be held responsible for the enthusiasm with which western governments have embraced financial deregulation, they must surely have recognised that the task of monitoring a de-regulated credit system would become far more difficult.

Apparently not.

Mr Warburton's remarks look eerily prescient from the perspective of 2008. But for more than two decades, the risks inherent in the 'new environment' were either blithely ignored by the New Olympians, dismissed as a small price to pay for a more efficient global economy or simply swept under the carpet.

There were good reasons for this, not least that the policies underpinning the Goldilocks economy allowed the New

Olympians to grab a bigger share of the porridge for themselves. The history of the past three decades is of a profound
change in the balance of power, with capital gaining a bigger
share of the proceeds of growth at the expense of labour; of
labour's diminished share increasingly captured by those on
the highest incomes at the expense of the unskilled; of management increasing its control in the workplace at the expense
of trade unions; and finance replacing manufacturing as the
hub of Western economies. In his book on the post-war history
of the global economy (*Capitalism Unleashed;* Oxford; 2006),
Andrew Glyn, who died early in 2008, notes that in the early
1970s it looked, as far as the British variant of capitalism was
concerned, that 'this time the wolf is really at the door' but
that the response was a ferocious struggle to combat the
strengthening of labour and the squeeze on profits in the
Golden Age.

*We now know that the outcome of this struggle was the radical weakening
of the labour movement, macroeconomic stabilisation and domination of
free market ideas. It was the comprehensive victory of capital in the struggle
with labour – not just in developed western countries but in those parts of
the world formerly under communist rule – that fostered the belief that
mankind had reached 'the end of history'.*

This was a world that had initial appeal to wage earners
and salaried staff who were not trade unionists, many of whom
had been repelled by the labour militancy of the 1960s and
1970s. As time went on, however, it became clear that every
strata of Western society bar the New Olympians had something to fear, even something to lose, from the new order.
There was the risk that the burgeoning, unfettered and ever-
more complex financial system would blow up; there was the
threat not just to blue-collar but also to white-collar jobs;
and there was the mounting pressure on welfare states (from
which the middle classes had always gained as much as low-
income workers).

It also became clear to those in the leading developing

countries that in times of trouble, the New Olympians would ensure – partly through the brute force power of capital flight and partly through the agency of the IMF – that it would be poor people in poor countries that bore the heaviest brunt of the 'adjustment' and not the Wall Street banks that had lent them money to finance unsustainable booms. Eventually, it became clear – even to some of the New Olympians themselves – that the unshackling of the financial markets had sent a Frankenstein's monster rampaging around the globe. Mervyn King, the governor of the Bank of England, argued that the message from the Latin American debt crisis of 1982, the Mexican peso crisis of 1994–1995 and the Asian financial crisis of 1997–1998 was that the West would always engineer a bail-out for Goldman Sachs, Morgan Stanley and Citigroup, even if it meant austerity packages for Thailand and Indonesia that had a real impact – death – on those deprived of life-saving drugs as a result of health cutbacks. Mr King was not alone in his criticism. Joseph Stiglitz, eased out of his job as chief economist of the World Bank by the then US Treasury Secretary Larry Summers for being too critical of the Washington consensus, took his revenge in a hatchet job on the IMF in the *New Republic*, calling those at the Fund responsible for the policies imposed on poor countries in 1997–1998 third-class brains from first-class universities. 'These economists frequently lack extensive knowledge in the country; they are more likely to have firsthand knowledge of its five-star hotels than of the villages that dot the countryside,' Professor Stiglitz noted, adding that the Fund likes to go about its business in the shadows. 'In theory, the Fund supports democratic institutions in the nations it assits, in practice, it undermines the democratic process by imposing policies' ('What I saw at the Devaluation'; *New Republic*; April 2000).

The Stiglitz article was a seminal work. Published at precisely the time the dotcom boom of the late 1990s was in its final, frenetic stages, the piece not only castigated the unholy troika of Wall Street, the US Treasury and the IMF for imposing recessionary policies on Asian countries, but also highlighted the *coup d'état* mounted by the New Olympians.

Since the end of the Cold War tremendous power has flowed to the people entrusted to bring the gospel of the market to the far corners of the globe. These economists, bureaucrats and officials act in the name of the United States and the other advanced industrial countries, and yet they speak a language that few average citizens understand and that few policymakers bother to translate. Economic policy is today the most important part of America's interaction with the rest of the world. And yet the culture of international economic policy in the world's most powerful democracy is not democratic.

The New Olympians saw Professor Stiglitz's attack as an act of treachery. He was, after all, one of them; a former economic adviser to Bill Clinton before moving to the World Bank. New Olympians were supposed to stick together, and by going public with his critique Professor Stiglitz had betrayed his own class. It would, however, take more than half a decade for Americans to wake up to the fact that Professor Stiglitz had been right and that there were profound implications for themselves from the triumph of the New Olympians. In the meantime, the lessons of 1997 and 1998 were immediately digested by millions of poor people in east and south-east Asia. One lesson was that the nations that had been at best agnostic about the gospel of financial market deregulation preached by the New Olympians – China and India – had avoided the recession that swept across the region. A second was that Malaysia, which imposed strict curbs on captial movements during the summer of 1997, saw its economy suffer far less grievously than Thailand, which followed the policies demanded by the Fund to the letter. A third lesson was that the fast-growing nations of Asia should never again be at the mercy of the Washington consensus. And when the Washington consensus strangled at birth an attempt by Asian countries to develop their own Asian Monetary Fund to rival the IMF, the region used its fast-growing export industries to build up a war chest of foreign exchange reserves big enough to burn the fingers of speculators and so make the Fund redundant.

Asian countries had, up until the crisis of 1997, been hefty borrowers on the world's capital markets. After 1997, that borrowing became taboo and Asian countries became lenders instead. As Brian Reading of Lombard Street Research put it: 'They have no wish to repeat the wrenching 1997–8 recessions that followed the switch from currency inflows to outflows.' Instead, they watched as the US itself became a debtor nation, with all the vulnerability that entailed to a sudden flight of capital.

What happened was this. Asian countries had massive trade surpluses, which meant that they were saving – in the parlance of the economics profession – more than they invested. They could have expanded domestic spending to soak up the glut of savings, but that would have deprived them of the funds to build up their reserves. Instead, they allowed America and – to a lesser extent – Britain to solve the problem for them by spending (investing) more than they produced (saved). The process had four stages. The first was that manufacturing was already being moved progressively to low-cost countries, leading to a hollowing-out of industry in the West, lowering potential productive capacity and leading to trade deficits. The second stage was that people in Western deficit countries were called upon to spend more than their incomes in order to prevent the savings glut in the East from tipping the world into recession. Central bankers like Alan Greenspan in the US and Lord George in the UK cut interest rates to stimulate spending, fearing that the alternative would be recession. Lord George admitted that this meant the UK economy was un-balanced but said unbalanced growth was better than no growth. Up to a point, Mr Greenspan and Lord George were right. At a global level, savings and investment have to balance each other out, so if the East was saving more (building up current account surpluses) the West had to spend more than it was saving (run current account deficits) or risk a global recession caused by a lack of demand for the goods being supplied by the world economy.

The third stage was the recycling of the Asian current account surpluses into the West, pushing up asset prices – shares, bonds and property – and making people in deficit countries feel wealthier. The fourth and final stage was that the flows of capital tended to find their way to countries with sophisticated financial systems, who by chance also happened to be those countries running the biggest current account deficits. For the New Olympians this seemed to be a case of porridge all round. The part of the economy where they were most heavily concentrated – the financial sector – was thriving. The flow of capital from the East pushed up asset prices, and they held more lucrative assets than anybody else. And their income and wealth went further than it did before because goods from the East were not only cheap but made cheaper still because all the hot money flooding in to London and New York pushed up the value of the pound and the dollar, making imports even less expensive (but, of course, making life even more difficult for those exporting manufactured goods and services).

This, then, was the Goldilocks economy. Strictly speaking, it was not a Goldilocks economy at all, since half the bowl of porridge was too hot and the other half was too cold, but for many years that did not seem to matter. Low inflation meant low interest rates, which in turn meant high levels of consumption and increases in asset values, which in turn brought a new pulse of hot money into Western economies. But if it all looked too good to be true, that is because it most certainly was.

The Asian crisis of 1997 was followed a year later by the Russian debt default and the collapse of the New York-based hedge fund Long Term Capital Management, run by two Nobel Prize-winning economists who claimed to have found the financial market equivalent of a perpetual motion machine. In September 1998, it emerged that Myron Scholes and Robert Merton (the two aforementioned Nobel Prize winners) might have been somewhat hubristic with their fool-proof plan for valuing options when LTCM went bust and threatened to bring a host of the top names on Wall Street and the City down with it. Mr Greenspan cut interest rates to boost confidence and the markets picked up again. Goldilocks slept on.

DANCING WITH BEARS: THE END OF THE PARTY

It took time, however, for the arrival of the three bears to disrupt the slumber of our heroine. Baby Bear arrived in the shape of rising commodity prices. At the end of the 1990s, oil prices were below $10 a barrel and were still hovering just above $20 a barrel when George Bush and Tony Blair were planning to invade Iraq in the early months of 2003. As Alan Greenspan admitted in 2007, once he had retired from the Federal Reserve, the war against Saddam Hussein was linked to the fact that Iraq's reserves are currently second only to those of Saudi Arabia. But if the aim was to provide America with cheap and secure supplies of crude oil from the Middle East, the war was a spectacular failure. The subsequent war had a more prolonged impact on Iraq's oil production than expected, and also helped to create a risk of terrorist attacks on oil installations in the region, thus pushing up prices. An even bigger factor in quadrupling the cost of crude oil to a record level in the early months of 2008 was the heavy demand for oil – and other commodities – from China, India and other rapidly industrialising Asian countries. Oil prices rose above $103 a barrel in the February, despite signs of recession in the US, comfortably the highest ever in nominal terms but also breaking the previous inflation-adjusted peak reached during the outbreak of the Iran–Iraq war in 1980. Ominously, bullion prices were also rising, traditionally a sign of trouble ahead as investors sought the fabled protection against inflation offered by precious metal. By the end of March 2008, gold had topped $1,000 a troy ounce, a 28-year high. Inflationary pressures had started to reappear back in 2004 and built up a head of steam in the years that followed, but Goldilocks had slept on.

Mother Bear arrived in the shape of booming real estate prices. We shall have more to say about this in later chapters, but suffice it to say here that the cuts in interest rates sanctioned by the Fed and the Bank of England led to property prices rising rapidly in both the United States and the UK. In America, Mr Greenspan's determination to make the recession that followed the collapse of the dotcom bubble a short lived one resulted in interest rates being cut to 1 per cent – a level not seen since the late 1950s – and thus ensured that the solution to one popped bubble was to inflate another one. By the time the US was experiencing the most pronounced real estate bubble in its history, even the New Olympians started to get concerned, and Mr Greenspan proceeded to raise interest rates by a quarter point at 17 successive meetings of the Fed's Open Market Committee. The ratcheting up of borrowing costs made mortgages less affordable, speculation riskier and consumers less happy about borrowing money against the value of their homes. Mother Bear roared but Goldilocks slept on.

The failure of central banks – and in particular, the Federal Reserve in the United States – to comprehend that the Goldilocks economy might be polluted with contaminated ingredients was all the more surprising given that the umbrella body for central banks, the Bank for International Settlements, was well aware of the risks that were involved. Bill White, chief economist at the BIS, could hardly have been blunter. While noting the benefits of reducing inflation from its previous high levels, White added: 'At the same time, history also teaches that the stability of consumer prices might not be sufficient to ensure macroeconomic stability. Past experience is replete with examples of major economic and financial crises that were not preceded by inflationary pressures.' The lesson from history that seemed to concern White was the period from 1929 to

1932, when a financial and economic crisis was spawned by an era characterised by low inflation but massive speculation and excessive debt. 'We are increasingly distant from the highly regulated period following the Great Depression and the Second World War, when our current policy frameworks were developed. Indeed, the structural landscape looks more and more like that seen in in the 1920s and the decades prior to World War 1. It would not seem implausible, in the light of this underlying change, that our policy frameworks might also need revision' (William White; *Is Price Stability enough?*; BIS working paper no. 205; April 2006).

Less than six months later the BIS issued a fresh warning. A paper written by Claudio Borio (*Monetary and prudential policies at a crossroads? New challenges in the new century*; BIS working paper no. 216; September 2006) noted that 'the establishment of credible anti-inflation monetary policies and (real-side) globalisation have resulted in subtle but profound changes in the dynamics of the economy and in the challenges faced by policymakers. In the new environment which has gradually been taking shape, the main "structural" risk may not be so much runaway inflation. Rather, it may be the damage caused by the unwinding of financial imbalances that occasionally build up over the longer expansion phases of the economy, typically spanning more than one higher-frequency business cycle. Depending on its intensity, the unwinding can lead to economic weakness, unwelcome disinflation and possibly financial strains.'

The BIS, apparently concerned that Goldilocks was not just sleeping but had ingested a mind-bending drug, decided that it was time to be even more blunt. In its annual report of June 2007, it described the four main features of the Goldilocks economy: unusually high levels of real growth; unusually low levels of inflation; uncharacteristically low real interest rates and risk premiums for buying what would once have been considered less safe assets; and the fact that record trade imbalances had so far been easily financed with exchange rates remaining quite stable. 'In isolation, each of these outcomes might be welcomed without further reflection. However, the combination of developments is so extraordinary that it must raise questions about the source and, closely related, the sustain-ablilty of all this good fortune.'

This was the equivalent of the BIS stooping down to bellow: 'Wake up, Goldilocks! We've warned you time and again you stupid girl, but the three bears are now plodding up the garden path.'

That was June 24 2007. Just over two weeks later, as we saw earlier, Chuck Prince, the chairman and chief executive of Citigroup, the world's biggest bank, made it clear that he thought the BIS was being a bit of a drama queen. 'When the music stops, in terms of liquidity, things will be complicated. But as long as the music is playing, you've got to get up and dance. We're still dancing.'

It was at this point that Father Bear arrived home. He came in the shape of a crisis in the financial system itself. This was the moment when the palace on Olympus found itself under the sort of attack its inhabitants had always claimed was impossible. Low inflation and low interest rates had bred complacency, the notion that the good times were perman-ent rather than cyclical and that therefore what were once risky bets were now sure-fire successes. Pension funds and other institutional investors avidly lapped up this message; with people living longer and annuity rates falling because of lower interest rates they were looking for punts that offered higher returns than they could expect on government bonds. Globalised financial markets duly obliged them with an array of product lines such as the yen 'carry trade', which allowed speculators to borrow money in Japan, where interest rates were virtually zero, and reinvest it in jurisdictions, such as New Zealand and the UK, where interest rates were higher. The impact of this, of course, was to push up the value of the New Zealand dollar and sterling, making exports from those countries still pricier and making the global imbalances still worse. A second product line involved derivatives based on mortgages granted to borrowers with less than marvel-lous track records in the US. We shall look at the travails of subprime lenders in the US in a later chapter. Suffice it to say here, though, that these derivatives were as toxic as the products associated with every get-rich-quick scheme dating back to Dutch tulips and the South Sea bubble. Within a month of Mr Prince putting on his dancing shoes, Father Bear roared and Goldilocks finally woke up.

The rest of this book will be devoted to seeing whether our fairy story has a happy ending. Some say that Goldilocks was lucky and escaped in the nick of time. Others say that a five-year-old girl, lost in a deep and impenetrable wood, would be no match for three ferocious bears, who were desperately cross at having no breakfast on the table when they returned home so ate Goldilocks instead. If it helps, Mr Prince was fired three months later. Citigroup had stopped dancing. Its executives were too busy counting their losses on subprime mortgages.

5

The Rainy Season:
Rising damp in Middle Britain

There are many more people today who could ask with George Orwell: 'I have a middle class education and a working class income – what class am I?'
  – Conservative Central Office; *The Right Approach;* 1976

Corporate greed is destroying the middle class, corporate greed is destroying our children's future.
  – John Edwards, US presidential candidate, speaking at Iowa State University; January 1 2008 (reported in the *Daily Telegraph;* January 3 2008)

You're not at the bottom yet. There is a lot further you can fall.
  – Martin Amis; *Success;* Jonathan Cape; 1978

The British summer of 2007 was a washout, literally so for people in Gloucestershire and Herefordshire, who suffered severe flooding. Autumn weather alternated between further rainfall and plunging temperatures. The glorious summer days and fiery autumn colours in 2005 and 2006 seemed a fond memory.

Poor weather was matched by growing unease in the British

middle class as 2007 turned into 2008. On every front, its living standards, status and career prospects were threatened, along with such objects of affection as the value of its homes and its children's education.

Across the broad centre of British society, that union of the traditional professional middle class and the much wider group of 'aspirant', or 'striving' households – the union best described, in short, as Middle Britain – was facing the stark possibility that 15 or more years of prosperity were drawing to a close. Worse, its members could have been forgiven for a sneaking feeling that they had been 'had' and were now themselves the target of the sort of asset stripping that had been visited on the nation's factory workers, on those employed in 'primary' industries such as farming, fishing, mining and quarrying and on the nation's small shopkeepers, thousands of whom had been driven out of business by supermarkets.

Indeed, on the subject of supermarkets, the nation's lawyers would have learned on June 3 that they had a new competitor:

Tesco, the UK's largest retailer, is plotting to take on high street solicitors by launching a property conveyancing service . . . The move . . . follows the recent liberalisation of the £20 billion legal market allowing companies such as supermarkets to offer legal services to the public . . . Tesco has approached a number of different conveyancing providers to develop a 'white label' service for it. The move is likely to see a call centre-type operation offering shoppers a low-cost, computerised service. (Sunday Telegraph)

One obvious point to suggest itself from this short extract from a news report is that anyone referring to 'the £20 billion legal market' (and we would blame here official sources rather than the newspaper) has a conception of the law and of legal advice that would have been incomprehensible to generations of distinguished jurists. A more obscure point, to those of a certain generation, is the 180-degree redefinition of the phrase 'white label'. Originally used to refer to very rare (thus valuable) records unavailable to the music-buying public and pressed only for distribution to radio stations and disc jockeys, it now describes any product supplied by mass manufacturers to retailers who then slap their own name on it.

But lest anyone comfort themselves with the thought that property conveyancing is a pretty standardised service, and that Tesco's incursion into the market was nothing about which to get excited, beware. The Labour government's 'liberalisation' of the 'legal market', due to take full effect by 2011, aimed to allow all legal advice, not merely conveyancing, to be dispensed from booths in supermarkets. Not for nothing were the 'reforms' dubbed 'Tesco law'.

As with the City of London's 'Big Bang' changes in 1986, 'Tesco law' allowed firms of solicitors to seek outside investment and even to have their shares listed on a stock market. This parallel was made explicit in an authoritative news report on November 9, headed 'Law firms gear up for their own Big Bang':

Observers inside and outside the profession say the very act of selling out would destroy the value of the business, as young lawyers who had been aiming to become partners would immediately leave and go into a better paid industry such as banking. Young lawyers would stay only if the new owners raised pay sharply so that salaries and bonuses were competitive with those at leading investment banks. (Financial Times)

This, of course, is precisely what happened to the stockbroking and stock-jobbing professions after Big Bang. Their partners sold out for huge sums and the firms were absorbed into anonymous, all-purpose 'investment banks'. With the checks and balances of the partnership system replaced by bonus-driven salary packages, the way was clear for 'rogue traders', most famously Nick Leeson, whose reckless gambles brought historic Barings Bank to its knees. Furthermore, deregulation in the City led to the American takeover of many British financial services businesses, while the demutualisation, parallel to the shake-up in the City, of many of Britian's building societies broke the link between local savings and local mortgages. While the societies had not been charitable enterprises, they knew their customers, avoided the impersonal excesses seen at Northern Rock and provided solid middle-class careers for their employees, as opposed to call-centre jobs.

With this sort of roaring success to its credit, no wonder the Big Bang model was now being replicated in the legal profession.

Nor was the law the only middle-class profession to face the asset strippers in 2007. In early November, the Heart of Birmingham Primary Care Trust announced plans to franchise general practitioners' surgeries to private firms. These firms would win National Health Service contracts from the trust to provide services to patients. According to the trust, Asda and (it's that shop again!) Tesco had expressed an interest, as had Sir Richard Branson's Virgin group. According to one news report:

[T]he trust said the non-health organisations . . . were confident they can replicate the best aspects of the GP partnership's relationship with its patients.

They do this with their customers on a daily basis.

But the British Medical Association slammed the proposal. Dr Robert Morley, who sits on the GP Committee, said the 'continuity of care' for patients would be disrupted if the private firms took over GPs' surgeries. Some smaller practices would also be forced out of business.

He said: 'Small GP surgeries are not going to be able to compete with the retail giants.' (Sun; 'Tesco "to run doc surgery"', November 9 2007)

As with the above-mentioned 'reforms' to the legal profession, there is little sign that the Heart of Birmingham Primary Care Trust had the first glimmering of the real nature of the 'business' with which it was dealing.

By the early weeks of 2008, the government was in a confrontation with family doctors over extended opening hours for surgeries. From the doctors' ranks came murmurings that this was meely a dummy run for a much bigger battle, started by ministers, to force doctors into anonymous 'polyclinics' run by private companies. On January 29 2008, London's *Evening Standard* reported:

A private American health firm has won control of three GP surgeries in London. The deal with United Health Europe opens the way to the privatisation of family doctors' practices. It comes after a Government push to put primary care into corporate hands.

'Doctors have warned that patients could suffer as conglomerates offer "cut price deals to win contracts".'

If that sounded an extraordinary sell-out by a supposedly Labour government, it was of a piece with the news on January 28 2008 that commercial companies were for the first time to be allowed to award nationally recognised qualifications based on their own work-place training schemes. In a parody-defying move, the government announced that the first three accredited schemes would be run by the burger chain McDonald's, the airline Flybe and the train track oper ator Network Rail.

The *Guardian* that day reported: 'Staff at McDonald's will gain the equivalent of A-levels in running burger restaurants after the fast-food giant won Government approval to become an exam board.'

Elsewhere in those long, rainy 18 months, plans to slash the Post Office network were being finalised. Of the 14,000-strong branch network, 2,500 were to close, leaving customers and communities stranded. Commentator Philip Johnston wrote:

Their locations read like a gazetteer of Middle England: Hawkhurst, Bidborough and Rodmersham Green in Kent; Long Eaton, Eggington and Eastwood in the East Midlands; South Somercotes, Bennetthorpe and New Hexthorpe in Lincolnshire and Yorkshire. They are among the first 180 or so post office branches to be earmarked for closure as part of an act of community vandalism that almost beggars belief. We knew it was coming . . . But now that it has started, it is still hard to believe that, as a country, we are preparing to rip the hearts out of many of our small towns and villages. (Daily Telegraph; October 8 2007)

For generations, the job of sub-postmaster and sub-postmistress had been part of the very backbone of middle-class respectability. Yet despite the terrible sadness of the destruction now being wreaked on the Royal Mail, the way it came about is instructive. The Conservative government of the early 1990s announced plans to privatise the Post Office, but backed down in the face of enormous public protest. Undaunted, British ministers and bureaucrats merely put the country's name to a European Union scheme to liberalise all EU postal services, which would have much the same effect without too much in the way of pesky public debate. When the branch closure programme – coupled with the abolition of second deliveries – evoked protest, the Royal Mail and the government were able to claim they had no choice, as the service had to be made leaner and fitter in order to compete with both private delivery organisations and foreign post offices.

Lawyers, GPs, sub-postmasters . . . like bewildered characters in a superior television thriller, all seemed destined by some shadowy authority for punishment for crimes the nature of which was never really spelled out. Nor were they alone. The bank manager, in times gone by a pillar of the community (for once, that overused phrase has some merit), had virtually disappeared in his old form. Lending decisions had been almost entirely centralised, using complex computer risk-assessment systems. Given the only real money to be made from overdrafts, mortgages and consumer credit relates to borderline cases (the bad risks are easily rejected and the good ones will attract the best terms, i.e. the least profitable terms from a bank's point of view), it was deemed best to let software make these fine judgements among these borderline cases.

Managers and staff ought to concentrate on selling financial products – assurance, insurance, savings, investments and the like.

Journalism, meanwhile, was a trade allegedly now in

competition with its own customers. The *Business* magazine, in its edition of July 21, carried an article on the subject of 'user-generated content', the phenomenon whereby readers, listeners and viewers employ camera-phones and other digital devices to supply 'citizen journalism' to publications, radio stations and television channels. You could tell this was an article about user-generated content because it was illustrated by a photograph of a young woman squirting water at the camera while pulling a silly face, such antics being something of a theme in the world of user-generated content. Alongside the hope that customers would fill media space was the already existing use of public relations companies to provide large quantities of uncontroversial material, presumably helpful to their clients. Needles to say, the élite preferred the expensive but scrupulously accurate services of Bloomberg, Reuters, the *Financial Times*, the *Wall Street Journal* and other sources.

Beyond journalism, the traditionally grander world of book authorship saw, on November 19 2007, the launch of the oddly named Kindle, an electronic book reader from the Amazon on-line bookselling group. Touted as book publishing's answer to the iPod music player, the Kindle at least raised the prospect, however remote, for authors and publishers of the same sort of large-scale consumer piracy that was wreaking such havoc with recorded music.

If the unrestrained free market – or indeed black market, in the case of illegal copying of intellectual property – threatened the status and earnings of the middle class on one flank, the activities of government mandarins posed quite a different threat on another.

Next in the affections of the denizens of Middle Britain to the value of their homes (and often linked intimately with that value) has been their children's education. Since the late 1980s, the official emphasis has been on parental choice within the state system. Labour fought the three elections of 1997, 2001 and 2005 on this platform. By 2007, however, it was becoming clear that, in the wonderful world of public education, 'choice' was not meant to involve actually choosing anything. Indeed, making effective school choices was thought to be vaguely reprehensible:

Schools should select pupils by lottery to prevent middle-class parents monopolising the best comprehensives, an official watchdog said yesterday. Dr Philip Hunter, the admissions regulator, said the policy should be used even if 'deeply unpopular with groups of articulate parents'.

A new admissions code was introduced this year to prevent the wealthy dominating the best schools by buying homes inside a catchment area. (Daily Telegraph; November 2 2007)

The Department for Children, Schools and Families – Prime Minister Gordon Brown's twee new name for the Department for Education and Skills – broadly agreed with Dr Hunter. That in doing so it was tacitly admitting that parents, rich and poor, would try to avoid like the plague a large number of the schools for which it was directly responsible would not be lost on Dr Hunter's 'articulate parents' – or even, perhaps, on the inarticulate ones.

At this point, the neutral observer may find his sympathies starting to drift. Does not the school lottery affair highlight a problem with going to the defence of Middle Britain at this time? Is not the whole of this chapter so far merely a defence of semi-closed shop arrangements – in the law, medicine and other professions and vocations and in the distribution of places at good schools – that may be agreeable to those on the inside but less so to those who are not? After all, if Tesco can provide cheap legal advice from a corner booth and medical services in a similar (albeit, one would hope, rather more private) location, what is so wrong with that?

We would argue on four grounds that there is likely to be a great deal wrong with it. First, from the customers' point of view there is little – indeed, no – reason to believe that the public, as a whole, will enjoy better or cheaper professional services from corporate providers than they do from local partnerships. Some of these providers will doubtless seek to cherry-pick the best customers, as (quite legitimately) did the pioneering telephone insurance service Direct Line and its banking equivalent First Direct. Those customers will receive favourable offers. The others will not, being offered instead standardised 'quickie' services. In law and medicine, in particular, where personal advice and consultation are so vital to the provision of the service, this could prove a very bad deal indeed.

Second, the transformation of independent professionals, effectively self-employed, into salaried corporate employees will be bad for everybody. It will rob ordinary people of sources of confidential service and bloat further the power of large corporations. Professionals provide an important counterweight to other forms of power, and can assert their independence in ways that corporate employees are not able to match. *Pro bono* work is different in kind from PR-driven 'corporate social responsibility'.

Third, an independent professional class has value beyond its utility as a source of advice and as a bulwark against the power of companies and the state. It provides a continuum within which aspirations can be satisfied while delivering a public service. If social tranquillity matters more than shareholder value (and we believe very strongly that it does), then the independent professional class should be shielded from corporate and other depredations, not exposed to them, as they have been by government 'reforms'.

At present, the professions offer an arena where discipline and hard work are not only rewarded with a decent salary. They offer autonomy and public recognition and gratitude. If professionals become corporate employees, albeit well-paid ones, they will lose that claim to public trust.

Fourth, as we have said before, if these dumbed-down, commoditised, supposedly cheap, corporately owned services are so good, why do we rarely hear of members of the wealthy élite using them? Why do they prefer to stick with the traditional one-to-one relationship with doctors or solicitors? The reply could be that they can afford it, but so, at present,

can most people, thanks to the ways in which the National
Health Service and the legal profession are structured. The
local GP's surgery may be down at heel compared to the
Harley Street consulting room, but the two are fundamentally the same *thing*.

Of course, our reference to school lotteries does not, on
the face of it, fit into our remarks here, concerning as it does
the middle class solely as a user of one particular type of
public servce: state education. But the neat symmetry of the
whole affair is a near-perfect illustration of the theme of this
chapter, that Middle Britain has been 'had'. For ten years, the
government supported the whole notion of parental choice
while suggesting it would become increasingly irrelevant as
all schools were steadily improved. With the lottery, the illusion is ended – the government opposes the whole notion of
parental choice precisely because it exposes the fact that there
has been no such improvement.

Middle Britain has been conned, well and truly. Enlisted
on the side of the financial interests to help defeat organised
labour, it had been promised – as are all footsoldiers –
generous booty once the battle was won, and a secure and
prosperous future. Now that future is crumbling at the edges.
In a prescient article in the autumn 2007 newsletter of Essex
University's Institute for Social and Economic Research, Ray
Pahl, David Rose and Liz Spencer noted that, at the time of
writing: 'There is little evidence of serious resentment of the
rich when people make social comparisons . . . As long as
others have worked hard for their success and do not become
arrogant or disdainful of their old friends, it is a case of "good
luck to them".'

But the authors end on a warning note: 'Such a conclusion
may be reassuring to politicians anxious to co-opt the "middle
mass" into managerialist policies. But it might be unwise to
be too complacent. People in the middle mass may consume
individually and have similar lifestyle aspirations, but they are
collectively and seriously in debt. Capitalism could return to
bite' *(Inequality: who cares?)*.

It could indeed – and by 2008 was beginning to do so. But then, if we assume the co-option of the 'middle mass' was a confidence trick, it is necessary to examine the structure of this particular fraud.

BUILDING MIDDLE BRITAIN: THATCHER, MAJOR, BLAIR, BROWN

There is a fairly conventional narrative as to the construction of today's prosperous Middle British majority. You can read it in newspaper and news magazine think-pieces, catch it on television or radio whenever one of those three-part series about the way we live now is being aired or you can read it in chunky books of the type that get serialised in the press.

Here it is, in a nutshell. Thirty years ago, large parts of our social infrastructure were not working: housing, the nationalised industries, the public utilities. Margaret Thatcher broke them into small pieces and sold them to the people who had allegedly owned them all along – the British public. In the case of council houses, this was a direct sale of the asset concerned. In other cases, the sale was of shares in the organisation in question. Large numbers of people thought this could not work and that the whole idea was potty. They were to be proved wrong. Whatever one's original position on this question, whatever one's current position on the political spectrum, it has to be admitted that, broadly speaking, three great benefits have flowed from this social revolution.

First, the ranks of what may loosely be described as the middle class (what we in this book call Middle Britain) have been greatly swelled, by the simple fact of the extension of the ownership of assets to millions more people. Second, some of the sold-off entities were previously state monopolies, a status denied them in the private sector. This is excellent news for Middle Britain, because it now has a choice of products and suppliers where previously there was none. To take one small example, until 1980 the only permitted supplier of telephone answering machines was the state-owned British Telecom. Third, asset ownership and the newly competitive nature of the privatised industries gave people a new self-respect and self-reliance; no longer dependent on council housing officials, surly telephone engineers, tardy British Gas employees or similar personnel, they could move house, switch their business to other suppliers and generally behave with the sort of blithe disregard for the 'jobsworth' fraternity that had previously been the prerogative of only the chilliest of upper-middle-class housewives.

On this reckoning, the real story of the last quarter-century has been the emergence not of the New Olympians of whom we write, whether in finance and banking or in central banks and governmental and quasi governmental organisations, but this 'New Yeomanry' of independent, resourceful and property-owning Middle Britons. True believers in this revived, expanded and resilient new middle class included some of the brightest rising stars of the British Conservative Party in the 1980s, some from instinct and experience, such as Norman Tebbit, formerly a member of one of the smarter professional trade unions, the British Air Line Pilots Association, some from intellectual conviction, such as John Redwood.

Of course, from the start, three decades ago, this new Middle Britain was defined to a considerable extent in contrast to the losers in the new economic order. 'So long as success and ability are rewarded – as they must be if we are not all to become paupers – there will be classes, as there are even in Soviet Russia. And how can it be in the general interest to encourage envy and hatred of ability and success?' (Conservative Central Office; *The Right Approach;* 1976)

Or, put rather differently:

One of the most obvious achievements of western society since the Second World War has been its ability to eliminate poverty; and its failure to do so. The survival of poverty has been a project second only in importance to the conservation of wealth by the rich . . . The persistence of poverty in spite of the capacity for enormous material advances shows that the poor are there for reasons that have nothing to do with scarcity of resources (in any way that scarcity could be interpreted by common sense) but everything to do with ideology.

The very idea of sufficiency is one which capitalism cannot acknowledge. The possibility that a society could produce enough to ensure the well-being and comfort of all its people is a terible blasphemy against the deep purposes of capitalism. The drive for more, for accumulation, for increase, the generation of wealth, imply dearth, wants and loss elsewhere; and the unchanging symbiosis of rich and poor only reflects this simple equation.

(Jeremy Seabrook; Unemployment; *Quartet Books; 1982)*

Sometimes losers and winners could be divided within industrial groups, with a 'winner' group that could expect success in the new economic order being split from the hinterland of losers. Sometimes the 'winner' status related to higher levels of skills, as with the toolmakers in the breakaway United Craft Organisation at the British Leyland vehicle maker in the late 1970s. Sometimes it was merely that the prospects of the winners looked better than those of their fellows, as with the Nottinghamshire miners, who refused to join the miners' strike of 1984–1985. A variation on this was seen in the dispute centred on the News International newspaper printing plant at Wapping in East London, to which the company's four main titles – *The Times,* the *Sunday Times,* the *Sun* and the *News of the World* – decamped overnight in January 1986 leaving a striking print workforce of about 7,000 people picketing now-obsolete premises in central London. The strikers, members of the two print unions, were replaced with what amounted to a job lot of about 700 members of a third union with, traditionally, a limited presence in the industry, the electricians. These new 'printers' were to work longer hours for less money than their predecessors but were still to enjoy reasonably paid, reasonably secure work at a time when unemployment was still very high. In short, they were winners.

Furthermore, if the need for losers in the new economic paradigm is rarely mentioned, there is even less acknowledgement that this 'free market' model is also in need of enormous quanities of public money. Council house sales, for example, have left us with a bill for housing benefit of about £15 billion in 2006/2007, equivalent to more than 1 per cent of Gross Domestic Product (GDP), in part the price we pay for having sold all that social housing. Furthermore, such housing is having to be partly reinvented at some expense, with the government trying to provide lower-cost homes for 'key workers' in London and the south-east. Rail privatisation has involved governments paying about double the subsidy received during the British Rail era for a similar level of service. The savings 'products' that define Middle Britain (chiefly pension schemes and individual savings accounts) come complete with tax breaks. Many, perhaps most, of the privatised industries had to be stuffed like Strasbourg geese full of taxpayers' money to ensure the sale 'got away'; either that, or the sale had to be ludicrously under-priced, which is a subsidy by another name.

And when economic trouble threatened, free-market principles were rapidly abandoned. In April 1995, with many homes stuck in 'negative equity' (the mortgage was worth more than the resale value), John Redwood, then Welsh Secretary, wrote a memorandum to Prime Minister John Major proposing an expensive and complex package of tax reliefs to get the housing market moving again (reprinted in *Guilty Men* by Hywel Williams; Aurum Press; 1998).

On the other hand, one large chunk of the new socio-economic order was permanently attached to the public teat. As market forces started to disrupt the Gordon Brown 'economic miracle', there was one way of ensuring one's place in Middle Britain, which was to leave altogether both productive industry and those parts of the public sector providing a measurable service and shift instead to a class of public 'servants' whom we have mentioned before, the 'new functionaries' (what a less polite age would have called 'jacks in office' or, hyperbolically, 'Little Hitlers') charged with monitoring and changing people's lifestyles and 'attitudes', rather than with actually providing a recognisable service, in the manners of tens of thousands of doctors, nurses, police officers and others. It is to this group of winners in the New Olympian age that we now turn.

ROOM AT THE TOP: PUBLIC SERVICE, PRIVATE PROFIT

For both Labour and the Conservatives, the 1970s have become the equivalent of the Dark Ages. Even almost three decades after the event, the first whiff of industrial action in the public sector is the cue for Tory politicians to talk about a return to the 'Winter of Discontent'. For Labour, the 1970s represent the past the party is glad to have put behind it; a decade of strikes, spending cuts and the arrival of the International Monetary Fund to provide financial support to the Labour government at the end of 1976. As one senior civil servant put it (in conversation with the authors): 'The mood in Whitehall is different now. The 1970s were all about managing decline. Today, we expect the economy to do well and we expect to win things like the 2012 Olympics.'

Yet there is something of a paradox here. Britain was a much poorer country in the 1970s and suffered wild swings in the economy from boom to bust. The governments of Tony Blair and Gordon Brown, by contrast, have enjoyed a benign economic climate and, after a self-imposed moratorium on spending in the first two years after the 1997 election, have sanctioned a rapid increase in public expenditure. In the eight years between 1999–2000 and 2007–2008, public spending when adjusted for inflation rose from £407.8 billion to £570.5 billion, an increase of 29 per cent. The share of the economy accounted for by the state jumped by five percentage points (from 37 per cent to 42 per cent); the sort of increase normally associated with recessions, when the government seeks to use its own spending to compensate for weakness in the private sector. By no stretch of the imagination could the public sector in Britain be considered, by 2008, to be starved of cash; spending was pretty much in line with the average across the European Union.

Even so, the neighbourhood police station that had been open 24 hours a day seven days a week in the 'dark days' of the 1970s (the 1970s are always described as dark days) was now only open between 8am and 4pm and closed all day Monday. The local sub post office was now closing for good, the library was short of books, the weekly refuse collection was now fortnightly and the state of the roads akin to those in the poorest developing country.

Voters had supported the increase in spending; they had been unhappy at the shabby state of the public realm in 1997 and wanted to see extra investment in the services they needed and used. Understandably they wanted to know what had happened to all the money.

The government's answer was twofold. Firstly, it said the money had led to an improvement in services, which was true but only up to a point. Given the colossal increase in spending – particularly on health and education – it would have been miraculous had there not been some benefits to the public; the question was whether the improvement matched the scale of the investment. Sadly, it did not. In the National Health Service, for example, the Office for National Statistics said productivity had been falling; in education, there was no evidence that extra money had meant higher achievement. To use a sporting analogy, it was as if a philanthropic owner had signed the entire Brazilian soccer team to play for the team languishing at the bottom of the premiership, but instead of seeing it leap to the top of the table had watched it struggle in mid-table mediocrity. One think tank, Reform, said that instead of a planned irrigation, the extra billions pumped into the public sector had been like a flash flood, and that 'much of the spending has resulted in doing the same thing at an extra cost' (*A Lost Decade;* March 2008).

The government disputed this. Its argument was that, after the hard rations of the 18 years of Conservative rule, it would take time for the extra money to show up in higher productivity. Reforms of the public sector to make them more responsive to their users (or customers, as they were now known) would speed up this process.

While stretching the boundaries of plausibility, this explanation was a lot more convincing than the second reason for the economies made by ministers, namely that it had duty to make sure that precious resources were spent as wisely and efficiently as possible. If that meant temporary opening hours at police stations that might have only two callers a day, the closure of 'uneconomic' post offices and other reductions in the quality of service, then so be it.

This was undermined, to say the least, by the glaring examples of New Labour's non efficiency drive once big corporate and financial interests became involved. These included the £2 billion bail-out for the failed Underground maintenance contractor, Metronet; the more than three fold increase in the budget for Whitehall press officers; the doubling of the cost of the new IT system for the NHS from £6 billion to £12 billion; the systematic closure of hospital beds to pay the annual fees on Public Finance Initiative contracts (generous deals under which private firms were paid large amounts of money in return for supplying and running public facilities); the siphoning off of lottery fund money to pay for the burgeoning cost of hosting the two-week Olympics (£9 billion and rising) and the extra coaches shunted annually on to the gravy train for management consultants hired to tell civil servants and local government officers what to do.

However, in some ways the smaller examples of profligacy rankled just as much. There was the case of the Financial Services Authority holding a strategy meeting at Mosimann's, one of London's swankiest dining clubs, in the summer of 2007, when it might have been better turning its attention from the *foie gras* and white truffles to the problems of Northern Rock. There was the Treasury's decision to hand out 60 per cent bonuses to its senior officials (who already rank among the highest paid civil servants in Europe) despite having had a year that included the loss of the personal details of 25 million taxpayers and the first bank run in almost a century and a half. And there was the South East Development Agency, which found it necessary to send 13 members of staff to a gathering of property developers – not in Tunbridge Wells or Margate, but in Cannes – to explore the possibility of a firm building a new conference centre in Ashford. At the time of writing, the exploration process, rather like Stanley's hunt for Livingstone, looks like being a lengthy one, since despite the tedious necessity of the agency's staff having to quaff large quantities of champagne on luxury yachts, there is, as yet, no centre nor even a firm proposal for one.

It was a far cry from the traditionally downbeat and worthy image of public service in general and local government in particular. Joe Lampton, the anti-hero in John Braine's seminal post-war novel *Room at the Top* (Eyre & Spottiswoode; 1957) had to woo a rich businessman's daughter to taste the full fruits of affluence. Nowadays, he could simply move over to a regional development agency.

Clearly, there have been beneficiaries of the surge in public spending over the past eight years. It is, however, not immediately apparent that the real gainers have been either the public or those at the sharp end – the nurses, the refuse collectors, the librarians, the prison officers or the police. Labour used to be accused of allowing producer interests to 'capture' the public sector. It is still open to that charge. All that is different is that the producer interests in question have bigger salaries, drive more expensive cars, enjoy extremely pleasant lifestyles and – so far at least – appear to have been singularly unsuccessful in delivering for the public.

This should come as no surprise. Like the old Olympians, the New Olympians know how to look after themselves. Waste is not really waste if it involves expensive new IT systems that do not work or spending on weekend bonding exercises in country house hotels. The British state has embraced New Olympian principles and is now more or less incapable of managing anything other than its unnervingly prestigious secret intelligence and surveillance apparatus – one sector of the public realm never subject to efficiency drives. It is also one of the few parts of the state machine to operate with anything approaching dynamism.

Some Sunday newspapers on March 9 2008 reported that a 33-year-old fast-stream civil servant was writing a blog entitled 'Civil Serf', exposing the chaos and incompetence of Whitehall under New Labour, and that an official inquiry was under way to establish her identity. By that evening, anyone idly browsing the internet and clicking on to 'Civil Serf' would have seen the curt message 'This page does not exist' appear on the screen.

The New Olympians of the public realm have even developed their own means of communication that is for the initiated only. Ealing Borough Council, for example, placed an advertisement in 2008 for a Decision Support Manager, and only someone in the know would understand that a DSM was in reality an accountant. But this particular officer was not there to do the accounts: he or she would have the task – for £52,000 a year – of 'overseeing the development and ongoing assessment of overhead re-charging modelling activities'.

So while the public might have wanted to have their libraries better stocked with books, what the New Olympians gave them was a Lifestyle Support Service Manager to 'support people who want to make positive changes to their lifestyle' (Stoke-on-Trent; £31,600) or an Ethnic Minority Achievement Consultant 'to work cross-phase supporting pupils, schools and the local authority to address barriers to achievement that face black and minority ethnic pupils, including those who are learning English as an additional language'.

Now, it is clear that under-achievement of black and ethnic minority children is a problem in Britain. In which case, a better use of the £44,000 salary might have been to pay the teachers more, particularly since the council advertising the job was the Royal Borough of Kingston-upon-Thames, which has one of the whitest populations in London.

Beneath the lavishly rewarded consultants and top managers was a layer of public servants working for any number of outfits in Whitehall and across the country whose main purpose is to tell people what to do. Indeed, as wet and chilly 2007 turned into 2008, here was one arena in which the Middle Britain ideal ('dream' sounds a little too American) of job security and pleasant housing could continue to be pursued, almost regardless of the gathering economic stormclouds. For those interested, there was, for example, the prospect of employment with the Food Standards Agency (FSA), the super-quango set up to supervise the nation's food. On November 21 2007, the FSA announced: 'Tighter controls on baby milk', adding that it would prohibit 'baby milk being advertised directly to parents'. As there is no way in a free society of preventing new parents from seeing such advertisements, presumably all advertising will shortly be prohibited as part of the 'further action' that the FSA said may be taken when the issue is reviewed a year from now.

But for those uninterested in joining the state-funded breast-feeding zealots, many other opportunities beckoned: in enforcing the prohibition of smoking in public places, in policing the Ministry of Justice's proposed 'thought crime' (sorry, 'hate speech') legislation and in the ranks of the nag-ocracy (those forever going on at their fellow citizens to take more exercise, eat more fruit, drink 'sensibly' and reduce their salt intake).

Not that there was much rhyme or reason to the intrusions of the state into private life. On the same day, February 7 2008, the *Daily Telegraph* reported that the Home Office was cracking down on alcohol misuse by teenagers and the Department of Health was promoting contraceptives dispensed through vending machines aimed at that self-same age group. In a parallel universe, perhaps, these latter-day functionaries would be cracking down furiously on teenage sex while supplying hangover cures to young drinkers via the above-mentioned machines.

But perhaps the whole point was simply to boss people about. On May 21 2007, the *Daily Telegraph* reported sociology professor Frank Furedi of Kent University thus:

At the time Jack Straw was Home Secretary . . . according to Professor Furedi . . . 'they [the government] started issuing documents telling mothers how to mother and fathers how to father . . . The assumption was that parents were morons, that we were incompetent and had to be told how to cuddle a child. It was patronising and based on the assumption that civil servants knew more about how to be parents.' ('Parenting experts "ruining family life"')

One flourishing branch of this social engineering industry is involved in moral uplift, especially in relation to 'community cohesion' (a sort of latter-day version of the 'Dunkirk Spirit'). In the wake of the July 7 2005 London bombings, the Mayor of London, in partnership with Capital Radio and British Gas, plastered the capital with posters declaring: 'We are Londoners', with the letters 'Lond' and 'rs' rendered in a different colour, thus sending the second message: 'We are one'. Only the deeply sceptical would point out that were this to be the case, there would be little need to advertise the fact. There are not many posters declaring that London is south of Aberdeen and north of Paris.

Not everyone wants to work on such high-profile campaigns. For the less ambitious, the social-engineering industry contains niches for those content to bring about fairly minor changes in attitude or lifestyle. In late 2007, spotted in a London Tube carriage, was a poster issued jointly by the Mayor of London and by the Tube operator Transport for London.

Its entire message ran as follows: 'Please use all carriage space'.

Whatever would we do without people like that to watch over us?

To sum up, we believe the current cold climate in most of Middle Britain is no accident, but part of the inevitable working out of the New Olympian system. For nations such as Britain that took the free-market road from the 1980s onwards, the early benefits, of the sort that would have been enjoyed by the middle earners in society, seemed to be just fine – an end to mortgage rationing, easier credit, the scrapping of restrictions on taking currency abroad and a wider range of consumer products and services from which to choose. Only by the mid-1990s would the truth be dawning that the 'reform' or 'adjustment' process was still under way, that, indeed, it would never really end, and that cherished entities such as local hospitals, Post Offices, transport services and schools were under threat – not to mention the career prospects of the middle class. All had to be asset-stripped to feed the maw of the New Olympians and their appetite for deals and profits. It is somewhat reminiscent of the children's story in which a man buys a magnificent stove for the cabin in which he lives, but, in order to keep it operating at full blast, he has to burn his entire stock of firewood, then his furniture and eventually the walls and roof of the cabin.

This is the 'reform' we are discussing; it cares not what we use for fuel as long as its hunger is satisfied.

A typical exposition of this sort of capitalistic 'permanent revolution' comes from Johnny Munkhammar in his 2007 book *The Guide to Reform: How policymakers can pursue real change, achieve great results and win re-election* (Timbro with the Institute of Economic Affairs).

Mr Munkhammar praises those countries that have gone furthest down the free-market road. New Zealand is one of them: 'Some small steps had been initiated already before the new government took office in 1984, but that year was the breakthrough for reform.' Labour markets were duly liberalised, taxes cut and welfare benefits reduced.

Job done? Not at all. Mr Munkhammar warns: 'New Zealand needs further reform. Considerable time has elapsed since the two successful reform waves and the positive effects are waning.'

We wonder whether this prospect of never-ending 'reform' was spelled out to the people of New Zealand back in 1984.

6

'Never Break the Chain': Debt and delusion in the British economy

I don't want a loan, father. I want a great deal of money, not on loan. Nothing else will do.
   – Iris Murdoch; *An Unofficial Rose;* Chatto & Windus; 1962

For Britain's part, our openness has enabled us to benefit from low cost goods exported from Asia, while at the same time enabling us to expand our own strength in the high value added industries and become the world's financial centre leading in exporting services to all parts of the world.
   Our openness, alongside all our economic and labour market reforms – matching flexibility with fairness – have helped keep inflation low, while enabling the economy and employment to grow.
   – Alistair Darling, Chancellor of the Exchequer, speaking at the London Business School; July 25 2007

'My dear Mister Bond, England is a sick nation by any standards.'
   – Ian Fleming; *You Only Live Twice;* Jonathan Cape; 1964

Just as it seemed things could get no worse for the British Treasury, they did. Ministers and mandarins were already grappling with the future of troubled mortgage lender Northern Rock, the loss of the personal details of 25 million child benefit claimants and their children and criticism of the financial regulatory system, of which the Treasury is the sponsoring ministry. They would have been less than human had they not hoped the countdown to the now-traditional Great British Christmas Shutdown would allow them to slip, however briefly, out of the limelight.

It was not to be. On December 20, a set of official statistics laid bare what seemed the truly shocking state of the British economy. Like a snap raid on a dodgy restaurant by health inspectors, the data shone a light on something very rotten behind the respectable façade.

The British people, and their government, were living far beyond their means. According to the Office for National Statistics, Britain's current account deficit during the third quarter of 2007 had hit a record £20 billion, equivalent to 5.7 per cent of gross domestic product and the largest such deficit of all the Group of Seven rich nations.

On the same day, public finance figures showed a sharp deterioration. In the 2007–2008 financial year up to November, public sector net borrowing stood at £36.2 billion. The government was on track to borrow more in the full year than the Major administration had done in 1993–1994, when borrowing in the full financial year had reached a record £51.1 billion.

Against the background of a global liquidity squeeze, the desperately bad figures were ominous. The country was not in recession as it had been when borrowing had last been this high. The economy had been growing for a decade. If the economy stalled, the government would find itself in deep trouble. Michael Saunders, a Citigroup economist, commented: 'All this looks pretty ugly: rising twin deficit and a credit crunch' (quoted in *Financial Times*, December 21 2007). Other City analysts commented in similar terms. But then, they as a group had been scrambling to keep abreast of Britain's rapidly developing economic problems.

Earlier in the month, the e-mail baskets of British financial journalists piled up with 'revised' predictions for the immediate path of UK interest rates flashed from some of the analysts and economists employed by the big banks, fund managers and independent consultancies. These analysts 'corrected' their previous predictions that there would be no change in the official Bank Rate when the Bank of England's Monetary Policy Committee made its monthly decision on the following day, December 6 2007. Now they were seized suddenly by another vision of the future. Now, they decided, there would be a cut, from the present level of 5.75 per cent to 5.5 per cent.

In other words, they changed their minds on the likely level of interest rates to the tune of more than 4 per cent. Never had speculator-turned-author Max Gunther's jibe about financial analysts' circulars – that they are revised so frequently that they are like a theatre ticket 'that is scheduled to expire before the play is performed' – seemed so apposite (*The Zurich Axioms*; Souvenir Press; 1985). It is worth noting that the City analysts themselves are part of the New Olympian élite, as are the money-market traders whose own changes of heart on the likely movements of interest rates in the mid-2000s resembled 'a near-perfect V-shape', in the word of one City strategist who preferred not to be named. They are not only supposed to forecast rate changes, but help to bring them about, given that the official rate is deemed to be driven by money-market changes. The recent record has not exactly been stellar, to put it mildly.

So what lay behind the December 2007 opinion swing?

Well, suggestions of weaker house prices from the Halifax bank and a four-and-a-half-year low in the index of Britain's dominant services sector produced by the Chartered Institute of Purchasing & Supply and the Royal Bank of Scotland seemed to have tipped the balance. It could hardly have been anything connected with the Bank's actual remit in setting interest rates – that of hitting a target of 2 per cent inflation as measured by the Consumer Prices Index (CPI). On the most recent reading, the CPI had risen from 1.8 per cent in the 12 months to September to 2.1 per cent in the 12 months to October. Furthermore, monetary policy was hardly restrictive – quite the opposite. A so-called 'neutral' level for official interest rates, one that neither stimulates the economy nor seeks to rein it in, can be defined as the sum of real-terms (i.e. discounted for the effects of inflation) annual economic growth plus the current level of the broadest measure of inflation, the GDP Deflator. At the time of the MPC's December meeting, the economy was expanding at 3.2 per cent a year and the GDP Deflator was at 3.7 per cent. Even adjusting for the fact that these two numbers covered slightly different time periods, which gives a 3 per cent growth figure, the neutral rate of interest would be well over 6.5 per cent.

In other words, at 5.75 per cent, the rate had already been expansionary on any conventional measure. With the economy already being stimulated, a rate reduction hardly seemed the obvious method of stopping inflation continuing to float off above its target rate.

True, the Bank's remit refers to the level of CPI inflation two years in the future, and that two-year horizon – like all horizons – is never reached, but always remains two years in the future. But a second rule prevents the MPC membership from playing fast and loose with inflation in the here and now while solemnly affirming their belief that inflation will be at 2 per cent two years hence. Should the actual inflation rate *at any time* deviate more than one percentage point either side of the 2 per cent target rate, then the governor of the Bank is required to explain publicly to the chancellor, in an open letter, what has gone wrong and what he plans to do about it.

So the analysts' forecast was certainly not based on the notion that an over-restrictive monetary policy was threatening a below-target inflation rate. Far from it – a loose monetary policy had, as one would have expected, delivered slightly above-target inflation. To be fair, the Bank was well aware of the risks of inflation. The February 2008 Inflation Report made the point that cuts in Bank Rate to boost the economy would be limited by the expected sharp increase in the cost of living over the coming months.

Had the MPC stayed put at 5.75 per cent, all this forecasting would be of little or no interest. But, as history records, Bank Rate was cut at the December meeting by a quarter of a percentage point, and was cut again in February 2008, taking the rate to 5.25 cent.

In its edition of December 8 2007, *The Economist* explained the December cut thus: 'The economy is on the brink of a painful tumble, which is why interest rates have been cut.'

Well, part of the economy – the housing market – certainly seemed to be on the slide; the influential Halifax house-price index's fall of 1.1 per cent in November was its third monthly decline in a row. Housing finance is the most important expression at the household level of the City of London's vast credit machine, thus it was unsurprising that the credit crunch that followed the so-called subprime lending crisis of 2007, which we cover in detail elsewhere, should have choked the supply of funds for mortgages.

On December 20, the day of the dreadful current account and public finance data, figures from the Council for Mortgage Lenders made it a hat-trick of bad news, stating that loans for house purchase in November 2007 had dived 22 per cent on the figure seen in November 2006.

For the New Olympians in Westminster, Whitehall and the Bank of England, all of this must have been deeply disturbing. For them, perhaps, the realisation was dawning that Britian's recovery from the horrors of the early 1980s, was in large part an optical illusion. The freeing of the financial interest had unleashed a tidal bore of asset stripping and 'creative destruction' (actually, 'destructive destruction' would be closer to the mark) on Britain's productive economic assets. But the plunge in living standards that would normally be associated with this pillaging and ransacking can be held at bay by the very same financial interest extending large amounts of credit to the public, much of it secured on houses. In this way, the country can live well beyond its means (as seen in December 20 current account figures), as can its government (as seen in December 20 public finance data), because tax revenue is inflated by debt-generated economic activity.

High house prices are essential to maintaining this illusion of prosperity, particularly as growth in earnings had been subdued for years. But as storm clouds were building over the housing market, a climatic depression had already settled on growth in the standard of living.

According to the government's National Accounts, real household disposable income grew by just 0.5 per cent in the 12 months to the end of June 2007. Using a different measure, government figures showed average weekly earnings rose 2.9 per cent in the year to April. Prices as measured by the Retail Prices Index, rose 3.6 per cent and by 2.8 per cent on the Consumer Prices Index.

Earnings had long been under downward pressure, but consumer borrowing had taken up the slack, borrowing often fuelled by rising house prices. Time was when the British talked about 'second mortgages', a disapproving term for what was thought to be the somewhat louche practice of raising a second home loan. Now even the Bank of England prefers to talk of 'housing equity withdrawal', a neutral term that manages to avoid any mention of 'borrowing' or 'debt'. According to the Bank, the sums thus raised reached the equivalent of 6 per cent of post-tax income in the last quarter of 2006, up from 5.3 per cent in the third quarter. To put that in perspective, the figure averaged 0.8 per cent in 1977, 5 per cent in 1987 and dropped by an average 0.3 per cent in 1997 as a result of net repayment of such loans.

Back in the present, the total stayed at 6 per cent in the first quarter of 2007 before slumping to 4.5 per cent in the second quarter.

Since then, there has been rather less 'equity' to 'withdraw'. House prices dropped 0.5 per cent in October, according to the Halifax; the Nationwide was marginally more cheerful, with a 1.1 per cent rise during the month.

This was ominous for consumer borrowing. In 2006, analysts at investment bank Société Générale in London figured out that changes in housing equity withdrawal as a percentage of net income were, in the words of Dhaval Joshi, then a strategist at the bank, 'the biggest single driver of changes in consumption patterns' (interviewed by the authors, November 21 2007).

But it does go some way to explaining the Bank of England's December rate decision.

At this stage, those uninitiated in the double-speak (and, indeed, treble-speak) of Britain's 'miracle economy' of the 1990s and the 2000s may have spotted that the 'stability' so prized by Prime Minister and former Chancellor Gordon Brown relied on a number of highly unstable factors all supporting each other.

Thus the economy depends to a large extent upon consumer spending, which in turns depends on consumer borrowing. This borrowing is underpinned by high house prices, which allow homeowners to raise finance against the part of their property's value that is unencumbered by a mortgage. Obviously, this slice of the value grows with the growth of house prices generally, which in turn depends on high levels of mortgage borrowing.

So one type of borrowing essential to economic growth, mortgage equity withdrawal, ultimately depends on another type of borrowing, mortgages raised for house purchase. The same people tend to be engaged in both sorts of borrowing, and the borrowing has to be officially encouraged because otherwise the economy will shudder to a halt. That is why the Bank cut borrowing costs in December 2007 in defiance of rising inflation. But, as with the tightrope walker, the indebted public must never be allowed to 'look down' – infusions of cheap money, as seen in December 2007, are intended to ensure that they do not. Nor must there be much by way of questioning the thinking behind this self-validating spiral of mortgage and consumer debt. Any answer is likely to run along the lines that consumer borrowing is 'secured on home equity withdrawal' and that home equity withdrawal is itself made possible by higher house prices. As, indeed, are high levels of mortgage borrowing; these, you will be told, are 'secured on the asset side', i.e. on the same inflated prices that the 'secured' mortgage borrowing made possible in the first place.

It is all vaguely reminiscent of a proper definition of the much-misused phrase 'begging the question': 'Strictly, it means that he [your opponent] is arguing from an assumption that is itself open to argument, or is drawing unjustified conclusions, e.g. in an argument on the merits of a Prime Minister, it is begging the question to say: "'Of course he's a good leader, he would not be in the job otherwise.'" (*Collins Gem Dictionary of English Usage*; Collins; 1971)

In other words, the circularity of the whole business is rather like the fabled perpetual motion machine of yesteryear. Rising asset prices support increased borrowing which supports economic growth and rising asset prices. These rising asset prices support yet more borrowing, which supports more economic growth and even higher house prices. Everything runs smoothly as long as we keep borrowing ever more money against ever more expensive houses while spending some part of the notional real-estate profits on goods and services. Before long the average property will cost dizzying multiples of the average wage. To keep people buying at ever-higher prices requires even lower interest rates.

Eventually, if the machine keeps going for long enough, even at very low interest rates, the cost of debt becomes unsustainable. At that point, perhaps, economists and others will remember that perpetual motion machines can never work.

Put another way, the multiple instabilities of the British economy, when added together, provide at least the simulacrum of a form of stability. In a similar way, the coach perched on the edge of a cliff at the end of the comedy bank-robbery film *The Italian Job* (1969), with the robbers at one end and the stolen loot at the other, is perfectly stable – as long as nobody moves.

By Christmas 2007, the coach was starting, alarmingly, to sway.

GHOST STORIES: RATTLING CHAINS AT THE TREASURY

For Gordon Brown and his lieutenants, the events of the winter of 2007–2008 will have been about more than simply bad economic figures, about more even than the ghastly prospect of an incipient economic 'feel-bad factor' among the electorate, something New Labour had successfully fended off for more than ten years.

Fittingly, for the season of ghost stories, Mr Brown and his colleagues now faced – in inflation, the current account gap and crisis in the public finances – horrors they were sure they had laid to rest. Or, to vary the metaphor, Mr Brown had, like Oscar Wilde's fictional Dorian Gray, nerved himself to inspect the portrait in the attic, only to find, staring back at him, the saturnine features of his Tory predecessor at the Treasury, Nigel Lawson.

The legacy of Lord Lawson, chancellor between June 1983 and October 1989, has appeared to be an object of both fascination and repugnance to Gordon Brown during his ten years at the Treasury. But then, the parallels between the two men were remarkably (perhaps, for Mr Brown, worryingly) similar. Both were pugnacious, self-confident, sometimes arrogant and intellectually capable of holding their own. Neither was in awe of Treasury mandarins or of officials of the Bank of England. Both chancellorships opened with iron-fisted financial rectitude – the swingeing spending cuts of summer 1983, the Labour pledge to stick to Conservative spending limits in the late 1990s. Both became convinced they had transformed the British economy for the better and enjoyed playing on the world stage alongside finance ministers from less happy lands.

Both men promoted schemes to pull poor countries out of debt. Both took the same line in their respective Mais lectures (Mr Lawson in 1984, Mr Brown in 1999), namely that the object of macro-economic policy was to keep inflation low as opposed to maintaining total demand, the position from the 1940s to the 1970s. Both opened the public-spending taps later on in their chancellorships, both presided over an explosion in consumer credit and a house-price boom, both had difficulties with their prime ministers, both seemed to believe (without much evidence) that they had prompted a boom in entrepreneurial activity and both found it hard to hide their contempt for predecessors in the job who had failed to match their brilliance and thus had failed to deliver economic prosperity.

But there, in the conventional view, the parallels end and the big differences open up. Things went Nigel Lawson's way for only about 18 months, the 'long year' from the autumn of 1986 to the early summer of 1988 taking in his *annus mirabilis*, 1987. Gordon Brown enjoyed ten years of uninterrupted growth. Nigel Lawson's first three years were marked by chronic unemployment and the plunge in sterling's value to close on $1 in January 1985. The dole queues shrank during Gordon Brown's first three years and sterling was strong. Nigel Lawson's last year in office was a miserable affair, marked by rows with the then prime minister Margaret Thatcher and strenuous attempts to get his own runaway economic boom under control. Gordon Brown's last year in office was a stately progress towards 10 Downing Street.

We imagine that Gordon Brown likes this conventional view. Who would not? It casts Lord Lawson as an early, flawed prototype of Mr Brown, brilliant mind and plenty of self-belief, but flawed nonetheless. And it would seem Mr Brown long ago identified the fatal flaw in the Mark One model – a loss of 'grip' at the wrong moment. Nigel Lawson, as chancellor, let rip between 1986 and 1988, cutting both taxes and interest rates while boosting public spending. Inflation, painfully reduced over several years, took off once more.

Mr Brown would not make the same mistake. He would

pass responsibility for interest rates to the Bank of England and impose fiscal rules on himself and his successors mandating that current budgets would be in balance over the economic cycle and that the national debt would stay below 40 per cent of gross domestic product. Every time Mr Brown talked of 'prudence', 'stability', 'cautious assumptions' and the rest, he was, in effect, saying: 'I may have thick black hair, a huge brain and enjoy knocking seven bells out of my opponents, but I am not Nigel Lawson.' This, surely, was the real meaning behind the oft-repeated pledge that there would be 'no return to boom and bust'?

During Mr Brown's chancellorship, most commentators treated his 'devotion to prudence' as a bit of a joke, an excessive protestation of something that was pretty self-evident anyway, rather like the teenage boy who, spooked by the sudden fear that his parents may think he is gay, starts ostentatiously wearing football scarves and leaving 'girlie' magazines lying round his bedroom.

By the winter of 2007–2008, however, as the parlous state of the economy came into focus, the parallels with the Lawson years would have been becoming increasingly uncomfortable. Nigel Lawson famously came to steer policy using those indicators – such as the exchange rate and the M0 measure of notes and coins in circulation – that pointed to the need to pump up growth while ignoring those that suggested the need for a cooling-off period. Mr Brown has selected an inflation measure, the Consumer Prices Index, that excludes the costs of home ownership and, as we shall see, adopted an apparently infinitely flexible 'rule' on public borrowing and spending. Both men, as their chancellorships developed, seemed to have acquired a taste for soft options.

It is our contention that the conventional view is right – up to a point. Nigel Lawson was the prototype, and Mr Brown was the more smoothly running 'advanced' model. But it is wrong, we believe, when it goes on to suggest the record in office of Mr Lawson and Mr Brown is chalk and cheese. Mr Brown has not, we suggest, eschewed Lawsonite policies. On the contrary, he has simply found more effective ways of implementing them.

Nigel Lawson was the first chancellor of the New Olympian age. Indeed, he transformed the chancellorship into an Olympian position in its own right. His predecessor, Sir Geoffrey Howe, had practised a much more old-fashioned form of economic management, with a windfall tax on clearing banks in 1981 and, in the same year, a tax rise in the middle of a recession that cleared the way for some interest rate cuts later. Sir Geoffrey, as he was then, was a veteran of the Heath government's titanic struggles with the trade unions, having, as Solicitor General, drafted the Industrial Relations Bill, that government's key weapon in the battle. Indeed, even after leaving the Treasury he could, apparently, not resist a pop at the old enemy. In January 1984, he removed the right to join a trade union that had been enjoyed by staff at the secret Government Communications Headquarters, for which he, as foreign secretary, was responsible. By contrast, Nigel Lawson, once the 1984–1985 miners' strike was over, early in his chancellorship, seemed bored by the trade unions and much keener on the red meat of tax cuts and 'enterprise'. He had inherited, in 1983, what was recognisably still the British economy of the 1970s, albeit with higher unemployment, and bequeathed in 1989 what was recognisably the economy of today, with a powerful City of London, permanently fragile manufacturing and production industries, an essentially white-collar rather than blue-collar public sector and high levels of personal indebtedness. Running through this new economy is the belief that New Olympians will deliver prosperity provided not only that they are left to their own devices but that public policy is tailored to their requirements, whether in terms of the setting of interest rates or the provision of public money to bail out failed financial institutions such as Northern Rock. It was, as we noted earlier, Nigel Lawson who, in October 1987, ordered the Bank of England to stand by as buyer of last resort for shares in British Petroleum after a privatisation issue was hit by a worldwide stock-market plunge. Had he not done so, the big Wall Street banks that had underwritten the issue would have lost money. And that would never do.

That vignette, and the stock-market turbulence that was its historical context, was a perfect example of the New Olympians in action. They promised stability, and delivered instability. They preached financial rectitude and 'small government', and demanded hand-outs the minute they hit trouble. They preached the unleashing of market forces against 'cosseted' business and industry, but – and here is the rub – they demanded protection from such forces for themselves.

Less than ten years since the so-called 'winter of discontent' in 1978–1979, trade union 'barons' had been replaced by a new aristocracy, richer, more powerful and with sympathetic fellow grandees in the political and central banking machinery.

This – rather than a hazy, half-nostalgic image of double-breasted power suits, a house-price boom, 'yuppies' and a pop chart showcasing the offerings of Bananarama, Aztec Camera and Belinda Carlisle – is the real legacy of Nigel Lawson. It is a legacy that has blossomed in the last ten years. And it is our belief that it has left us in a frighteningly unstable position.

TRAVELS IN NEVER-NEVERLAND: BRITAIN AND THE BORROWING BUG

Debt has long been the dirty secret of Britain's 'economic miracle'. By freeing finance from its post-war controls, the authorities had opened the door to grand-scale asset stripping and deal making, elevating the City – or the 'financial intermediation sector', to use its prosaic official name – above all other economic actors. Put another way: '[O]ne section of society, chiefly concerned with moving money, has cheated the other sections. It has been one of the greatest "scams" ever pulled' (Robin Ramsay; *Prawn Cocktail Party;* Vision; 1998).

As noted above, one might have expected this widespread destruction of productive assets would have caused widespread misery, as indeed it did for a while in the early 1980s.

But liberalised finance could also package up the fact of subdued earnings and unfulfilled aspirations into a booming mortgage and consumer-finance industry. For some time, this giant extension of credit to the general public provided a substitute for real prosperity. Politicians, for whom a sense of history is, like reading, very much an optional extra these days, conclude that financial liberalisation has 'worked'. They slap their thighs in merriment at the recollection of how things used to be, when governments tried to control capital. Everyone is better off now. The proof of the pudding, surely, is in the eating? The City does not disabuse them.

But like any drug, liberalised finance wreaks more damage with every dose. Thus easy credit sucks in more cheap imports, weakening further Britain's manufacturing position with regard to the rest of the world. It inflates the value of property, thus bloating this 'asset class' at the expense of productive investment. It makes vast amounts of money available for 'private equity' operations (asset stripping), damaging further the productive sector of the economy. Above all, the financial sector insists that economic policy in general and monetary policy in particular remains geared to its own needs, with interest rates always supportive of inflated asset prices.

Politicians, convinced that all this 'prosperity' is the fruit of their own foresight in freeing the financial interest, have it drummed into them (not that it would seem to need much drumming) that the worst thing they could do would be to tamper with the City's New Olympians.

But we believe the UK economy is about to have a very nasty reality check. Two or three years ago, we had few other people for company. Today, we have no shortage of companions. Indeed, the only people exuding serene confidence about Britain's economic prospects seem to be Mr Brown, his sidekick, the schools secretary Ed Balls, and his successor, the unfortunate Mr Darling. Elsewhere, once-maverick views are becoming mainstream. Jonathan Loynes, chief UK economist at Capital Economics – probably the country's most successful independent economic consultancy – made this comment on the figures released on December 20:

This morning's flurry of UK data paints a worrying picture of a dangerously unbalanced economy. Although annual GDP growth in the third quarter was revised up again from 3.2 per cent to 3.3 per cent, this solid performance disguises a number of major stresses and strains. For a start, the household saving ratio fell again in the third quarter from 4 per cent to 3.4 per cent, suggesting that households are still overstretching themselves. Second, the balance of payments release revealed a huge current account deficit in the third quarter . . . The UK's external position now looks pretty much as bad as that in the US, suggesting that the pound needs to fall sharply like the US dollar. And finally, this morning's public finances data revealed another hefty budget . . . Overall, a pretty ugly picture, supporting our view that the coming economic slowdown will be a prolonged period of adjustment rather than a short pause for breath like that seen in 2005.

When an economist speaks of a 'prolonged period of adjustment' it is rather like a diplomat referring to 'a full and frank exchange of views'. The reality is rather bloodier than the calm phrasing may suggest.

Official figures go some way to highlighting the chronic dependence of the economy on borrowing. In the second quarter of 2007, according to national statistics, real household disposable income had risen by an average of just 0.5 per cent since the second quarter of 2006. In the 12 months to the end of June 2007, according to the Bank of England, net lending to individuals rose by 10.2 per cent. Within that figure, mortgage lending rose by a net 11.5 per cent and consumer credit by 5.8 per cent. At £1,344 billion in June 2007, the total stock of individual debt, both mortgages and consumer credit, was broadly equivalent to one year's gross domestic product.

All of this is the result of unbridled credit creation, the unleashing of so-called fractional reserve banking. As with so much about high finance, this is a boring-sounding expression for something that is ultimately about power. In contrast to credit unions and the most basic types of savings banks, the clearing banks have long been allowed to lend out more than they have in their care, simply because it is an observable fact that most deposits are not withdrawn on any one day. Furthermore, money lent usually becomes itself the basis for new deposits, thus the basis again for more lending. The ratio has tended to be that £100 can be lent out for every £8 held by the bank. This extraordinary privilege was strictly controlled during the decades immediately after the war, for good reason. Without controls, the only check on credit creation would be the rate of interest, and that was hardly a discpline for the banks, as they would at the least recoup the higher cost of borrowing from those to whom they had lent money.

Fractional reserve banking has a magical quality in that it conjures money into existence. For 25 years after the Second World War, this magical power was strictly controlled by the state. Since 1971, however, these controls were progressively dismantled. The results in terms of a huge credit bubble are only too visible.

LABOUR'S ECONOMIC RECORD: THE CASE FOR THE PROSECUTION

To the dwindling fan club of Labour's economic record, the current crisis is merely a replay of 1997–1998. Then, currency turmoil in the Far East and Russia threatened to capsize the world economy. Britain was thought to be particularly vulnerable, because of the openness of the City and because it had a reputation as a crisis-prone economy – Black Wednesday was only six years in the past. But Britain weathered the storm and emerged stronger. The reason, according to Mr Brown and his lieutenants, was not hard to find:

This has been a difficult time for the global economy – a quarter of the world is now in recession and world growth has halved. Exports to parts of Asia are down more than 50 per cent. The turbulence of last autumn has eased but it is too early to say that the period of global financial instability is over. But as a result of tough and decisive action to build a platform of stability, I believe we can now say that the government has been able to steer a course of stability – based on low inflation and sound public finances – and we are now laying the foundations for sustainable growth.

That was Gordon Brown as chancellor speaking to the annual dinner of the Confederation of British Industry on May 18 1999. Institutional 'stability' was the centrepiece of his economic policy, and any charge sheet against Mr Brown and his colleagues should start here.

How stable is the monetary and fiscal policy framework? 'Independence' for the Bank of England (espoused by Nigel Lawson after he left office) was based on the notion that the 'right' thing to do in terms of raising or lowering interest rates was easy to discern but politically difficult to do. Removing the decision from elected politicians and giving it to New Olympian technocrats would ensure the 'correct', albeit sometimes painful, changes in interest rates would be made. But as we saw earlier in this chapter, the December 2007 decision was taken against a background of conflicting economic indicators – rising inflation against stalling house prices, for example.

So, an already expansionary rate was reduced further, despite rising inflation to sustain consumer confidence and higher house prices. The machine has to be kept going perpetually. Eventually interest rates will reach zero, the pound will collapse and inflation will take off. Unlike Japan in its stagnation years, Britain has very little to sell in export markets, meaning that our own position would be much worse were the wheel really to fall off.

On the fiscal side, the search for the much-vaunted 'stability' is an even tougher assignment. After Labour's 1997 election victory, Mr Brown had pledged in his so-called 'golden rule' to balance the budget for 'current' (i.e. day to day) expenditure over the length of the economic cycle. The exact length of this cycle was chopped and changed during the Brown years, and when he became prime minister in summer 2007, the latest official version stated that the cycle had begun in 1997 and had yet to end. There may have been a hint of playing for time in all this; if so, a glance at the public finances might have explained why.

Mr Darling announced that the borrowing on the current budget for 2007–2008 was £4 billion greater than had been expected in the spring, taking the total to £8.3 billion. Adjusted for the economic cycle, the borrowing on the current budget as a percentage of gross domestic product had worsened from 0.3 per cent in the spring to 0.7 per cent. That is quite impressive considering that the whole point of the golden rule is that the cyclically adjusted figure ought always to be zero at worst, and possibly in surplus.

Undaunted by all this, the chancellor explained that everything was going swimmingly. Mr Darling even had the effrontery to claim that, although the present economic cycle had not yet ended, and thus it was impossible to tell whether the golden rule had been met, he was confident of meeting the rule in the next economic cycle, the one whose start date, let alone whose finishing date, is unknown. This was what the Treasury wrote: 'At this early stage, and based on cautious assumptions, the Government is therefore on course to meet the golden rule in the next economic cycle' (2007 Pre-Budget Report and Comprehensive Spending Review).

But then, the economy had become partially dependent on public spending to keep the motor turning.

[G]overnment expenditure . . . has risen by 2.7 per cent a year, far faster than the 1.9 per cent a year between 1964 and 1970 and 1974 to 1979 [the two previous periods of Labour government], when the Treasury was allegedly under the control of tax and spend devotees. (Frank Wilkinson; 'Neo-liberalism and New Labour Policy'; Cambridge Journal of Economics; November 2007)

Unfortunately, as the December 20 public finance figures showed, the government had failed to squirrel away money during the good years so would be unable to use public spending to any great extent to stabilise the economy during any downturn. Far from it – Mr Darling would be reining in his own spending just as the public would be reining in its own, a pro-cyclical move the result of which would be anything but stability.

But if the use of government expenditure as a stimulant for economic growth has undermined the whole notion of the 'platform of stability', the use of consumer indebtedness has done so to a very much greater extent. By the end of 2007, the figures were staggering, even to professionals in banking, finance, the media and the law whose job involved routine acquaintance with the statistics behind Britain's borrowing binge.

Lending to individuals in October 2007 added up as follows: £1,200 billion outstanding on mortgage debt and £222 billion outstanding on unsecured consumer credit, giving a grand total, in round numbers, of £1.4 trillion. In other words, using an admittedly imperfect statistic of 46 million for the adult population of the UK gives an average mortgage debt per adult of £26,086 and average consumer credit debt of just under £5,000.

Seven years earlier, in October 2000, the figures looked like this: on mortgages, £525 billion was outstanding, and on consumer credit £125 billion, giving a grand total, in round figures, of £650 billion. The increase, in other words, has been of the order of 115 per cent in seven years.

During those same seven years, earnings rose on average by less than 30 per cent.

[E]conomic growth has been sustained by high levels of consumption, which have been driven by easily available credit, which in turn has led to high levels of debt and insolvency. At the macroeconomic level the growth of consumption has outstripped the growth of domestic production and has been sustained by import growth and by persistent balance of payments

deficits. (Michael Kitson and Frank Wilkinson; 'The Economics of New Labour'; Cambridge Journal of Economics; November 2007)

As the economy's addiction to consumer and housing debt and government spending were making a mockery of the notion of a 'platform of stability', the headlong decline of manufacturing has cast a lurid light on Labour's economic record.

The most striking aspect of structural change under Labour has been the continued decline of manufacturing against a background of rapid growth in the service sector. The shift of jobs from manufacturing to services is a feature of virtually all advanced economies and has been under way in this country for approximately four decades. However, the pace of change has accelerated under Labour and manufacturing jobs have been lost at a faster rate in parts of the country where there was already a surplus of labour. (Ken Coutts, Andrew Glyn and Bob Rowthorn; 'Structural Change Under New Labour'; Cambridge Journal of Economics; November 2007)

The authors estimate imports from low wage countries have resulted in the loss of 300,000 manufacturing jobs under New Labour.

So if the platform of stability has its base in the shifting sands of an opaque monetary and fiscal policy, excessive reliance on consumer indebtedness and public expenditure and on an ever-shrinking manufacturing sector, where do Messrs Brown and Darling imagine they can compensate for these unstable factors and anchor the economy?

In their above-mentioned article, Kitson and Wilkinson give us a clue:

As far as innovation is concerned, much policy uses a narrow notion that science and technology will generate economic growth.

There is an excessive focus of high-technology industries – such as information technology, biotechnology and nanotechnology. These activities are currently a relatively small part of the national economy and tend to be concentrated in the south and east of England. Furthermore, the notion that such activities are independent development blocks that will generate economic growth ignores the important inter-sectoral linkages that feed the products of 'new industries' into old industries, generating innovation there and generalising the benefits of knowledge advance.

Yes, it is time (briefly) to revisit the 'creative economy'.

TURNING ON THE CHARM: CREATIVITY, CREDULITY AND CREDIT

Of all the myths sedulously fostered by New Labour – aided and abetted by New Olympians in both the public and private sectors – one of the most important is the notion that Britain is, or is about to become, a 'creative' or 'knowledge-based' economy. We may not make things any more, but we are world leaders in making things up. In our previous book, *Fantasy Island* (Constable; 2007) we explored (and, we hope, exploded) this notion at some length. This is not the place for an extensive reprise of the theme. But the 'creative/knowledge economy' is central to the Gordon Brown legacy. It is about much more than having Tony Blair photographed with the members of Oasis in the early days of his premiership. It is supposed to be the escape hatch from all our economic conditions.

Briefly, we are told the British economy can behave quite differently to most other economies because it is not like other economies. No, indeed. We have a 'creative/knowledge economy' very different from the traditional economy, the one inhabited by girls serving behind the counter at Woolworths and lads in safety goggles cutting up sheet metal on industrial estates.

As it is so different, the old rules do not apply. From Gordon Brown and Tony Blair downwards, senior people told us that the creative/knowledge economy would be such a bountiful source of 'value added' that our economic policy could be configured differently.

The state sector's own version of the creative/knowledge economy is called 'transformational government'. The origins of this phrase are not easy to discern but it has been ascribed (plausibly enough) to Tony Blair. One day very soon, the staggering sums of money being spent by the government on information technology contracts will come good, and there will be a giant release of efficiency, of energy (on the part of the public servants) and of contentment (on the part of the public itself).

Well, as a 'theory of everything', the creative/knowledge economy is certainly an enticing one. We are constantly told we live in a 'globalised world'. And this in turn raises the question of our ability to pay our way in the world. But paying our way in the world would become a lot easier of we had access to something no other country possessed but which the world economy needed.

Platinum or gold, for instance. Oil, it goes without saying. But for an endlessly renewable resource, creativity takes some beating. They want it – we've got it. At this point, the obvious question is – haven't they got it too? No, we are led to believe that Taiwan, or India, or China are, apparently, at a lower stage of economic evolution than we are. One hundred or more years ago, our prejudice was that 'mysterious Orientals' were jolly good at arty stuff, at imagery and making fabulous carpets and so forth, not to mention spell-binding poetry and jewellery fabrication. We Westerners, on the other hand, and the British in particular, were the hard-headed types who could run factories, build steam locomotives and battleships and generally run an economy. We were practical; they, at best, were 'charming', in a childlike and rather untrustworthy way. Now, they are the drones who can not only turn out factory-made goods but lend us their savings in order that we may buy these goods. Not to worry, however, because we have the artists, the designers and the creative brains. We have also those personable if somewhat slippery characters in advertising, public relations, marketing and the City.

Who are the charming, feckless, childlike Orientals now?

China and other Asian countries in centuries past ran up unsustainable debts to buy the products of modernity from Western manufacturers and to pay for grandiose vanity projects. In this they were encouraged by easy money on easy terms from bankers in London and Paris. Of course eventually the debt spiralled out of control and the European powers had to step in, albeit reluctantly, to run countries that their own inhabitants were too creative and imaginative to run for themselves.

But if it pays the bills, not to worry. Does it?

Here is the good news: we ran a surplus in our trade on 'audiovisual and related services' in 2006 of £1.28 billion. The bad news is that this was a fall on the £1.39 billion clocked up the previous year (*The Pink Book 2007;* Office for National Statistics).

Now, it could be argued that all exportable service industries – whether shipping insurance, tourism, general financial services or films and television programmes – are 'knowledge' industries. How did this overall category of all services, creative or not, perform?

On the face of it, not badly – there was a surplus in 2006 of £29 billion, up from £25 billion the previous year.

As to whether it pays the bills or not, that question is easily answered. The surplus on services came nowhere near wiping out the deficit on goods of £84 billion, leaving a trade deficit of more than £54 billion once the surplus on services was deducted from the deficit on goods.

To be fair, there is a sort of external version of the creative economy – the notion that we make better investments abroad than foreigners do here. Indeed, a third section of the balance of payments, after trade in goods and in services, is the bit counting net investment income, and this has been strong in recent years.

That is quite surprising, on the face of it, given that these earnings are perched on top of a *negative* international asset position of minus £291.9 billion in 2006, a worsening on the minus £143.5 billion seen in 2005. In other words, foreigners own more of the UK than the UK owns of 'abroad'. How do we manage to out-earn them from this unpromising position?

There are two possible answers to that. One – we are naturally more brilliant investors than foreigners. Or two – we have been making riskier bets, which provide higher returns, for as long as the hot streak lasts. Let us assume, for the sake of argument, that the second explanation is rather more likely than the first. If so, the danger is that the hot streak can go cold. And, indeed, that is just what seems to be happening.

The investment income surplus in the third quarter of 2007 was non-existent. In fact, it was a deficit of £3.6 billion, against a £1 billion surplus a year earlier and a small £6 million surplus the previous quarter. So our creative, brained-up service sector is not delivering the goods, and we had a balance of payments deficit of £20 billion in the third quarter of 2007, from £13.2 billion in the third quarter of 2006, the balance of payments being arrived at after taking into account trade in goods and services, investment income and a small category for transfer payments, such as Britian's payments to the European Union or the sending home to the UK of money earned abroad.

What of the public sector's version of the creative/knowledge economy, 'transformational government'? Here, developments were, if anything, even less encouraging.

As we mentioned earlier in this chapter, on November 20 2007, Chancellor Alistair Darling informed MPs that two computer discs, containing details of 25 million child-benefit claimants and their children, had been lost in the post. This did more than merely make the Treasury, through its best-known subsidiary, HM Revenue & Customs, look incompetent. It thrust the department into the front line of the huge, simmering row over identity cards, the computerisation of the National Health Service and ContactPoint, a new computer index of all children in England, a place where Treasury mandarins would prefer not to be.

Together, these three projects are cornerstones of the 'transformational government', agenda. Mr Darling's announcement cast a lurid light on all three projects, in particular the largest of them all, the identity card scheme.

Less well known was ContactPoint, which has been at the centre of a great deal of consultation. In November 2007, Roger Morgan, children's rights director for England for the Office for Standards in Education, Children's Services and Skills (Ofsted), published his own consultation with children about the scheme. He described it thus: 'ContactPoint will be a new list, on computer, of every child in England. For each child it will list their name, address, date of birth, how to contact their parents or carers, their school, doctor and other people working with the child.'

Given the major role of local authorities in running ContactPoint, the scope for data to get into the wrong hands was obvious.

Much the same could be said about the £12 billion-plus National Health Service scheme to computerise all patients' records and store them on a database to which about 300,000 people would have access. The good news, for those spooked by such an idea, was that patients would be able to opt out.

So the state sector version of the creative/knowledge economy was looking even shakier than the private sector sort. Unable to function properly without access to vast amounts of personal data, New Labour's new model government was then apparently incapable of safeguarding that data. The surrender of personal privacy in return for personal security, defence against terrorism and the smooth delivery of government services was looking rather like a devil's bargain with a spectacularly incompetent devil.

The official explanation as to how Britain's economic circle can be squared does not stand up to scrutiny. We do not inhabit a creative/knowledge economy in which the old rulebook has been torn up. That being the case, how are we resolving all the above-mentioned contradictions? Put another way, we seem to be getting away with it, and if the creative/knowledge economy is not the escape hatch, then what is?

The answer, as we saw earlier in this chapter, is simple.

Borrowed money – a lot of it. An unproductive economy, asset-stripped of most of the resources that would have enabled it to pay its way in the world, was unable to provide the level of earnings to which the public and the government felt entitled. The obvious, if dangerous, answer was to borrow the difference.

PUTTING OUT THE EMPTIES: ENFORCED SOBRIETY AND THE BRITISH ECONOMY

What of business, in whose name New Olympian economic policy is frequently claimed to have been moulded? For much of the 2000s, the business sector, in contrast to households and government, had, overall, been saving money rather than borrowing it. This 'overall' picture concealed a lot of differences at the level of the individual firm, not least with regard to mediocre businesses. The global credit bubble – both cause and effect of a driving down of interest rates and, thus, of returns to investors – had created what the Bank of England described as 'the search for yield' (Bank publications *passim*, 2005–2007), in which investors took on higher than usual levels of risk in return for yields that did not fully reflect that risk. In this climate, mediocre businesses could be endlessly refinanced; 'creative destruction', the process identified by economist Joseph Schumpeter through which capitalism renews itself, had been put on hold. By the end of 2007, however, time was running out for such businesses. 'Corporate insolvencies are set to hit seven-year highs in 2008 . . . Insolvency and restructuring professionals are braced for the sort of level of business failures last seen in 2000–2012, when the dotcom boom turned to bust, and some are recruiting more staff to help cope' (*Mail on Sunday*; December 9 2007).

On top of the drying-up of credit, firms were confronted with a feared slowdown in consumer spending, if not during the Christmas period then shortly afterwards, and with a new attitude to auditing among accountancy firms, who were reportedly toughening up their criteria for declaring a business to be a 'going concern'. Even blameless small and medium-sized enterprises with sensible medium-term financing arrangements in place were facing a bleak new year. Professor Peter Spencer, of York University, is economist to the independent Item forecasting club. Sponsored by accountant Ernst & Young, it uses the Treasury's computer model of the economy. On December 10 2007, Professor Spencer warned: 'A lot has been written about the 1.4 million people whose mortgages come up for refinancing this coming year and the fact they face higher rates because of the credit crunch. But small and medium-sized enterprises are in a similar position.

'They borrow huge amounts from banks on three to five-year terms. What will happen when these firms go back to their lenders?' (Interview with the authors.)

And for the smallest businesses, personal and company credit are often the same thing. On December 12 2007, Tracy Hoather, a trustee of the Small Business Research Trust and director of courier firm Sameday, sounded the alarm. 'A lot of very small firms use personal credit cards and mortgages as a source of finance. When that bomb goes off, there will be shock waves' (interview with the authors).

In fact, the early tremors had already started. Figures from the Insolvency Service for the third quarter of 2007 in England and Wales were, on the face of it, none too alarming. Company liquidations, at 3,106, were lower than they had been in the third quarter of 2006, when they stood at 3,250. Individual bankruptcies were up a little on the same period a year earlier, at 15,833 against 15,486, but they were down on the second quarter of 2007's total of 16,170. Above all, the rise in so-called individual voluntary arrangements (IVAs), an alternative to bankruptcy under which the debtor agrees to repay some of the money owed in return for having the rest written off, seemed to have been stemmed. The growth in IVAs had caused alarm, and not only in banking circles, at the prospect of a moral shift being under way, one that would undermine the principle that debts ought, in usual circumstances, to be repaid.

But the supply of good cheer to be had from these figures was strictly limited. For a start, given the bureaucratic delays necessarily involved in bankruptcy, liquidation and so on, the figures covered insolvencies that would have been in train before the credit crunch took effect.

Then there is the fact that while company liquidations were lower than a year earlier, they had risen slightly on the second quarter figure of 3,051.

True, the bankruptcy figures were down on the previous quarter. But they sat within a range of between 15,486 and 17,070 a quarter since the third quarter of 2006. They were nothing special.

Most worryingly of all, however, was the reality behind the apparent decline in the number of IVAs. This was very largely artificial and had been caused by a 'creditors' strike' by the banks earlier in the year. They had taken umbrage at what they saw as expensive IVA providers misleading people into walking away from what they owed, and had used their position as the (usually) largest creditor to block large numbers of IVAs. Talks between the banks and the providers led to a peace deal in December 2007 that would not merely clear the backlog but, according to one senior insolvency source, return the level of IVAs to their previous rate of about 50,000 a year.

So what of the New Labour 'economic miracle'? Kitson and Williamson's paper concludes that Labour's record is not nearly as good as it looks:

First, the growth of the UK economy can be traced back to the early 1990s, starting under the previous Tory Government following the expulsion from the Exchange Rate Mechanism that enabled a loosening of monetary policy and a more competitive exchange rate. Second, the UK economy has been expanding during a period of rapid global economic growth, although there is some evidence that the UK has improved its relative performance compared to other industrialised countries. Third, economic growth has been sustained by high levels of consumption, which have been driven by easily available credit, which in turn has led to high levels of private debt and insolvency. At the macroeconomic level the growth of consumption has outstripped the growth of domestic production and has been sustained by import growth and persistent balance of payments deficits. Fourth, productivity in the UK still lags behind many of the other major industrialized countries.

They conclude:

New Labour economics refined and developed the Thatcherism that preceded it. It embraced neo-liberal economics and accepted the notion that government demand management would not work. And it has washed its hands of rising inequality. The paradox is that while New Labour dismissed the role of demand, it was the expansion of demand that has led to increased economic growth, falling unemployment and raising job quality since 1997. But the expansion of demand was not largely due to the deliberate acts of government policy – although fiscal policy was relaxed after 2000. Demand has been driven by a consumption binge that has been NICE (non-inflationary continual expansion) while it lasted – but the hangover may be worse.

As 2007 became 2008, there were signs that the party still had an hour or so of heavy drinking to go before the dreadful 'morning after'. Professor Spencer said: 'Christmas will see heavy spending, I would guess, as it always does. I am looking to next year for people to cut back.'

Former BBC business editor Jeff Randall was more graphic: 'The message, it seems, [from the Bank of England] is that if inebriates are shivering and shaking, the best and quickest remedy is the re-introduction of Happy Hour. Pull the pints, mix the cocktails, uncork the vino – all drinks a pound' (*Daily Telegraph*; December 14 2007).

Tracy Hoather saw only limited concern as the New Year approached. Her remarks were aimed at the business community, but they could well have applied to the country as a whole: 'There is a lot of complacency. I do not get any feeling of panic. I want to say to business people "No, this can happen, guys. You should be hunkering down."' They were to do so soon enough. The British economy was like a chain letter that was running out of subscribers. Soon, there would be no more names to go on the list.

7

Here There be Monsters:

The perils lurking in the uncharted waters of the financial markets

Speculation is the romance of trade, and casts contempt upon all its sober realities. It renders the stock-jobber a magician, and the Exchange a region of enchantment. It elevates the merchant into a kind of knight-errant, or rather a commercial Quixote. The slow but sure gains of snug percentage become despicable in his eyes; no 'operation' is thought worthy of attention that does not double or treble the investment. No business is worth following that does not promise an immediate fortune.

– Washington Irving; *A Time of Unexampled Prosperity*

'I'm in capital markets. I arrange swaps.'

'Swaps?' The word reminded her of Basil when he was her kid brother, a gangling boy in scuffed shoes and a stained blazer, sorting conkers or gloating over his stamp collection.

'Yes. Suppose a corporate has borrowed x thousands at a fixed rate of interest. If they think that interest rates are going to fall, they could execute a swap transaction whereby we pay them a fixed rate and they pay us LIBOR, that's the London Interbank Offered Rate, which is variable . . .'

– David Lodge; *Nice Work;* Secker & Warburg; 1988

Speculation is a round game: the players see little or nothing of their cards at first starting; gains *may* be great – and so may losses. The run of luck went against Mr Nickleby; a mania prevailed, a bubble burst, four stock brokers took villa residences at Florence, four hundred nobodies were ruined, and among them Mr Nickleby.
    – Charles Dickens; *Nicholas Nickleby*; (1839)

With the benefit of hindsight, it was clear that the bubble went through four distinct phases. In the first place, there was a change in the economic climate caused by financial innovation. Asset prices rose as a result, and with good reason. In the second phase, overseas speculators noticed what was happening and demanded a piece of the action, driving up prices still further. In the third phase, all ideas of basing investment decisions on economic rationality were dispensed with as buyers assumed they would always be able to sell for a higher price. Finally, and inevitably, there was a collapse caused by the unwinding of speculative positions prompted by the tightening of credit.

If it all seems familiar, then it would have been – to Isaac Newton, Daniel Defoe and Robert Walpole. For this was how economic historians summed up the conditions that led to the South Sea bubble crisis of 1720. The story of the past three centuries is the story of how little life has changed. Financial markets are endlessly innovative, always coming up with new money-making ideas. The public is eternally credulous, suspicious only in the immediate aftermath of a crash, but soon convinced by those selling tulips, shares in railroads, dotcom stock or real estate that 'it is different this time'.

Historians would counter that the records show that this is the triumph of hope over experience, and that financial markets eventually realise as much. One sure sign that a bubble is about to burst is when financial commentators start to warn that 'it is different this time' are the five most dangerous words in the lexicon of markets. At that point, they dust down their history books and find that futures trading was common in the tulip mania that convulsed the Netherlands in the first half of the 17th century, that financial engineering was key to the fortunes of the South Sea Company and that widespread insider trading and crooked share tipping was revealed in the financial post-mortem examination conducted after the Wall Street crash.

In the end, little changes. The coffee houses become internet cafés, the powdered wigs become Armani suits, the millions become trillions but the song remains the same. Just like most of the companies that saw their shares ramped up in the dotcom boom of the late 1990s, the South Sea Company did little actual trading and made no profits. As with so much of the New Olympians' financial system, the South Sea bubble was inflated less by any sort of hard-headed analysis by investors as by a quasi-mystical faith. And as with most of the financial crises of the past quarter-century, the South Sea bubble had an international dimension: stock markets in Paris, Amsterdam, Lisbon and Hamburg were affected when the shares collapsed. And just as with the build-up to the 2007–2008 credit crunch, the South Sea bubble originated in a novel form of financing – converting government debt into equity in the South Sea Company in return for a monopoly on trade with South America – that seemed to offer risk-free returns for all involved.

And, just as today, there was no shortage of commentators in 18th-century London who insisted that lessons needed to be learned from the speculative madness. This, for example, was Adam Anderson, the first historian of the South Sea bubble, writing in 1764. 'The unaccountable frenzy in stocks and projects of this year 1720 may by some be thought to have taken up too much room in this work; but we are persuaded that others of superior judgement, will approve of the perpetuating . . . the remembrance thereof, as a warning to after ages' (quoted in *The First Crash;* Richard Dale; Princeton Press; 2004).

Alan Greenspan expressed similar sentiments when he gave evidence to Congress following the collapse of the dotcom boom at the turn of the millennium. 'At root was the rapid enlargement of stock-market capitalisations in the latter part of the 1990s that arguably engendered an outsized increase in opportunities for avarice. Our historical guardians of financial information were overwhelmed.'

Warming to his theme, Mr Greenspan sought to reassure senators by insisting that the weeds had been pulled up and that everything in the garden was rosy once again. 'Perhaps the recent breakdown of protective barriers resulted from a once-in-a-generation frenzy of speculation that is now over. With profitable opportunities for malfeasance markedly diminished, far fewer questionable practices are likely to be initiated in the immediate future' (Mr Greenspan's testimony before the Senate Committee on Banking, Housing and Urban Affairs; July 16 2002).

Mr Greenspan was wrong on two counts. Firstly, the dotcom frenzy was far from a one-off; since his arrival at the Federal Reserve there had been the global stock crash of 1987, the Japanese financial and real estate bubble of the early 1990s when, according to unsubstantiated reports, the land occupied by the imperial palace in Tokyo was worth more than the whole of California; and the various bubbles in the developing economies in the 1990s. These last had seen a speculative frenzy as foreign capital flooded into and then out of Thailand, Malaysia, South Korea and elsewhere. In the UK, the boom of the late 1980s was reaching its peak just as Chairman Greenspan was getting his feet under the desk, marked by soaring prices for residential and commercial property, ludicrous over-valuation of business assets and feverish demand for art, antiques and 'collectibles'. In the US, deregulation of the country's mortgage banks, the Savings & Loan institutions, in the 1980s paved the way for a disaster that cost the US government about $200 billion. The S&Ls (or 'thrifts') had been hit by high interest rates and high inflation, both of which eroded the value of mortgages advanced in quieter times. 'Reform' removed controls on interest rates and investments; stupidity and sometimes outright fraud were among the results.

For Mr Greenspan, the words 'once-in-a-generation' appeared to have a different meaning from the dictionary definition. Unless, that is, that when he talked about 'once-in-a-generation', Mr Greenspan was referring to a more than averagely long-lived insect of some kind. For 'once in a generation', read 'every few years'.

Even were a casuist to point out that the 1987 crash was not really the result of a bubble and that all the other examples of frenzied behaviour had taken place beyond the shores of the United States, as he spoke to Congress in the summer of 2002, Mr Greenspan's Fed was ensuring that the American housing market would see many 'profitable opportunities for malfeasance'.

Given that he has been a strong supporter of the deregulation of financial markets on his watch, it is perhaps unsurprising that Mr Greenspan believes that crises are the result of individual wrong-doing rather than system failure. Not all chroniclers of bubbles agree with this interpretation, even in instances where there has been bountiful evidence of both cupidity and fraud. Historian Larry Neal (in *The Rise of Financial Capitalism: International Capital Markets in the Age of Reason;* Cambridge University Press; 1990) says the South Sea bubble appeared 'to be a tale less about the perpetual folly of mankind and more about the continual difficulties of the adjustments of financial markets to an array of innovations'. This book has much to say about the 'perpetual folly of mankind' and also the dubious dealings of those who would exploit that folly. In this chapter, however, we will try to explain in simple language the 'array of innovations' that made possible the 2007–2008 subprime mortgage crisis and liquidity crunch.

We ought to point out that no housing market is ever entirely rational. In the absence of not only unlimited development land but of unlimited development land near places of employment and general amenity, there are bound to be short-run booms and busts. This is as true in a relatively empty country, such as the US, as in a relatively crowded country, such as Britain. What ought to keep such a market in trim is a fairly steady supply of money for house purchase rationed out on a reasonably unchanging set of criteria, in terms of the multiples of salary the lenders are prepared to make available, the quality of property against which they are prepared to lend, and so forth. Those unable to obtain housing finance have traditionally departed that particular housing market, heading either for the rented sector, for accommodation with family or friends or even for a very much cheaper area. This may sound harsh, but almost nobody in any country is living in their absolute first choice of house, or location – or both. And, as we shall see, the alternative was to prove less than impressive.

The selling of subprime mortgages was a classic New Olympian project that involved all the various chapters of the organisation. Central banks, ratings agencies, investment banks, hedge funds, the financial media; all were fully implicated in the manufacture of the new products.

What happened was this. At the very start of the process, a family in the United States decided to buy a home and went looking for a mortgage. Some of these people were already home-owners and had mortgages that were small in relation to the value of their properties. These people, most of whom were also in full-time, well-paid employment, are known as prime borrowers who are at very low risk of defaulting on their loans. Another group of prospective buyers were not so well placed financially; they tended to be first-time buyers and so had no equity in their existing properties. They were also much more likely to be in part-time employment and often on low wages, even assuming they were in work at all. This group was known as subprime borrowers, and loans extended to this section of the public were obviously riskier than those provided to prime borrowers.

On the face of it, this presented a problem for the American real estate sector, since it needed a supply of first-time buyers to keep the market humming. Without first-time buyers, property markets seize up, because those higher up the ladder cannot move to new homes unless a new entrant forms the first rung in the chain. This, in turn, cools down the rise in house prices, which in turn shrinks the potential size of the assets on which the lending is secured, making such loans less attractive to lenders.

Fortunately help was at hand, in terms of throwing the gears of the housing market out of neutral or even reverse and into overdrive. The US way of managing home-loan finance had moved on since the days when small-town bankers had operated their '3-6-3' model (take in deposits at 3 per cent, lend out on mortgages at 6 per cent, hit the golf course by 3pm). In the new world, the real estate industry would sign up a subprime borrower with an attractive-looking introductory offer and then sell on the loans to an investment bank.

Investment banks were happy to do this, because they could bundle up mortgages of varying qualities into securities that could be traded in the financial markets. This was a process known as securitisation, with the securities given the ugly name of collateralised debt obligations (CDOs). Everybody was a winner: the subprime borrowers got their mortgages and hence a foot on the housing ladder; the rest of the home-owning population saw the breakneck pace of activity in the real estate market maintained, with prices rising strongly as a result; the real estate brokers picked up fat commissions; and Wall Street found itself with a new and lucrative means of speculation ideal for an environment in which low interest rates had made returns on safe investments such as government bonds extremely low.

The International Monetary Fund, given the role of acting like the Oracle at Delphi for this new offering from the Olympion heroes, purred with pleasure, noting that deregulation and technological advances had revolutionised financial systems in the developed world.

'The changes that have occurred in financial systems have transformed the opportunities for borrowing and saving facing households and firms,' it said in its October 2006 *World Economic Outlook*. Households now had a broader array of borrowing options to choose from and could invest in a wider range of financial instruments. Firms were no longer so dependent on banks for their financing because they were able to raise bonds on the world's capital markets. Banks, too, were changing the way they made their money, moving away from simply taking deposits and lending money to activities for which they could charge fees, such as the securitisation of loans.

All this was one aspect of Washington economist Thomas Palley's concept of 'financialisation', which we encountered in the first chapter. In a paper in December 2007, he defined it thus:

Financialisation is a process whereby financial markets, financial institutions, and financial élites gain greater influence over economic policy and economic outcomes. Financialisation transforms the functioning of economic systems at both the macro and micro levels.

Its principal impacts are to (1) elevate the significance of the financial sector relative to the real sector, (2) transfer income from the real sector to the financial sector, and (3) increase income inequality and contribute to wage stagnation. Additionally, there are reasons to believe that financialisation may put the economy at risk of debt deflation and prolonged recession.

Financialisation operates through three different conduits: changes in the structure and operation of financial markets, changes in the behaviour of non-financial corporations, and changes in economic policy. (Financialisation: What it is and why it matters; *The Levy Economics Institute and Economics for Democratic and Open Societies*)

A final sting in the tail of financialisation – a final absurdity, in fact – has been the creation of financial instruments that give a creditor a vested interest in the *failure* of a company that owes them money. These are the credit default swaps (CDS), a type of insurance policy on a piece of lending, usually issued by a bank, which can be traded on the open market.

In any attempt to restructure a troubled company, most creditors will be prepared to write off some of what they are owed in order to get the firm back on its feet. But CDS holders are better off if the company goes bust, because this will trigger repayment of what is owed under the terms of the CDS. Alongside the CDS are more straightforward debt securities that give creditors first refusal of a company's assets in the event of a liquidation. As with the CDS, this can give a creditor an incentive to block a rescue and means a fifth column can be present at business restructuring meetings.

TALLY-HO!: THE HUNT FOR YIELD

As is clear from the IMF's above-mentioned encomium to the new world financial order, subprime mortgages were merely one of a range of what were inevitably described as 'innovative financial products' aimed at both households and companies. Since the creation of the 'Eurodollar' market in London in the late 1960s – which took dollars held in sleepy accounts outside the US and bundled them into higher-earning loans – the New Olympians had sought ways of making money 'work harder', to use the cliché beloved of financial advertising. But by the early 2000s, there was a new urgency to their efforts. The joint effect of the dotcom crash, the September 11 attacks on New York and Washington and the continuing *marasme* in Japan was to predispose central bankers to keep official interest rates at very low levels. They were further encouraged to do so by the downward pressure on the price of consumer goods exerted by the exports of developing countries, chiefly China.

The Olympians may have preached price stability but they had actually profited from high inflation. True, as Margaret Thatcher's Tories had pointed out in the 1970s, high inflation was bad for *savings*. According to the 2003 Barclays' Equity Gilt Study from the eponymous bank, £100 parked with a building society in January 1975 would have shown a 'real' (i.e. inflation-adjusted) value of just £92 by the end of December 1980. But it was much kinder to share prices and other paper assets. Over the same six years, £100 invested in shares would have risen in real terms to £132 – and that figure includes *all* shares, the duds as well as the winners, so the 'higher-risk, higher-reward' argument does not really apply.

Furthermore, even low-risk government stock outperformed savings; £100-worth of gilts in January 1975 would have become £108 by the end of 1980.

High inflation has the effect of silently redistributing wealth from some people and giving it to others. In the 1970s, members of those trade unions with powerful bargaining positions were held up as winners, and pensioners on fixed incomes as losers. Less noted was the 'winner' status of those holding shares and other securities. In the opening years of the new century, however, the New Olympians were granted what they (or at least their apologists in academia and the media) had claimed they had wanted all along: low inflation and low interest rates.

The bubble of money puffed up by Alan Greenspan and his central bankers had to be invested somewhere. By keeping interest rates low and letting banks use their 'fractional reserve' powers to create money out of thin air, central banks generated huge amount of cash. This poured into safer investments, such as government securities, so returns, naturally, fell. Great rafts of capital roamed the world, looking for above-average rewards. What the Bank of England was to refer to repeatedly as 'the search for yield', sometimes known as the 'hunt for yield', was under way in earnest.

In many cases, companies that would have gone bust in normal times were able to refinance themselves, sometimes more than once. It is a sobering thought that some of the high-profile casualties of the dotcom collapse, such as Clickmango or boo.com, might still be with us had they hit trouble a year or two later than they did. In some cases, the money bubble bankrolled 'private equity investors' to take over and then asset-strip companies that had previously been listed on one or more stock markets. And, of course, in other cases this flood of cheap money was bundled up into loans – for both consumer and house-purchase purposes – to people who were quite likely to have difficulty in meeting the repayments. This was the infamous 'subprime lending'.

What these and other investment types have in common is that they are, by definition, more risky than gilt-edged stock or blue-chip shares. In the hunt for yield, investors, such as fund managers or offshore hedge funds, could not be choosers. To top up their returns in a climate of very low yields, they needed to assume more risk. Indeed, the very act of making the higher-yielding investment would bring the risk into existence. For example, imagine a person with a poor credit history and a patchy employment record applying for a home loan in 1970, or 1980, or even 1995. As they would almost certainly be refused, the file would be closed and there would be no continuing implications for the lender.

But should this application be accepted, the lender is taking on to its books, along with the potential reward of this higher-yielding (because riskier) home loan, the potential risk of default. In an absolutely rational world, the overall financial position of the lender would be unchanged, because the default risk would cancel out the yield potential. Only when the home loan had run its course – or gone into default – would it be possible to figure out whether it had proved a good bet. Even then, assuming the lender made a very large number of such loans, the yield on these loans overall ought to adjust itself to the default risk.

Markets and prices are not, of course, absolutely (or even, sometimes, approximately) rational. In the real world, impaired borrowers of all types – corporate and individual – could probably be persuaded to pay even more above the odds than usual for the privilege of borrowing money, thus bolstering the lenders' real-term yields, at least until some sharp competitors turned up. This over-the-odds cost for poorer borrowers is not affected by the ultra-low rates on which many of them were tempted to take out subprime mortgages, as those rates applied only to the earlier part of the life of the loan. Over its whole life, the borrower would be expected to pay at least enough to reflect in full the risk that they represented.

That said, life would be a lot easier for the lenders if all that risk could simply be made to disappear. Happily, some of the brightest minds in the City, Wall Street and elsewhere had been perfecting precisely this sort of disappearing trick for at least two decades.

Looked at from one angle, the whole history of financial institutions is that of trying to secure the rewards of a particular investment while passing the risk of that investment to someone else. Put another way, they pursue the rewards that come from risky position-taking (of which declaring a buying or selling price is the pre-eminent example) with the security that comes from simply earning fees. You could call this a creative dynamic, or you could call it something less complimentary. For decades, the principle means of achieving this was the so-called 'greater fool' method, whereby institutions would routinely sell over-priced assets either directly to individual investors or to pooled investment funds such as pension schemes, unit trusts, savings plans and so forth. It remains the case that, by the time the fruit reaches the general public, it has been pretty well sucked dry.

But from the 1980s onwards, new, intricate forms of financial engineering seemed to promise something far less crude than this sort of pump-and-dump activity in terms of getting the risk to disappear while hanging on to the rewards. So-called derivative products had been available in the commodity markets for years, allowing producers such as farmers, mining firms and oil companies to 'hedge' their risks by selling future production at a price fixed in the present. By the early 1990s, however, this sort of homely and wholesome activity was only about 2 per cent or less of a derivatives market that had ballooned into a vast, speculative card game.

Derivatives come in two forms: futures (which confer the *obligation* to buy or sell a commodity or financial asset at a fixed point in the future) and options (which confer the *right* to buy or sell a commodity or financial asset at a fixed point in the future). Because options, unlike futures, allow holders simply to walk away should prices have moved against them, they are more expensive than futures. That said, in the overwhelming majority of cases neither futures nor options contracts ever run to actual delivery of the specified commodity or security – in the market there are enough equal and opposite contracts to cancel them out. It is simply gambling.

Collaterised debt obligations were not, strictly speaking, derivative products. But they emerged from the same financial-engineering industry and radiated the same reassuring sense that risk could be almost infinitely dissipated while the rewards could be pocketed. They, like derivatives, were premised on the idea that breaking something up into the right-shaped pieces or slices would increase its value and diminish its riskiness. CDOs were, in fact, an example of the other great invention of the financial engineers – 'securitisation'.

This is one of those words that sounds reassuring, deriving as it does from the word 'security', but describes something that is anything but. It covers the process whereby a large number of IOUs, all of which are slightly different from one another, can be rolled up into one monster IOU and sold on the capital markets. One example would be hire-purchase loans, the income stream of which could be sold to major investors – provided enough loans had been aggregated to make the sums involved worthwhile.

Another would be mortgages. In the US, Salomon Brothers pioneered the trading of mortgage-backed securities, thus was ideally placed when, in October 1981, a change in American law saw the country's savings and loans institutions, the so-called 'thrifts' responsible for much mortgage lending, offload $1 trillion of home loans on the capital market. As former Salomon employee Michael Lewis recorded, the thrifts were in deep trouble after US interest rates shot up in 1979 because the thrifts were restricted in the rates they themselves could charge. So Congress changed both the tax and accounting rules to allow them to offload their now-unprofitable mortgages to Wall Street and other investors and to replace them with new ones, more profitably priced.

Mr Lewis noted: '[It] amounted to a massive subsidy to Wall Street from Congress. Long live motherhood and home ownership!' (*Liar's Poker*; Hodder & Stoughton; 1989)

Perhaps ironically, Salomon's top mortgage trader Lewis Ranieri became convinced his activities had something to do with spreading the benefits of home ownership, putting big finance on the side of the little person. He was not to be the last to plug this theme.

Lewie Ranieri, formerly of the Salomon Brothers' mail room and utility bond trading desk, had become the champion of the American homeowner. It was a far more appealing persona than that of the slick, profiteering Wall Street trader.

'Lewie had this spiel about building homes for America,' says Bob Dall [a colleague at Salomon Brothers]. 'When we'd come out of those meetings, I'd say, "C'mon, you don't think anyone believes that crap do you?" But that was what made Ranieri so convincing. He believed that crap.'

Ranieri was perhaps the first populist in the history of Wall Street. (Lewis; ibid)

Alas, it was not long before the forerunner of the CDO financial engineers arrived.

'The nature of the trader changed,' says long-time mortgage bond salesman Samuel Sachs. 'They wheeled in rocket scientists, who started to carve up mortgage securities into itty bitty pieces.' (Lewis; *ibid*)

Yes, indeed.

Regardless of the source of the income stream – mortgages,

hire-purchase debt, student loans or, in one celebrated case, ten years' worth of revenues from the first 25 albums of the singer David Bowie – securitisation involves taking the debt off the books of the originating institution (such as a mortgage lender), putting it together with a large number of similar debts and selling it on to an institution or individual unconnected with the original transaction.

Securitisation, according to the IMF, was a good thing. It allowed the 'unbundling' of financial risks, which could be 'repackaged' into portfolios of financial instruments and transferred to investors willing to assume such risks.

Here, in a nutshell, is the justification not only for CDOs and securitisation, but also for derivatives and for most of the other exotic financial products that have proliferated in recent years. They are said to relieve workaday businesses of the risks involved in recovering what they are owed and transfer that risk to the broad shoulders of New Olympian investors and institutions only too happy to assume it, on the principle enunciated by Raymond Chandler's fictional private eye Philip Marlowe that 'trouble is my business'.

Sad to say, the current gathering storm of lawsuits from these institutions in relation to having been sold many of the flakier securities belies somewhat this notion of the hedge funds and the more buccaneering investment banks as the unflappable hard men of high finance.

Furthermore, it is far from clear that the most dangerous of the exotic financial instruments – whether CDOs or anything else – did, in fact, end up with these super-cool, ultra-professional investors. In 1997, Frank Partnoy, a former First Boston and Morgan Stanley derivatives trader, wrote of life on Wall Street. In one passage, Mr Partnoy is asking an experienced derivatives salesmen who it is who actually buys First Boston's derivatives. Is it hedge funds?

'"No way. Are you kidding me?" It was a stupid question. The top hedge funds were much too sophisticated to buy this trade from First Boston. They could place such bets on their own.'

Mr Partnoy tries again. Other investment banks? No. Investment funds? No. Commercial banks? No.

'I was running out of choices.'

Finally, the salesman enlightens him.

'He said: "State pension funds and insurance companies." "What?" I was shocked. He just smiled.' (*FIASCO*; Profile Books)

SUBPRIME MORTGAGES: INSIDE, OUTSIDE, USA . . .

In its modern form, securitisation has its origins in the early 1970s with the first appearance of asset-backed securities (ABSs), but from modest beginnings it had become a huge business by 2007. New issues of asset-backed securities amounted to $3.07 trillion in the US alone in 2005.

We mentioned earlier that securitisation takes the risk away from the originator of a piece of business, a car loan, for example, and transfers it to an individual or institution with an appetite for risk. Key to this is transforming an asset that was illiquid (that is to say, it could not easily be traded) and turning it into an asset that could be traded freely. This is achieved by taking individual financial transactions – mortgage debt, student loans or aircraft leases, for example – and pooling them. The pool of assets produces a stream of income – the interest payments on the mortgages, for example – and the bank that has created the pool can turn that stream of income into a lump sum by selling the rights to the income stream.

Leigh Skene, of Lombard Street Research, notes there is still a credit risk, but the bank seeks to remove that by setting up a structured investment vehicle (SIV), or a conduit, a type of what are known as special purpose vehicles (SPVs). He notes that securitisation involves three key characteristics: the pooling of assets, the de-linking of the credit risk of the pool of assets from the credit risk of the originating lender through a special purpose vehicle and, finally, a trust that either passes the cash flow from the assets straight to investors or creates different tranches with different risks and returns.

For instance, mortgage company X has originated $1 billion nominal value of mortgages from which it receives a cash flow. It can turn that income stream into a lump sum today by selling the rights to that cash flow to an SPV. The SPV puts the cash flow into a trust so it cannot be distributed to Company X's creditors if it goes into bankruptcy. The trust then pays for the rights to the mortgages by issuing bonds that receive the cash flow from the assets less administrative costs.
(Credit and Credibility; *Lombard Street Research; September 2007)*

If the average layman found all that esoteric, there was an added complexity. The next innovation was to leverage, to increase the potential profit (or loss) by slicing and dicing the asset-backed securities into tranches, some of which were more risky than others. These financial instruments are the above-mentioned collateralised debt obligations (CDOs).

'The senior bonds have first claim on cash flows, and are usually rated AAA to A,' said Mr Skene *(LSR; ibid)*. 'Mezzanine bonds have a subordinate claim on cash flows and are usually rated BBB to B. The equity class is the most junior, unrated and receives the residual proceeds of the collateral – but also absorbs the initial losses. The high risk of the equity class has led to allegations of mis-selling and commentators have called it "Toxic Waste", so the originator of the loans or the underwriter of the securities issued under the trust usually retains it.'

In 2006 and early 2007 there was big money to be made from asset-backed securities and CDOs. In the US, around $6 trillion of the $10 trillion mortgages outstanding had been packaged into mortgage-backed securities, while the issuance of CDOs rose by almost 100 per cent in 2006 to almost $1.2 trillion. As one commentator noted, this was an industrial-style process: raw materials (loans) were sent down the assembly line to be turned into an array of products

(CDO tranches). The quality assurance department (rating agencies) inspected the goods, which were then shipped out. There were top-of-the-range products (AAA-rated tranches) for the pension funds and mutual funds, while the mezzanine tranches were snapped up by those with an appetite for something a bit riskier, such as hedge funds.

They often did so by treating an SPV as a glorified hedge fund, to take the toxic waste off the balance sheet of the parent bank. ('Sudden Debt'; http://suddendebt.blogspot.com/2007/12/here-there-be-monsters.html).

That just left the toxic waste, and that was where the parallel with a big manufacturing firm broke down. When an industrial conglomerate is left with waste it either recycles it into a new source of raw materials, finds somewhere to make it safe or harmless, or in the case of the more unscrupulous firms, dumps it in the environment. None of these options was open to the banks with their 'toxic waste'; instead they either had to find speculators willing to bear the high risks involved or keep the waste 'on site' and hope that it did not contaminate the rest of the plant.

One of the reasons the credit crunch proved so serious was that nobody knows for sure quite how much toxic waste was produced, although one estimate for 2004 alone – before CDOs became really popular in the markets – puts the total at $100bn or more (suddendebt; *ibid*). 'Trying to navigate through the *terra incognita* of structured finance holdings at banks and hedge funds is a near impossibility,' says one internet site specialising in CDOs. 'They are so heavily annotated with Class II and Class III markings – plus unknown off-balance sheet exposures – as to be the equivalent of "Here There Be Monsters" in old maps. It is little wonder that the credit market has seized: mariners are unwilling to steer by such maps; the few that do ask for pay commensurate to the risk' ('Hellasious'; blog entry December 14 2007; suddendebt *ibid*).

In the good times, it didn't seem to matter much that the ship was being steered with incomplete maps, a dodgy compass and a captain rather too fond of his grog. So long as house prices were going up and mortgage defaults were low, the banks found that they could make big money by selling toxic waste to their own special purpose vehicles.

Unlike, say, the sterling-dollar exchange rate or shares in Tesco, there was no readily available market price for CDOs. The banks, therefore, employed the very brightest mathematicians to construct fiendishly clever models that would enable them to put a price on the CDOs. In a rising market, the message from the models was that holding toxic waste was advantageous, since the lowest-rated tranches of the CDOs benefited disproportionately when asset prices were going up, because investors secured higher returns for the extra risk they were taking. These pricing models, therefore, marked up the value of the toxic waste, which the hedge funds and SPVs could use as collateral to buy still more toxic waste.

It was, of course, a completely different story when asset prices turned down. The first thing that happened was that banks found there was a big gap between the value of toxic waste according to their carefully constructed models and the actual price they could get for the waste from a buyer, even assuming they could find one. The second thing that happened was that the toxic waste tranches lost just as heavily on the way down as they had gained on the way up, leading to the banks that had lent to the hedge funds demanding extra collateral to compensate for the lower valuations. As had been the case with LTCM in 1998, the hedge funds were fully leveraged and could raise the additional collateral only through a fire sale of assets. To their horror, the lending banks found that they couldn't sell this collateral – much of which was in the form of highly rated bonds – at anything like the valuations put on it by the models. Within days, banks decided they were no longer happy with maps that merely said: 'Here there be monsters.' On the contrary, they insisted that they would not leave port without assurances that they had the very latest charts on which all wrecks were marked, that the seas would remain calm for the foreseeable future and that the government would act as underwriter for their voyage into the unknown.

And this was a global problem. The securitisation process had increasingly taken on an international dimension, since the markets for mortgage-backed securities were attracting a significant number of foreign investors. Again, this had met with the approval of the IMF. As with all Delphic utterances, however, there was a sting in the tail. Yes, the Fund approved of securitisation; that was hardly a surprise since it contained all the elements – financial liberalisation, deregulation and globalisation – guaranteed to make the IMF happy. But there was a need for policy makers to remain vigilant; otherwise there could be repercussions.

The key question for policymakers is how to maximise the benefits of this continuing move toward financial systems that are more reliant on arm's length transactions, while minimising the downside risks. Financial and regulatory policies have to adapt to changing financial systems in order to maintain stability. The greater speed and flexibility with which transactions can be executed and the higher degree of leverage in the household sector in more arm's length systems could become sources of financial instability with macroeconomic consequences, if not adequately monitored. Supervisors and regulators will therefore need to continually assess and upgrade their policy tools to match financial systems. (October 2006 World Economic Outlook, ibid)

Well, yes – if regulators cannot or will not keep a close eye on the novelty products being cooked up in the City and Wall Street, then the global economy could be in serious trouble. The Olympians had the deregulation they demanded. Now they prepared to blame the regulators for not having paid close enough attention. It is a fair bet that few of those involved in the buying and selling of CDOs in late 2006 and 2007 bothered to read what the IMF had to say about the possible risks of securitisation, and that even those who did probably paid little heed to the warning. The IMF's soporific language cannot have helped. But there seems little evidence that the regulators managed to grasp what the IMF was saying.

This was an environment in which a prolonged period of low – and in the case of the Bank of Japan, zero – interest rates had led to a rapid increase in the amount of money available for speculation, because this plunge in the price of money made it much easier for borrowers to demand more, thus generating more credit in the system. It was a period when there was a search for high-yielding investments. It was a time when securitisation, derivatives and leverage could be used to bypass any remaining regulations on speculation. And it was a time when markets remained supremely confident that central banks would bail them out in the unlikely event that the economic skies darkened.

From the perspective of a hedge fund manager, it had made perfect sense to load up with CDOs. For a while they had delivered profits. The term hedge fund was first inspired by Alfred Winslow Jones, a former editor of America's *Fortune* magazine, who decided that it was a good idea to take conflicting positions on pairs of stocks in order to limit his risk. Mr Jones took a punt on stocks he considered cheap, but limited his exposure to the bet going wrong by gambling that a stock he considered over-valued would go down. This strategy was not foolproof (both the cheap and the expensive sahare could go the wrong way) but it held out the hope of small, incremental gains that would multiply over time.

Today's hedge funds are a far cry from the model he envisaged. As one writer put it: 'Today's global macro funds are anything but hedged: they involve naked speculation, albeit extensively researched. Some are characterised by aggressive use of derivatives, such as swaps, futures and options which, like insurance contracts, require small down-payments for potentially big payouts' (Henry Tricks; 'The biggest bets in the world'; *Prospect* magazine; December 2006).

Long Term Capital Management had shown how things could go wrong for hedge funds. The Russian debt default of August 1998 had led to a divergence in bond yields as investors took the view that some countries were less creditworthy than others. LTCM had bet that bond spreads would narrow and found that it had to start selling assets to cover losses. On paper it had \$125 billion of assets, but \$120 billion of them were backed by borrowed money. The inevitable fire sale of assets followed, prompting a bail-out organised by the Federal Reserve as it became clear that the hedge fund would go bust.

But since neither LTCM or the much more serious dotcom collapse appeared to derail the global economy, hedge funds took the view that the combination of a benign macroeconomic backdrop and the availability of the new range of sophisticated financial products meant it really was 'different this time'. That view was reflected in credit spreads, the gap between the interest rates paid for rock-solid investments such as US Treasury bonds and those payable on riskier assets such as the bonds issued by developing countries. When financial markets are cautious, these spreads are wide; in 2006 and early 2007, the spreads had narrowed even though the quality of some of the products being offered – subprime mortgages most notably – were of deeply dubious quality.

Up until midsummer 2007, that was the sort of talk few in the City or Wall Street wished to hear.

NEW FRONTIERS FOR THE OLYMPIANS: THE GLOBAL IMBALANCES

The boom in CDOs, derivatives and other exotic instruments did not happen in isolation. True, Western central banks, such as the Federal Reserve Board in the US and the Bank of England, pursued very lax monetary policies during most of the 2000s. But easy money alone is no guarantee of even illusory prosperity: ask the people of Zimbabwe. Rather, these exotic, and frequently toxic, instruments were bobbing like corks on the surface of a vast tide of money, most of which was flowing in the wrong direction, from poor, young countries to rich, ageing ones.

Like the crumbling aristocrat forever borrowing from the butler to pay the gardener's wages, major Western economies have been borrowing money from developing countries in order to fund their purchases of goods from . . . developing countries. Figures published in the IMF's October 2007 World Economic Outlook make sobering reading. As a percentage of GDP, the US current account deficit was calculated to move as follows, from 6.2 per cent in 2006 to 5.7 per cent in 2007 to 5.5 per cent in 2008.

The figures for the UK are as follows: 3.2 per cent, 3.5 per cent and 3.6 per cent. Other so-called Anglo-Saxon 'miracle' economies are performing even more badly. For Australia, the figures are 5.5 per cent, 5.7 per cent and 5.6 per cent, and for New Zealand they are 8.7 per cent, 8.5 per cent and 8.6 per cent.

Nor is this Rake's Progress confined to the Anglo-Saxon countries. True, the IMF notes healthy current account surpluses for both Germany and the Netherlands, but elsewhere in the eurozone are some truly worrying figures. For Spain, the deficit is calculated to move from 8.6 per cent of GDP in 2006 to 9.8 per cent in 2007 and 10.2 per cent in 2008. For Greece, the figures are 9.6 per cent, 9.7 per cent and 9.6 per cent; for Portugal, they are 9.4 per cent, 9.2 per cent and 9.2 per cent and for the Republic of Ireland 4.2 per cent, 4.4 per cent and 3.3 per cent.

So these are some of the debtors. Who are the creditors?

China is one. The IMF has its surplus as moving from 9.4 per cent of GDP in 2006 to 11.7 per cent in 2007 and 12.2 per cent in 2008. China has suffered famine within living memory and millions of its people are living in grinding poverty, yet China is lending money to people in Dorking, Surrey, and McLean, Virginia.

Malaysia is another. The IMF has its current account surplus moving from 17.2 per cent of GDP in 2006 to 14.4 per cent in 2007 and 13.3 per cent in 2008. Malaysia may be an industrialisation success story, but many of its people have yet to share fully in the fruits of that success and there are racial and other tensions below the surface of society, yet Malaysia is lending money to people in Basildon, Essex, and Bantry, Co. Cork.

Then there is Singapore, where the numbers are 27.5 per cent, 27 per cent and 25.4 per cent; Taiwan, where the numbers are 6.8 per cent, 6.8 per cent and 7.1 per cent; Russia, where the numbers are a more modest 9.7 per cent, 5.98 per cent and 3.3 per cent and Saudi Arabia, where the numbers are 27.4 per cent, 22.2 per cent and 20.1 per cent.

These are what the IMF refers to delicately as the 'global imbalances', the process whereby developing countries in need of capital end up exporting their own savings to the very developed countries that ought, in classical capitalist economic theory, to be investing in the developing world. Not only, in classical theory, does this provide higher returns for the developing country investors (given their own, more mature, companies are unlikely to be growing as quickly), but those returns provide an income stream from which to pay the pensions of the ageing developed country population. Instead of this, the New Olympians have cheerfully sold to the developing countries vast quantities of assets, both paper securities, such as US Treasury bills, and, more recently, tangible assets such as companies and property. In doing so, of course, the New Olympians have earned fat fees, apparently oblivious to the fact that, when the last share, factory or acre of land has been sold, there will be no more of the 'deal flow' upon which the City and Wall Street rely.

Until that happens, however, the agreeable illusion is maintained that we can live beyond our means indefinitely, an illusion best summed up not by an economist but by the corrupt police chief played by Claude Rains in the film *Casablanca* (Warner Bros; 1942), who explains thus his ability to drink for free at a local watering hole: 'Please, Monsieur, it is a little game we play. They put it on the bill; I tear the bill up. It is very convenient.'

Of course, the convenience of the West will ultimately prove to have been a low priority of our creditors. Indeed, as senior British officials complain in private, and occasionally in public, we have an allegedly single global market that contains two incompatible systems, the free market in capital and goods beloved of the New Olympians, which reigns supreme in the developed world, and the nation-building system exemplified by China, which has constructed its economy using policies that have some similarities to those used by the West after the Second World War: capital controls, fixed exchange rates, industrial strategies. Furthermore, China and other Asian economies have been helped by the Olympian-inspired deindustrialisation of the West and by the willingness of the New Olympians to pretend that Britain and the US could permanently live beyond their means. In the autumn of 2007, a new battleground opened up between the Western system and the developing countries, the so-called sovereign wealth funds (SWFs). These entities are precisely what their name suggests: government investment schemes that buy up assets round the world that are then held on behalf of the country concerned. The SWFs tend to be concentrated in the creditor countries, and are looking to snap up assets in debtor countries. In the case of Norway, for example, such state supervised investment is likely to be largely benign from the point of view of the country in which the investment has taken place. In the cases of Russia or China, those on the receiving end of their investments may wonder as to the likely extent of political interference.

As a rule, finance ministers of the Group of Seven rich nations fear and loathe SWFs, which they regard as an expression of primitive and uncivilised thinking, like cannibalism or widow-burning. On the evening of October 19 2007 in Washington, G7 finance ministers invited to dinner representatives of some of the SWF countries. There were suggestions that a code of conduct was to be drawn up under which SWFs would behave themselves when operating in Western countries and act as if they were ordinary commercial investors.

Ahead of a policy statement in February 27 2008, Manuel Barroso, president of the European Commission, said that

Brussels could not allow non-European funds 'to be run in an opaque manner or used as an implement of geopolitical strategy'.

The Americans have been holding talks with SWFs and the IMF was expected to publish a voluntary code of conduct in time for the April 2008 spring meeting. And whereas the Davos meeting of the World Economic Forum in January 2007 had been dominated by shows of respect for the then ever-present private equity firms, the meeting of 2008 saw SWFs under the spotlight. The US was far more concerned about the activities of the latter (which it did not control) than of the former (most of which were American owned), but when the former treasury secretary Larry Summers called on SWFs to be more transparent and sign up to a code of conduct he was rebuffed. The Saudis accused him of double standards, asking why there were calls for regulation of SWFs by Washington but no calls for the regulation of hedge funds. Russia, which has already used the financial clout from its oil and gas reserves to bully its near neighbours, was equally blunt. It said Mr Summers's comments were 'unhelpful' – diplomat-speak for 'bang out of order'.

But given the 'imbalances' – the sums owned by key rich nations to poorer ones – the G7 was in no position to lay down the law. As British officials made clear in private conversation with the authors, the rise of the SWFs was a symptom, not a cause, of the rise of economic power outside the G7. They could have added that these new economic actors were not only outside the G7, but did not share the G7 dogma of free trade, open markets and unfettered capital-market activity.

In the battle for ideas between the free traders and the nation builders, the under-developed countries were a critical strategic objective. Although the poorer countries were helped in the first years after decolonisation by demand for their commodities in the long post-war boom, they were badly affected by the oil shocks of the 1970s, accumulating massive debts that they could not pay in an era of high interest rates.

Many of the poorest nations found themselves trapped in a cycle of low growth, high indebtedness and weak governance.

Come the 1980s and 1990s, and the New Olympians had an answer to the problems of the developing world. Unsurprisingly they were the same answers as those being promoted domestically. The Washington Consensus – the mindset of a coalition of the US Treasury, Wall Street, the World Bank and the IMF – insisted that the least-developed nations open up their markets to foreign imports, scrap capital controls, cut public spending and keep a tight rein on welfare projects. Precisely the opposite policies, in other words, to those used by every country in history that has developed successfully, including Britain, the United States, Germany and Japan.

By and large, the Washington Consensus did not travel well. Its failure to generate real benefits for poorer countries was summed up by Malawi's then trade minister Sam Mpasu, speaking at world trade talks in Cancun, Mexico, in September 2003: 'We have opened our economy. That is why we are flat on our back.'

But while many of those forced to swallow the New Olympian medicine in the 1980s and 1990s saw their economies go backwards, those that ignored the Washington Consensus, such as China and India, started to develop rapidly. True, they traded with other countries and, in some cases, dismantled capital controls, but they did so at their own speed and in their own way.

Professor Dani Rodrik, of Harvard University, wrote:

What is striking about China, Indian and a few other Asian countries that have done well recently, is that they have played the globalisation game by the Bretton Woods rulebook rather than the current rulebook. These countries did not significantly liberalise their import regimes until well after their economies had taken off, and they continue to restrict short-term capital inflows. They have used industrial policies – many of them banned by the World Trade Organisation – strategically to restructure their economies and to enable them to better take advantage of world markets. ('Saving Globalisation?'; newsletter of Leverhulme Centre, Nottingham University; Winter 2007 issue)

In less fortunate nations, the impact of failed policies has been twofold: it has proved to be a fertile breeding ground for terrorism and it has led to pressure for mass migration. In light of this, it is unsurprising that the assault on New Olympian policies came from the aid agencies and other non-governmental organisations that called for debt relief, higher aid flows, the right for poor countries to industrialise behind tariff barriers (just as the rich ones had done) and for the relaxation of stringent conditions for economic assistance.

But even within the G7, bubble-type activity has been thriving, as seen in the phenomenon that we mentioned earlier known as 'carry trading'. It sounds like some sort of take-away food, but in fact refers to the process whereby hedge funds and others exploited differences in interest rates in different countries, chiefly Japan. The Tokyo authorities, following the bursting of the country's bubble in the 1990s, had mandated extremely low official interest rates. The 'carry trade' involved borrowing in Japan at low levels – about 1 per cent on average – in order to lend in markets where interest rates were higher. Both New Zealand and the United Kingdom fell into this category, since they had interest rates of 5 per cent or more. The annual return of some four percentage points could be multiplied by leverage – i.e. borrowing – while the increase in the value of the New Zealand dollar and sterling caused by the influx of 'hot money' from overseas added to the profit from the carry trade.

The economic impact of the carry trade on a country like Britain was perverse; the size of the UK's trade deficit meant that the pound should have been depreciating in order to make imports dearer and exports cheaper, thus helping to bring the balance of payments into equilibrium. However, the profits from the carry trade were considerable and had the knock-on effect of bringing business into London's financial markets. The downside for the hedge funds was, of course, that the big returns also entailed big risks, since, as Leigh Skene of

Lombard Street Research has noted, an unexpected movement in a currency triggered by an economic or political event can wipe out a year's profit within a week.

Furthermore, the New Olympians may have reflected that the carry trade proved that the foreign currency market – routinely championed as a super-efficient Olympian institution – does not actually work properly. If it did, differences in interest rates would be cancelled out by differences in exchange rates, and there would be no profit.

They *may* have reflected that way. But in a world riven with imbalances, such reflections could be dangerous, in that they could lead to further reflection, and so on. Reflections on the nature of such a world, a place in which New Olympians have made fortunes from asset-stripping Western economies, and are making second fortunes from selling those assets to the gigantic pawn shop that is the developing world in return for our being able to buy goods from developing countries. Surfing the wave of money coming in (for now) from those developing countries, they became convinced of their ability to conjure up ever-greater wealth through types of financial engineering that allow rewards to be pocketed and risk to be massaged away.

No self-respecting New Olympian could face the ghastly truth that they had grown fat on a fantastical type of food for the gods and their hero-servants, a deadly form of ambrosia.

WAITING FOR THE BARBARIANS: THE LAST HELPINGS OF AMBROSIA

The yen carry trade was an early casualty of the credit crunch of 2007–2008, coming to a halt as soon as financial markets started to reassess risk. It was, however, merely a support act to the main event, the problems caused by an over-optimistic view of what securitisation and other financial engineering could deliver.

According to the Bank of England's Financial Stability Review of October 2007, there was no single cause for the outbreak of market turbulence but it said a key development was the impact of mounting expected losses in the American mortgage market on the toxic waste tranches of subprime residential mortgage-backed securities (RMBS). It had been clear for some time that the US housing bubble was deflating; what changed in the summer was that financial markets realised that the more highly rated tranches of subprime CDOs also contained toxic waste. The banks had the same problem as that faced by a food manufacturer who knows that an infected carcass has contaminated one in ten thousand tins of corned beef but doesn't know which one. In the food business, all tins of corned beef are taken off the shelves; in the financial world the same happened to CDOs.

Falling prices of highly rated RMBS put pressure on investors who in their search for yield had highly leveraged positions in what they believed to be low-risk debt. Losses also began to appear in AA and AAA tranches of so-called mezzanine collateralised debt obligations. As a direct result, two leveraged funds of Bear Stearns collapsed in late June. As losses mounted and exposed funds tried to de-leverage, secondary market liquidity in RMBS evaporated and prices fell further, amplifying mark-to-market losses.

The Bank's report added that by the end of June 2007 financial vehicles that funded long-term investments with short-term debt had accumulated assets of almost $2 trillion but were finding it hard to finance their activities as key investors, including money market mutual funds, were concerned about the true state of their finances. Like everybody else, Threadneedle Street struggled to put a figure on the likely scale of the losses.

The fundamental values of subprime RMBS depend on the prospective default losses on the mortgages to which they are linked. These appear particularly uncertain at present. It is unclear, for example, the extent to which weaker lending standards, increased fraud and the resetting of mortgage interest rates from teaser rates could raise the frequency of

*defaults. In addition, it is uncertain whether declining house prices could
lead to lower recovery rates in the event of default.*

Fittingly, it was left to *The Economist*, a cheerleader for the
New Olympians and all their works, to provide the coda to
the IMF's remarks about the potential perils of securitisation.
Writing in the autumn of 2007, hence with the immeasurable
benefit of hindsight, the world's premier business magazine
expressed surprise that anybody had been taken in by what
was obviously such a flawed concept ('Lessons from the Credit
Crunch'; October 20–26 2007).

*Imagine a country where a fifth of all mortgages are taken out by the
shakiest borrowers. About half of these loans are written by companies
that are almost entirely unregulated. The mortgages, on average are worth
almost 95% of the underlying house. Half of them demand no documen-
tation of the borrower's income.*

*These loans are then bundled and sliced into complicated debt instru-
ments. The risk of these is gauged by credit-rating agencies which are paid
by the very firms that created the securities and which make a lot of their
money from advising on how to win the best ratings. Many of these structured debt instruments are bought by banks in other countries using off-
balance sheet entities for which they make little capital provision and about
which banking supervisors know virtually nothing. Financial supervisors
tend to be sober and calm, but that tale ought to bring any half-competent
regulator out in a cold sweat.*

The first crisis to test the new glittering world of high
finance, said *The Economist*, had shown that markets were now
so interconnected and so global that poison could spread across
continents at dizzying speed. 'It is a long way from the shabby
hoardings of American subprime mortgages to the marbled
halls of the European interbank market. It was as if the ambush
of a few legionnaires in the forests of Germania had triggered
a revolution in ancient Rome.'
What *The Economist* could have added, of course, was that
in the end the tribes lurking on other side of the Rhine and

the Danube eventually swept down through Italy and brought Rome to its knees.

Nor is it clear that CDOs will be the last 'toxic security' to poison world markets. Indeed, compared to some instruments, CDOs were – strange as it may seem – relatively straight-forward. They may have ended up as the cause of instability, but they were not intended to be so. Some 'securities', however, would be almost certain to destabilise markets.

Frank Partnoy, whom we met earlier in this chapter, gives the example of one derivative product relating to the future level of the London Inter-Bank Offered Rate (the rate at which banks lend to each) *cubed*. Who, asks Mr Partnoy, could possibly have Libor cubed liabilities? The question answers itself. Such an instrument has lost contact entirely with reality. It has been designed with one end in mind, to earn large fees. And, as Mr Partnoy discovered, it is quite likely to be sold on to suppos-edly conservative institutions such as pension funds.

It is bad enough when CDOs, derivatives and other instru-ments are sold to such institutions, in the process transferring risk from New Olympian operators to, in effect, the general public. But at least there was some risk to transfer in the first place, however wrongfully we may believe that risk was gener-ated. But in this case, the risks against which it supposedly hedges do not exist. The product itself is the sole risk.

How many of these instruments are out there and what trigger will expose their real market value as being as badly impaired as that of the CDOs?

In summary, the New Olympians used financial deregula-tion from the 1970s onwards to asset-strip countries such as Britain, whose long-term current account position deterio-rated more or less consistently since the 1980s. With returns on our own productive assets and even on our service busi-nesses and overseas investments inadequate in terms of paying our way in the world, borrowed money has poured in, in the expectation that our New Olympians will be able to generate higher than average returns. In order to do so, the Olympians have had to make very much riskier bets – effectively, they have turned the UK into a vast hedge fund. Having assumed all this risk, the Olympians then used financial engineering to make it disappear again, with the result that banks, pension funds and others have found themselves stuffed with toxic securities.

Looked at in this light, the New Olympians' activities have been and continue to be absolutely terrifying, as are the already realised and the anticipated consequences.

8

Last Tango on Wall Street:

The fall of the 'American miracle'

Sgt Bilko: 'Pay? It's a word I seldom use. I have a rule in life, never pay what you can talk your way out of.'
  – from *The Phil Silvers Show*; CBS Television

Whether a bubble or a froth, the party was winding down by late 2005, when first-time buyers began to find prices increasingly out of reach . . . The heady days when buyers paid above offering price to bid away a house were over. Sellers' offering prices held up, but buyers pulled their bids. Sales volumes according fell sharply for both new and existing homes. The boom was over.
  – Alan Greenspan; *The Age of Turbulence*; Penguin; 2007

Slam! So it wasn't a game?
  – David Bowie; *Watch that man*; RCA (INTK 5067)

In the film *Trading Places* (Paramount Pictures and Cinema Group Ventures; 1983) Randolph and Mortimer Duke are two elderly but crooked commodity brokers who, while seeking to fix the market for frozen orange juice, strike a bet that it would be possible for a small-time hustler from the ghetto to replace the obnoxious yuppie running their company.

What is interesting about the film today – apart from the absurdly low sums involved when the plan goes predictably awry – is that the Dukes and their fellow financiers seem to spend more time lolling around in the wood-panelled luxury of their Philadelphia club than they do actually taking decisions that might make them money. To the filmgoer of today, *Trading Places* may appear to represent a world that no longer exists. New Olympians get up early and go to bed late because they operate in 24/7 markets that never sleep. Their BlackBerrys are with them night and day, blinking out the command to answer an e-mail that might make or break a deal. To be sure, they earn the sort of packages in a year that ordinary mortals could not dream of taking home in a lifetime, but the money is the reward for incisive decision-making and sheer hard graft.

In fact, the response of the New Olympians as the financial crisis of 2007 and 2008 evolved suggests that not much has changed since Jon Landis made Eddie Murphy a star in his film more than two decades ago, and indeed that life was pretty much what it had been for Wall Street's leisured class a century before. It was a fact lovingly documented by the magazines devoted to the glorification of conspicuous consumption that life for New York's wealthy was as good as it had been since the days of Vandebilt, Rockefeller and JP Morgan. Where once the monied rich would not think twice about hiring a symphony orchestra to serenade a new-born baby so today the New Olympians, eager to show that they are both hip and loaded rather than merely nouveau riche, might ring around to see if Elton John, perhaps even The Rolling Stones, might care to earn $5 million by playing at a bash for their wife or daughter. Few, though, were prepared to castigate the scions of Wall Street in the way that Walt Whitman did when he called New York society 'cankered, crude, superstitious, and rotten' (Walt Whitman quoted by Walter Fuller Taylor; *The Economic Novel in America;* Octagon Books; 1964). After all, these men and women were the true descendents of the frontiersmen who had blazed their trails across the West in the 19th century. The covered wagon had been replaced by a dealing screen, but the pioneering spirit principle remained the same. These were the men and women who made the dollars that kept the economy ticking over. These were the men and women who worked hard and played hard, and were a shining example of intelligence, self-reliance and doing things the American way. As it turned out, these were also men (not women, as it happens) who were driving their golf buggies across the well-manicured fairways of some of America's swankiest courses when the biggest financial crisis in their lifetime erupted in the summer of 2007.

REWARDS FOR FAILURE: FOOD FIT FOR HEROES

The first big bank on Wall Street to come clean about its exposure to the subprime crisis was Bear Stearns, which admitted in July 2007 that it was facing big losses at two of its hedge funds. In June, the month leading up to the crisis, it could hardly be said that James Cayne, the chief executive of Bear Stearns, was burning the midnight oil to remedy the situation, since he managed to find time for 13 rounds of golf. In August, when the credit markets froze up as banks refused to lend to each other, Mr Cayne obviously found the idea of golf a bit too strenuous and repaired to Nashville where by all accounts he thoroughly enjoyed himself at a bridge tournament. This bank was sold to JP Morgan Chase, in a US government-sponsored rescue, in March 2008.

Mr Cayne was not alone. Stan O'Neal, then the boss of Merrill Lynch, spent 20 days in the six weeks between the middle of August and the end of September honing his golf game. The bad news was that while Mr O'Neal was away from the office, Merrill Lynch was sitting on losses from subprime loans of $3.7 billion. The good news was that the practice paid off, since Mr O'Neal managed to reduce his handicap. The even better news was that this particular New Olympian would now have the time and the money to tinker with his swing and find his touch on the greens, since his reward for failure at Merrill Lynch was $160 million in pay-offs and pensions.

Sad to say, for those struggling to pay their mortgages in the trailer parks of Las Vegas or the scruffier parts of Bakersfield, California, real life was not like the movies. As the prospect of foreclosure rose steadily there was no sugar daddy – no Randolph or Mortimer Duke – prepared to exchange their life on the wrong side of the tracks for one of chauffeur-driven limousines, jacuzzis and five-star cuisine. As Mr Cayne was preparing to ruff a trump in Nashville and Mr O'Neal was splashing out of a bunker at the Vineyard golf club near Martha's Vineyard, the collapse of the American real estate market was threatening more than two million families with foreclosure. The rest of this chapter will explain how it was that loans provided to some of the poorest people in the US spread a fast-moving form of financial dry rot through the world's markets. But the story is essentially a simple one. For the past two decades, the United States has been living in a fantasy world, relying on an indulgent central bank to drop interest rates at the first sign of any discomfort and hence allow the economy to float along on a series of bubbles. One of Gordon Brown's favourite jokes was that there were only two types of chancellors of the exchequer: the ones who failed and the ones who got out in time. The same rule of thumb applies to chairmen of the Federal Reserve Board. Alan Greenspan, who presided over America's central bank for nigh on two decades certainly got out just as the unsustainable property boom he had engineered came to grief. Touring the world to publicise his self-regarding memoirs, Mr Greenspan suddenly found that the miracle economy he was supposed to have created perhaps wasn't so perfect after all, and he proceeded to give Ben Bernanke, the man given the unfortunate task of picking up the pieces, the benefit of his accumulated wisdom. In all truth, you did not need to be Adam Smith or John Maynard Keynes to work out what had gone wrong and why.

Indeed, as the crisis unfolded, Mr Greenspan's time at the Fed began eerily to echo the tenure as US Treasury secretary of Andrew Mellon, who held that position at the time of the Wall Street crash. Just like Mr Greenspan, Mr Mellon in the late 1920s kept interest rates low, much to the delight of Wall Stret. Like Mr Greenspan, Mr Mellon favoured the rich, in his case through his tax policies. Just like Mr Greenspan, Mr Mellon presided over a boom in mergers and takeovers. And just like Mr Greenspan, Mr Mellon ignored signs of distress in the economy outside the investment houses of Lower Manhattan.

Bountiful supplies of cheap money provided by Mr Greenspan allowed American consumers to borrow more money, which they used to buy real estate. Property prices rose rapidly, pushing home ownership out of the reach of many low-income families. The financial system decreed that this did not matter; ways could be found to provide these so-called subprime lenders to live the American dream. A modern version of the Wild West medicine show arrived in trailer park America, with real estate brokers displaying the full range of hucksterism as they gulled the poor, the old and the vulnerable with their once-in-a-lifetime, live-now-pay-later, special introductory offers. Where once the US mortgage industry had been a staid, conservative affair, it was now at the cutting edge of financial innovation. At first there were 'low doc' mortgages, where the normal high level of documentary proof that a borrower was financially sound was relaxed. When the next group of applicants was required to keep the boom going, 'low doc' mortgages became 'no doc' mortgages. The sin of omission became the sin of commission in the next stage of the real estate boom, with the advent of 'liar loans' in which individuals were encouraged to falsify the details of their employment, wages and savings. Those that lacked all three were offered 'ninja loans', which stood for no income no job or assets. As with all bubbles as far back as Tulip Mania in 17th-century Holland, the real estate market was rife with sharp practice and, in some cases, outright illegality.

In the Wild West, the snake-oil salesmen were often run out of town at the point of a gun. This time, though, they got clean away, helped by a rising real estate market which, for a time, made those who had taken out loans that they couldn't really afford think that all would be well. Indeed, the mortgage industry in the US resisted the implementation of new federal guidelines to tighten rules on lending, delaying their introduction during the last frenetic months of the boom between December 2005 and September 2006, on the grounds that there would be 'regulatory over-reach' and the stifling of 'innovation'. Subprime loans in the United States were not a new phenomenon. What was different, however, about the spate of loans extended as the market reached its zenith in 2005 and early 2006 was the aggressive nature of the lending and the recklessness with which the real financial situation of many borrowers was treated. As a result, a subprime loan taken out in 2005 was twice as risky as one taken out in 2002. 'Subprime loans originated in 2002 have a one-in-ten lifetime chance of foreclosing. For loans originated in 2005 and 2006, the probability shoots up to one in five'. (*Losing Ground;* Center for Responsible Lending; December 2006).

There is hard evidence for our medicine show analogy. A recent study by three IMF economists for the Centre for Economic Policy Research in London (not connected with the similarly named Washington institution) concluded that fewer people had been denied home loans and that the decline in lending standards had been greatest where competition for business was strongest. The paper identified four factors that explained the change in lending standards.

First, we find evidence that standards declined more where the credit boom was larger. This lends support to the assertions that rapid credit growth episodes tend to breed lax lending behaviour. Second, lower standards were associated with a past fast rate of house price appreciation, consistent with the notion that lenders were to some extent gambling on a continuing housing boom, relying on the fact that borrowers in default could always liquidate the collteral and repay the loan. Third, change in market structure mattered: lending standards declined more in regions where (large and aggressive) previously absent institutions entered the market. Finally, there is evidence that disintermediation played a role, with standards declining more in regions where larger portions of the lenders' loan portfolios were sold to third players. (Givoanni Dell'Ariccia, Deniz Igan and Luc Laeven; 'Credit Booms and Lending Standards: Evidence from the Subprime Mortgage Market'; CEPR; February 2008)

The increased popularity of subprime borrowing reflected the fact that house prices were going up much faster than earnings for the average American family. With real incomes squeezed, and the cost of health care and fuel rising rapidly, Americans had a choice; borrow more or give up hope of getting a foot on the housing ladder. Millions took the former option, even if it meant falsifying income records. In this, applicants were encouraged by the mortgage industry; more blind eyes were turned in this period in the US than at a Horatio Nelson look-alike convention.

Some saw the growth in subprime lending as a positive breakthrough in extending credit to the less well-off. Yet, as the Center for Responsible Lending put it:

This increased access has come at great cost to many families, since the highest rate of home foreclosures occurs among subprime loans. In many communities, the pressing issue today is less the availability of home-secured credit than the terms on which credit is offered. For the average American, building wealth through homeownership is the most accessible path to economic progress, but progress is not achieved when a family buys or refinances a home only to lose the home or get caught in a cycle of escalating debt.

Subprime borrowers in 2005 and 2006 were vulnerable for three reasons. The first was that those who took out loans in 2005 and 2006 bought at the top of the market, when the big increases in house prices had already occurred. They either had no equity in their homes or – in many cases – had taken out loans that were bigger than the value of their properties. The second reason was that they had been seduced by loan conditions that looked attractive on the surface but were in fact inherently risky. These included low initial fixed – or teaser – rates that would rise, often sharply, after a two-year period. At that point, lenders would pay the full cost of their mortgage plus a premium to compensate for the interest deferred in the first 24 months. Finally, the Federal Funds rate in 2006 was 5.25 per cent. In 2002, it had been on its way down to 1 per cent.

In the meantime, the subprime loans, riskier self-evidently than those granted to prime lenders who had well-paid employment or money in the bank, were then bundled up with better-quality loans and offered for sale in the financial markets. We looked at the process known as 'securitisation' in more depth in the previous chapter. Suffice it to say here that the complexity of modern financial markets meant that the initial bundle of mortgage-backed securities could be leveraged up many, many times – offering the prospect of easy money when real estate was booming but huge losses if and when the bubble burst, as it did from the summer of 2006 onwards. It was at this point that a slow-burning fuse was lit. A year later the flame reached the barrels of gunpowder hidden deep in the foundations of Western financial markets.

FROM MIRACLE TO MIRAGE: THE US ECONOMY

Securitisation in its modern form began in the early 1970s when the bright sparks in the financial markets realised that

they could make use of assets that were illiquid (or not easily
tradeable). It was, however, used back in the 1920s, during the
bull market in shares that ended famously with the Wall Street
Crash of 1929. What they did was create asset-backed securities, financial instruments that used as collateral the cash flow
from a specified pool of underlying assets, such as mortgages.
Gradually, the system became more sophisticated, with the
original asset-backed securities (ABS) spawning a variety of
financial derivatives, of which one was collateralised debt obligations (CDOs).

As Diana Choyleva of Lombard Street Research puts it:

Securitisation has allowed the banks to boost their income without
increasing their risk. They offered the loans from their balance sheet,
releasing capital for making new loans, but as well as fees from the orig-
ination of the loans they continue to earn the fees from their servicing,
and then from the next round of the same process. The more banks
securitise, the more profits they earn. Inevitably lending standards
fall as banks no longer hold the risk. Revenue is solely governed by
volume. ('US liquidity crunch – the slow motion crisis'; LSR monthly
review 219; August 2007)

The sense that these inherently risky trades were not risky
at all fostered complacency in the markets. Investors normally
expect to be offered far higher yields when they buy assets
that are traditionally not rock solid, but in the market frenzy
of 2005 and 2006 they allowed good judgement to be subsumed
by the classic trait of bubbles – greed.

The collapse of the US real estate market was an entirely
predictable crisis. Indeed, it had been predicted, frequently,
throughout 2006 and the first half of 2007 by a wide range
of economists. Each half year, for example, the International
Monetary Fund delivers its august view on the prospects for
both developed and developing nations in its *World Economic
Outlook*. While being a key part of the New Olympian movement, the *WEO* is a thoroughly research and unideological
piece of work. IMF economists tend to be poor at forecasting

precisely what is going to happen to the world economy, underestimating both the strength of booms and the savagery of downturns, but their assessment of longer-term trends tends to be accurate. In September 2006, when the IMF held its annual meeting in Singapore, the fund that the most likely source of a headwind for the US economy was the housing market (*IMF World Economic Outlook*; September 2006). Rising house prices, it said, had provided a significant boost to consumption, residential investment, and employment in recent years, but the market now looked over-valued and activity had slowed as the Fed had belatedly tightened monetary policy, pushing up interest rates from 1 per cent to 5.25 per cent in quarter-point jumps at 17 consecutive meetings of its open market committee. Rapidly declining applications for mortgages, a rising supply of unsold homes on the market, a decline in homebuilder confidence to a 15-year-low and a slowdown in the rate of house price inflation were all highlighted as possible signs of trouble ahead. The IMF stated that the world economy has been enjoying its longest spell of strong growth since the late 1960s and early 1970s, but stressed that 'an abrupt slowdown in the US housing market' was a notable source of uncertainty.

Six months later, the Fund returned to the same them. In the next *IMF World Economic Outlook*, released in April 2007, the Fund said that a particular concern was the 'potential for a sharper slowdown in the US if the housing sector continues to deteriorate'. For good measure, the IMF was also the harbinger of the credit crisis that was to affect global markets some three months later, raising concerns about 'the risk of a deeper and more sustained retrenchment from risky assets if financial markets remain volatile.'

At a time when shares on Wall Street were rising and the talk was of which company would be the next to be targeted by a private equity firm, the Fund was rather more concerned about what was going on in subprime land. 'The housing market downturn in the US has, if anything, been deeper than projected at the time of the September 2006 WEO,' it said, adding perceptively that there was worse to come. 'The housing correction still has a way to run. Housing starts and permits (to build) are still heading downward, while inventories of unsold homes are at their highest levels in 15 years.'

As to the cause of the problem, the Fund noted – somewhat belatedly perhaps – that there had clearly been 'an excessive relaxation of lending and underwriting standards'. It was equally clear to other analysts and commentators that the US housing market was an accident waiting to happen. The Cassandras included the analysts working for some of the big global investment houses that were heavily exposed to the vulnerable US housing market.

This was what HSBC bank had to say in September 2006, almost a full year before the crisis broke. In a paper bluntly titled 'US – recession warning issued', the bank's analysts noted that the 'miraculous' recovery in the world's biggest economy from the dotcom crash of 2000–2001 was ending.

The US has become a 'push-me, pull you' economy: companies may be profitable but households, who have been the key drivers of growth, are in trouble. A cocktail of higher energy prices, tighter monetary policy, an end to tax cuts and, more recently, a housing market that appears to be in free-fall threatens to poison the upswing. Economic growth in the early years of this decade appears to have built on the most fragile of foundations.

At the time, this was a somewhat heretical view. And given the losses racked up by HSBC in US mortgage, credit card and other lending it seems to have been ignored by some inside the bank itself.

Warren Buffet, the legendary investor, put it this way:

Nothing sedates rationality like large doses of effortless money. After a heady experience of that kind, normally sensible people drift into behavior akin to that of Cinderella at the ball. They know that overstaying the festivities – that is, continuing to speculate in companies that have gigantic valuations relative to the cash they are likely to generate in the future – will eventually bring on pumpkins and mice. But they nevertheless hate to miss a single minute of what is one helluva party. (Berkshire Hathaway chairman's letter, 2000)

The received wisdom about the US economy was that it had experienced a renaissance since the deindustrialisation of the rust-belt during the deep recession of the 1980s. Rather like Britain, America was supposed to have emerged from a decade that included Watergate, the withdrawal from Vietnam, the Iranian hostages crisis, double-digit inflation and the highest unemployment since the 1930s in a trans-formed state. When Bruce Springsteen was penning his songs of blue-collar melancholy, the US was convinced that it was at risk of losing its economic hegemony to Germany and Japan. By the early part of the current decade, the tables had been turned. Japan was struggling to emerge from 15 years of deflation; if Germany avoided being the exemplar of how not to run an economy, that was only because it was just one step up the ladder from the cheese-eating surrender monkeys west of the Rhine. The US, by contrast, was surfing the wave of the new technology. It had replaced the sunset industries of Ohio and Michigan with the sunrise industries of Texas and Arizona; it had boosted productivity and jobs; it had embraced the future at a time when Europe was stuck in the past.

In reality, the US productivity miracle was something of a myth. As one study showed, the real difference between the efficiency of the American and the European economies could be explained by higher productivity in retailing. The US retail sector used the interstate system to ferry goods between out-of-town distribution centres and hypermarkets using the latest IT equipment. Europe could only enjoy the same sort of productivity if it was prepared to abandon its more stringent planning laws, allow 40-ton lorries to invade the centres of medieval cities and perhaps knock down the odd Gothic cathedral or two. That, for some reason, the Europeans proved somewhat reluctant to do (Adair Turner; *What's Wrong with Europe's Economy?; Challenges for Europe;* Palgrave; 2005).

By 2007, the data suggested that there had been no sustained improvement in US productivity following the one-off boost provided by the widespread introduction of IT systems in the 1990s. One piece of research comparing the post-war Golden Age from 1947 to 1973 with the subsequent era concluded that there had been no evidence that trickle down economics had increased the economy's long-term growth rate.

Adusted productivity growth over the whole post-1973 period has badly trailed the pre-1973 rate. Even during the post-1995 speedup the adjusted annual rate of productivity growth was still more than a percentage point less than the 1947–73 average. In short, the economy has seen a sharp upward redistribution of income over the last three decades with little obvious growth dividend. Policies that redistribute income upward, yet fail to increase growth, are very costly to the vast majority of the US labour force (Dean Baker; The Productivity to Paycheck Gap: what the data show; *Centre for Economic and Policy Research; 2007)*

In another piece of research from the same institution – one of the few left-of-centre think tanks still swimming against the New Olympian tide in Washington – it was shown to be no longer true that the US was leaving Europe for dead in terms of employment (John Schmitt; *Whatever Happened to the American Jobs Machine?;* Centre for Economic and Policy Research; October 2006). 'In the 1990s, the United States developed an international reputation as a "jobs machine" capable of creating jobs at a far faster rate than the European Union. Remarkably, however, in the current decade, the United States has been creating jobs at a slower pace than the European Union.'

Mr Schmitt said this characterisation was true in the 1990s, particularly during the American boom of the second half of the decade. But in the first half of the current decade – between 2000 and 2005 – employment growth in the US was an annual 0.7 per cent, compared to 0.9 per cent a year for the European Union. True, the EU average was dragged upwards by the booming economies of Spain and Ireland – which had property bubbles to match those on the other side of the Atlantic Ocean, but American jobs growth was little better than that of allegedly 'sclerotic' France, which increased employment by 0.5 per cent a year.

Despite being exaggerated, the story of the US economy reborn was partly true. America, unlike Britain, retained a strong manufacturing base, with technological innovation helped by lavish military spending, and world leadership in computer hardware, aerospace and the audio-visual sector. It was this underlying strength that American policy makers took comfort in as the housing market weakened in late 2006 and early 2007. The fundamentals of the US economy were strong, they said. The problems of subprime would be contained, they insisted. There would be no contagion effects on the rest of the US economy let alone the rest of the world, they reassured.

But as the Bloomberg news agency reported on August 10 as the subprime tsunami crashed over Wall Street: 'Federal Reserve chairman Ben Bernanke was wrong. So were US Treasury Secretary Henry Paulson and Merrill Lynch chief executive officer Stanley O'Neal. The subprime mortgage industry's problems were contained, they all said. It turns out that the turmoil was contagious.'

With the benefit of perfect hindsight, many explanations were provided for the failure of the best brains in America – at the Fed, in the US Treasury and in the boardrooms of New York's investment banking community – to spot that something was seriously amiss. One was that sunny optimism is the natural disposition of Americans. Another, somewhat more politically pointed, was that those who extolled capitalism's ability to bounce back from any adversity had never themselves been at the sharp end of a factory closure or a wage cut.

A more convincing explanation, however, was that the US had experienced a 'Minsky moment'. In a paper for the Levy Institute based on the ideas of the late Hyman Minsky, Randall Wray, economics professor at the University of Missouri, said the long period of growth and long inflation had created an environment where markets were blind to the risks they were taking (L. Randall Wray, economics professor at the University of Missouri, Kansas City; *Lessons from the subprime meltdown; 2007*).

Minsky came up with a theory of financial instability based on two propositions. The first, not especially original, was that there are two types of regimes for financial markets – one that is conistent with stability and one which is not. The second proposition, however, was more striking because Minsky argued that stability was destabilising and carried the seeds of its own destruction because those operating in a stable world would take actions that would push the system towards instability.

Making a case not just for the sort of curbs put on Wall Street after its excesses of the late 1920s but for a state of constant supervisory vigilance, Minsky noted: 'Over a protracted period of good times, capitalist economies tend to move from a financial structure dominated by hedge finance units to a structure in which there is a large weight to units engaged in speculative and Ponzi finance.' *(The Financial Instability Hypothesis;* the Levy Institute; 1992).

Minsky argued that the strongest force in a capitalist economy operated towards an unfettered speculative boom and in his paper Wray argued that the subprime crisis in the US was a natural and inevitable outcome of those processes. 'Minsky would not blame irrational exuberance or manias or bubbles. Those who had been caught up in the boom behaved rationally, at least according to the "model or the model" they had developed to guide their behaviour.

'It is only in retrospect that we can see the boom for what

it was – mass delusion propagated in part by policy makers and those with vested interests who should have known better.'

America's vested interests, however, did not know better. Having created an economy in which the real incomes of the bulk of the population (but not their own) were constrained, they needed a new mechanism for keeping the recovery of the early 2000s going. They were convinced that what they were doing was foolproof. They had forgotten the lessons of the Great Depression. They had stripped away, bit by bit, the New Deal reforms such as the Glass-Steagal Act, which had limited their freedom of action. Above all, they believed in their heart of hearts that if times turned really rough the government would step in, with cheap money, higher public spending and an unlimited lender of last resort facility. In this last belief, Wall Street was right. The Great Depression had been the abiding American economic event of the 20th century; it was part of what Jung called the collective unconscious in just the same way as the hyper-inflation of 1923 haunted the Germans. Wall Street knew that the Fed tended to err on the side of caution when recession threatened, cutting interest rates to sustain growth.

So, as Minsky noted, a speculative boom became more difficult to control even as it became ever more likely. Responsibility for stripping away the constraints on finance was not Wall Street's alone. Certainly, there was strong lobbying from Lower Manhattan for deregulation, but it found a willing ear at the US Treasury and the Federal Reserve. Not only were so-called 'innovations' tolerated, they were in many cases actively encouraged.

Wall Street had a touching faith in the ability of the Fed – and of Mr Greenspan in particular – to keep the good times rolling. Precious few analysts paid attention to America's burgeoning trade deficit, the clearest evidence that the country was living beyond its means. Nor did investment banks appear concerned about the build-up in personal debt that was necessary to purchase all the imported goods. There was, Wall Street insisted, no reason to be worried. The dollar was the world's reserve currency so there would always be a demand for American financial assets. Foreign purchases of Treasury bills would finance the trade deficit and keep the dollar strong. A strong currency meant imports were cheap, and that in turn allowed Mr Greenspan to keep interest rates low. In turn, low interest rates allowed people to borrow at cheap rates, fuelling demand for real estate and so keeping property prices high. Rising property prices meant that there would be no problems with mortgage defaults and foreclosures, so all those securitised loans were sure-fire bets.

By the start of 2008, all Wall Street's comfort blankets were looking somewhat threadbare. Mr Greenspan had taken fright at the asset price bubble he had allowed to develop by cutting interest rates to 1 per cent in June 2003 and leaving them there for a year. Even then it was probably not too late to have controlled the wilder excesses of the real estate bubble, but instead of displaying to households and Wall Street that he was concerned that the boom might turn to bust, Mr Greenspan proceeded to tighten monetary policy slowly and steadily. As *The Economist* said (October 2007), pushing up rates in predictable quarter-point steps intensified the housing boom and made the eventual bust all the more painful.

Eventually, rising interest rates did have an effect and they exposed how the precarious state of family finances in heartland America had been camouflaged by cheap money. Adjusted for inflation, median US incomes have been falling for the past five years, yet consumption has been rising as a proportion of the economy. In the 1980s and 1990s, it hovered between 66 per cent and 68 per cent of GDP, but has since risen to almost 72 per cent. This could be achieved only by borrowing more and saving less. Household debt is now three times as large as the annual output of the US economy – higher than at any time since the Great Depression, while the savings ratio has been negative for more than two years, again without parallel since the slump of the 1930s.

As one commentator noted, Mr Greenspan (aided and abetted by the US Treasury) had solved the problem of high indebtedness in one sector of the US economy – the heavily exposed business sector at the time the dotcom boom ended – by shifting the debt to two other sectors, households and the government. (Brian Reading; 'The hangover'; *Lombard Street Monthly Review* 206; October 2006) 'After the Wall Street bubble burst the business sector retrenched savagely. Its financial balance went from a 2 per cent deficit to near 4 per cent surplus in the three years to mid-2003, a swing of 6 per cent of GDP that would have knocked the economy for six had no other sectors given ground. Cheap and easy money boosted house prices, inflating a consumer borrowing bubble that together with tax cuts and the sharp deterioration into deficit in public finances, ensured a shallow recession (if technically there was one at all) followed by a recovery.' The price of repairing corporate balance sheets was to impair those of households and the state.

THE DOLLAR: A SLOW-MOTION DISINTEGRATION

The next part of the fantasy to be exposed was the notion that foregin investors would allow the US to spend $107 for every $100 it produced – the difference being the country's trade deficit. Two Harvard economists, Ricardo Hausmann and Frederico Sturzenegger, found a novel way of getting round the problem by saying that the US current account was not a question of imports far exceeding exports but of measurement problems that had persisted since 1980. The current account need not trouble economists and potential investors in the US because it did not exist in the first place (Hausmann and Sturzenegger; *US and global imbalances: can dark matter prevent a big bang?*; November 2005).

There was no real evidence, however, that foreign exchange markets were convinced by this line of reasoning. On the contrary, the dollar fell by 30 per cent against the euro between 2004 and 2007 as investors took the view that the US current account deficit was fact not fiction, and that a drop in the value of the dollar to make exports cheaper and imports dearer was an inevitable part of any remedy. For a time, rising interest rates and strong US growth meant foreign buying of American assets remained high enough to cover the current account deficit. But the warning signs were there of what might happen were overseas investors to decide that the prospect of a sharply falling dollar made the purchase of Treasury bills too risky, and that the euro looked a safer bet. One academic study showed that interest rates would have been a percentage point higher were foreigners to cease buying US Treasury bonds and two points higher were they to reverse the inflows off capital into the US (Francis Warnock and Veronica Warnock; *International Capital Flows and US interest rates;* National Bureau of Economic Research paper no 12560).

Former Fed chairman Paul Volcker, writing in the *Washington Post* (April 10 2005) stated that he 'didn't know of any country that has managed to consume and invest 6 per cent more than it produces for long'. The deficit worsened subsequently to 7 per cent of GDP and despite improving in 2007 is still 6 per cent of GDP.

The risks of the dollar losing its reserve currency status were highlighted long before the crisis broke in 2007. Avinash Persaud noted in a speech in New York in 2006 that international currencies come and go (address to the annual Integrated Wealth Management Forum, Union League Club) and that by 2050 China and India were likely to have bigger economies – when judged by how much a dollar, a renminbi or a rupee would buy – than the US, Western Europe or Japan. Sterling had been a reserve currency in the first half of the 20th century, but had lost that status as a result of the cost of fighting two world wars and the debt and inflation that followed.

In the case of the US today, the process is also being accelerated by wars where the end is as elusive as the enemy and by a consumerism built on a property bubble. Perhaps we will not have to wait until 2050. In my life-time, the dollar will start to lose its reserve currency status, not to the euro, but to the renminbi or the rupee. The loss of reserve currency status for the US will bring economic and political crisis. If it was economically and politically painful for the UK, even though its international financial position did not begin from a position off heavy deficit, what will it be for the US which has become the world's largest debtor?

Mr Persaud said the time it took for the dollar to lose its reserve status would depend on what the Fed did. It would take quite a long time were the US central bank to tighten monetary policy in the face of inflation and currency weakness, but it would be accelerated should the Fed seek to boost short-term growth by cutting interest rates. 'The Fed may have to take that decision sooner rather than later.' That was September 2006. By the autumn of 2007, it was clear that the Fed had chosen the second option.

The climax of *Trading Places* is a scene on the dealing floor of the New York commodities exchange. Facing bankruptcy after being outsmarted by the hustler and the yuppie, the Duke brothers can see only one way out of their predicament. They demand that business be resumed on the by now deserted trading floor so that they can make good their losses. 'Turn those machines back on,' one of them screams.

Neither of us, sadly, knows Ben Bernanke, Henry Paulson or George Bush well enough to know whether any or all of them are big fans of *Trading Places*. What we do know is that from the moment the full extent of the subprime crisis became apparent in the summer of 2007, it was a case of 'turn those machines back on'.

It was not hard to see why this was the response of American policy makers. Belatedly, they had woken up to the fact that the ebb tide in the housing market for the past year had left millions of borrowers stranded on the rocks of debt. In 2006, the US mortgage market was worth

$10 trillion, with 80 per cent accounted for by prime loans, 15 per cent by subprime mortgages and 5 per cent by Alt-A loans, believed the least risky of loans considered not to be of the highest quality. Those figures, however, said more about what had happened to the US real estate market in previous years than it did about what was happening in 2006. Of the loans made in that year, 20 per cent were subprime and 14 per cent were Alt-A. A further 16 per cent were known as Jumbo loans, which meant they exceded the maximum loan amount established by the Federal Home Loan Mortgage Corporation (Freddie Mac, as it is commonly known). Default rates by the summer of 2007 were already running at 14 per cent, with the prospect of far worse to come in 2008 and 2009 as those borrowers enticed by low-cost 'teaser' loans had their monthly payments reset to much higher levels.

When Bear Stearns admitted that two of its hedge funds were no longer solvent as a result of the losses made on securities backed by subprime assets, there was the loud and unmistakable sound of stable doors being bolted. Wall Street realised that it did not know how big the losses were, nor who was sitting on them. It found that the highly complex models that its so-called 'rocket scientists' had constructed to value CDOs and the other fruits of securitisation were worthless, and it did what financial markets tend to do in those circumstances. It demanded help from the Big Government it normally affected to despise.

Help was not long in coming, with action proposed on several fronts simultaneously – a short-term injection of liquidity into the money markets to ensure that banks had enough cash to balance their books; cuts in short-term interest rates to boost confidence and help prevent the economy from slipping into recession; and a bail-out plan for subprime borrowers to limit the number of defaults and foreclosures, and so put a floor under the housing market. Fears proved groundless that Bernanke was keen to expunge the belief on Wall Street that Mr Greenspan's Fed had always

been ready to protect reckless investors from the consequences of their own bad decisions by cutting interest rates.
Instead, it was very much 'business as usual' when the Fed
told dealers in August that it would enter the money markets
as often as necessary and would accept high-quality
mortgage-backed securities as collateral for any financial
assistance given. According to the *Financial Times* (August
11 2007) it amounted to 'the most extensive liquidity support
operation undertaken by the US central bank since the 9/11
terrorist attacks and follows similar steps by the European
Central Bank and the Japanese central bank in the past two
days'.

At the September meeting of its open market committee,
the Fed cut interest rates by half a point, and then announced
quarter-point reductions in borrowing costs at its next two
meetings in October and December. On January 22 2008, it
announced an emergency 0.75 percentage point cut, followed
by a 0.5-point cut on January 30. Meanwhile, Treasury Secretary
Henry Paulson was busy with a plan that involved some of
Wall Street's biggest investment banks creating a $100 billion
fund into which all the worthless subprime loans could be
parked. The Bush administration announced in the autumn
that interest rates would be frozen on some subprime mortgages.

This burst of frenetic action – in sharp contrast to the
state of denial that had preceded it – was an attempt to
replicate the operation in 1998 that had prevented the
collapse of the hedge fund Long Term Capital Management
from contaminating the financial markets and the wider
economy. Some economists warned, however, that in 1998
the US economy was booming and consumers were not
nearly so deeply in debt. A quick and aggressive cut in
interest rates coupled with a meeting in which the Fed told
Wall Street that it had to bail out LTCM averted the crisis.
But as Nouriel Roubini, economics professor at the Stern
School of Business at New York University, wrote in his on-
line blog on August 9 2007, the difference between 1998 and

2007 was the difference between a cash flow problem and an insolvency problem.

First, you have hundreds of thousands of US households who are insolvent on their mortgages. And this is not a subprime problem; the same reckless lending practices used in subprime – no downpayment, no verification of income and assets, interest rate only loans, negative amortisation, teaser rates – were used for near prime Alt-A loans, hybrid prime ARMs, home equity loans, piggyback loans. More than 50 per cent of all mortgage originations in 2005 and 2006 had this toxic waste characteristic. That is why you will have hundreds of thousands – perhaps over a million – of subprime, near prime and prime borrowers who will end up in delinquency, default and foreclosure. Lots of insolvent borrowers.

But that was just the start, Professor Roubini noted. Insolvent borrowers meant insolvent lenders, insolvent builders and insolvent hedge funds – not just in the US but in Australia, Germany and France. All the signs were of a credit and insolvency crisis that would affect the US and the wider global economy.

We are indeed at a Minsky moment and this recent financial turmoil is the beginning of a much more serious and protracted US and global credit crunch. The risks of a systemic crisis are rising: liquidity injections and lender or last resort bail out of insolvent borrowers – however necessary and unavoidable during a liquidity panic – will not work; they will postpone and exacerbate the eventual and unavoidable insolvencies.

By the turn of the year, it was clear that Professor Roubini's assessment was right; the subprime crisis was proving far more intractable than the LTCM crisis of a decade earlier. The housing market remained in free fall, losses for the big financial institutions were still mounting, and economists were scrabbling to downgrade their forecasts for US growth. Some remained confident that the Fed could keep the economy moving, while others predicted a short recession.

One example of the downgrades came from the Economist Intelligence Unit, which in January 2008 said it expected US growth of 1.5 per cent in 2008 and 2 per cent in 2009, but lowered them to 0.8 per cent and 1.4 per cent a month later (February 20 2008).

There were signs, however, that it could be worse than that.

Firstly, there was the prospect of mortgage rates on $1 trillion of 'teaser' loans being reset in 2008 and 2009. Secondly, there was the fact that $6 trillion of mortgages had been securitised into mortgage-backed debt, and the rise in home-loan delinquencies meant that the price of that debt had fallen sharply. Thirdly, the sharp fall in the value of the dollar was leading to higher inflation, making it harder for the Fed to cut interest rates. Higher inflation was also eating into disposable incomes, making lower interest rates less effective as a stimulus to higher borrowing and spending. Fourthly, there were signs that foreign investors were becoming warier about increasing their exposure to US assets, particularly given the risk that the Fed would put a higher priority on growth than on controlling inflation or safeguarding the value of the dollar. Finally, there was the less than reassuring message from history that every previous crash in the housing market in the US had led to a full-blown recession and that by the end of 2007 the slump in real estate had only lasted about half as long as previous downturns, none of which were nearly so serious. Mr Bush's help for subprime borrowers was derided for being too little, too late since it would only help borrowers who were not yet behind with their monthly payments and had more than 3 per cent equity in the property. Bank of America calculated that this would leave around $500 billion of subprime and Alt-A loans untouched.

With the crisis four months old, Mr Persaud noted:

Subprime was merely where the first Molotov cocktail was thrown not its source. The source of today's problem was a long period of predatory lending and there will be many more petrol bombs erupting wherever lending growth was excessively strong over the past few years. Secondly, the insidious problem for the financial sector is that the attempt to combine securitisation with financial statistics that blithely assumed away strategic behaviour by investors has so contaminated the asset pool that it has undermined confidence in collateral and those who own it more generally. (We are at a riot point in the markets; November 27 2007; note from Mr Persaud).

By any measure, it was a serious situation, and one for which the New Olympian class stood indicted. The Federal Reserve had mismanaged the economy. Wall Street had ignored every warning sign as it enriched itself at the expense of ordinary Americans. The Bush administration had turned surplus into deficit, not just as a result of expensive wars, but also by pursuing tax policies that had favoured corporations and wealthy individuals.

The charge sheet was a long one. Perhaps the most serious accusation for the New Olympians is that despite the job insecurity, despite the pro-enterprise tax breaks, despite the IT revolution and two decades of growth, the US is not nearly as mobile a society as Americans believe it is, and is becoming less so. To be sure, more people own stocks and shares than they used to, but only because they are being forced to plan for their own retirement now that companies have closed final salary pension schemes. Although 52 per cent of households owned stock at the time of the dotcom meltdown in 2001, 70 per cent of the stock was in mutual funds or 401(k) pension plans. As in the UK, risk in retirement has been shifted from employers to employees.

Jeff Faux says that in the three decades following the Second World War America did become a more mobile society and the distribution of income became more equal. 'Labour unions gave greater bargaining power to workers, educational opportunities were expanded, and government-subsidised housing gave working-class Americans access to a wealth-building asset. Then, after the 1970s, both trends reversed.' Back in the 1970s, 74 per cent of people who were poor at the start of the decade were still poor at the end of the decade. In the 1990s, the comparable figure was 77 per cent. It was the same story for those at the top; 73 per cent of those who were rich in 1970 were still in the top 20 per cent of earners in 1980; in the 1990s that figure had risen to 77 per cent.

The political story of the US over the same period is not, however, of a populist backlash but of a successful diversion of blue-collar anger and discontent into conservative culture wars, there being no outlet for the left-wing economic outlook of working-class Americans. There is more likely to be a furore about a pop star exposing a breast during the half-time entertainment at the Super Bowl than there is about the fact that it is more than four decades since a president faced down the corporate lobby and forced business to do something it did not want to do. Even then, President Kennedy's insistence the major steel companies rescind planned simultaneous price increases in October 1962 co-incided with the Cuban missile crisis, a time when it would have been hard on patriotic grounds alone for the corporate interest to push its luck.

J.K. Galbraith once paid back-handed tribute to the way in which America's élite had managed to fashion the new consensus in which 'welfare queens' were demonised but the corporate dependency culture was not.

It is the nature of privileged position that it develops its own political justi-fication and often the economic and social doctrine that serves it best. No one likes to believe that his or her personal economic wellbeing is in conflict with the greater public need. To invent a plausible ideology in defence of self-interest is thus a natural course. A corps of willing and talented craftsmen is available for the task. (The Good Society; Houghton Mifflin; 1996)

Professor Galbraith was also sceptical about independent central banks. He argued that the almost religious belief in a technocratic institution 'removed from the pressures of democratic processes is a myth perpetuated by those' associated with large pools of money 'to perpetuate their economic comfort at the expense of others' (*The Good Society*).

America is central to this book. In part, that is because the financial crisis had its origins in the US housing market. In part, that is because it has been apparent for the past 15 years that the series of mini-tremors to the global economy were rippling back towards the epicentre of the global money system, Wall Street. In this respect, 2007 bore the hallmark of the period between 1890 and 1929, when problems first became apparent on the periphery of the global economy, in countries like Argentina, then affected rich developed nations like Germany, and ultimately spread to the hub of the system itself, with far-reaching consequences. But there's a third, and vital reason, why the role of America is crucial. Any populist fightback against the New Olympian hegemony is likely to begin in the United States, where – despite the conservative counter-revolution of the past 30 years – the deep-seated belief in local participatory democracy, states rights, equal rights before the law, provide the raw ingredients for political change, however unlikely that seems at present.

Populism in the US during the election year of 2008 was a much weaker beast than it had been in 1896, when William Jennings Bryan was the defeated Democratic candidate in the presidential race and fought the contest on the Jeffersonian principle that it was America's farmers, miners and labourers who created the real wealth in the country not 'the few financial magnates who, in a back room corner the money of the world'. The explanation for this was that the Democratic Party had pretty much given up on populism. True, one of the candidates seeking to be nominated for the party's ticket in 2008, John Edwards, was a self-styled populist. But Mr Edwards hardly looked capable of running a Harry Truman-style campaign. During his whistle-stop tour in 1948, Truman

conjured up memories of the Wall Street crash and the
Depression that followed, saying:

*You remember the big boom and the great crash of 1929. You remember
that in 1932 the position of the farmer had become so desperate that there
was actual violence in many farming communities. You remember that
insurance companies and banks took over much of the land of small independent farmers – 233,000 farmers lost their farms . . . I wonder how many
times you have to be hit on the head before you find out who's hitting you?
The Democratic party represents the people. It is pledged to work for agriculture . . . the Democratic party puts human rights and human welfare
first . . . These Republican gluttons of privilege are cold men. They are
cunning men . . . They want a return of the Wall Street economic dicta-
torship. (Quoted from Truman by David McCullough; Simon & Schuster;
1992; pages 658–9)*

Mr Edwards, as one commentator put it, was made of less
stern stuff. 'Campaigning as a populist, Edwards comes across
as a wealthy trial lawyer recycling his jury appeals to make
corporations pay' (John O'Sullivan; *Spectator*; December 2007).
By the standards of 1896 or 1948, Mr Edwards would have
been seen as a rather weak-kneed progressive; the state of the
Democratic Party's mainstream in 2008 made him look a
regular firebrand. Indeed, he proved far too radical for the
Democracts and dropped out early in the race. By contrast,
the personable but, in policy terms, elusive Barack Obama
stormed past him.

Wall Street had every reason to feel comfortable about
the idea of Hillary Clinton becoming the first woman president. After all, when Mrs Clinton's husband Bill had been
in the White House, the US Treasury had bailed America's
big banks out of every scrape they got into. And during Mr
Clinton's eight-year presidency, there were plenty of those –
from Mexico to Thailand, from South Korea to Russia. Mr
Clinton had the choice when he arrived in office to spend
his political capital either on pushing through health care
reform in the teeth of opposition from the big pharmaceutical

companies and the medical insurers or pushing through the NAFTA (North American Free Trade Agreement) free trade deal with Mexico and Canada in the teeth of opposition from the labour unions, who argued (correctly as it turned out) that the point of the treaty was not to make the individual countries more competitive but to make corporations more competitive and profitable. The loss of Congress by the Democrats in 1994 was in part attributable to Mr Clinton's decision to turn his back on his own natural supporters. It was a decision, however, entirely in keeping with the party's gradual shift over the past 40 years, away from politics of class to politics of identity. In the new politics, the big economic issues were settled. Open markets, free trade, capital liberalisation, labour market flexibility, reform of the welfare state, tax breaks to encourage innovation, higher investment on human capital, technological advance: these were the building blocks of the new economic orthodoxy and there was little difference between the two main parties. What separated them was culture: abortion, religion, gay marriage, race. As Faux rightly noted, the big shift came in 1968 and the years immediately afterwards.

The civil rights and Vietnam conflicts of the 1960s splintered the Democratic Party's broad-based New Deal coalition that had been united around issues of economic class. Since then, liberal identity has been defined by issues of gender, race, sexual preference, disability and other subclass categories that emphasise differences among their own core constituencies. The institutions that unite the traditional Democratic constituencies but make business uncomfortable, such as the labor unions and the local political clubs, were gradually marginalised by the party, a process that accelerated in the 1980s with the expanded influence of corporate money. The result was that liberalism's accomplishments have been aimed at niche political constituencies. Thus, notes Elaine Bernard, executive director of the Trade Union Program at Harvard University: 'The boss cannot fire you because of your race. He cannot fire you because of your gender. He cannot fire you because of your sexual preference or your disability. He can just fire you for no reason at all.'

The crisis of 2007 and 2008 provided the perfect conditions for a new populism. Americans had grudgingly accepted that the labour market dice were loaded in favour of the employers. They had responded to the top 1 per cent of earners grabbing 90 per cent of any increase in incomes not by taking to the streets but by taking another job. The threat of two million foreclosures was of a different order or magnitude, however. It conjured up memories of the dustbowl years of the 1930s and the last time Wall Street had been allowed to mess things up. It created the impression that America was facing an economic crisis unprecedented since the Great Depression. Which indeed it was.

9

Thunder in the West:
Scanning the horizon for the perfect storm

There is no cause for worry. The high tide of prosperity
will continue.
   – US Treasury Secretary Andrew Mellon; September
   1928

I expect to see the stock market a good deal higher than
it is today within a few months.
   – Professor Irving Fisher; October 15 1929

The global credit problem that started in America is now
the most immediate challenge for every economy, and
addressing it the most immediate priority. But just as we
withstood the Asia crisis, the American recession, the
end of the IT bubble and the trebling of oil prices and
continued to grow, Britain will meet and master this new
challenge by our determination to maintain stability and
low inflation.
   – Gordon Brown in his New Year message to Britain;
   January 2008

Each year Lake Superior's state university offers a prize to the
most overused word or phrase that has affronted the English

language over the past 12 months. There were no surprises when on January 1 2008 it was announced that the award for 2007 had been given to 'The perfect storm'.

Originally a perfect storm had a precise meteorological meaning; a mixture of tropical moisture with warm air from a low pressure weather system and cool air from a high pressure system converging on a single point. By the start of 2008, it had become a theory of everything. The *Financial Times* said Guy Hands, the private equity entrepreneur trying to revive the fortunes of EMI in the face of opposition not just from staff but the record label's roster of 'stars', was facing a 'perfect storm' (January 13 2008). After being caught flat-footed by Hillary Clinton's unexpected victory in the New Hampshire primaries, the media needed to find a way of explaining a forecasting *faux pas* on a par with the *Chicago Times* front page headline in 1948: 'Dewey Defeats Truman'. Rather than admit they simply got it wrong, the humbled psephologists said a combination of a trembling-lip, baby-boomer feminism and the alleged superficiality of Barack Obama had resulted in Hillary Clinton's victory. 'Barack's wave crashed in Hillary's perfect storm', said one headline (*Boston Globe*; January 10 2008). Perhaps best of all, however, was report in the *Los Angeles Times* the previous summer in which the mayor of the city described the drought conditions as – you guessed it – a perfect storm. The students of Lake Superior state university were right; the phrase was threatening to make the leap from meaning a confluence of warm air and cold air to signifying instead billowing gusts of hot air. The word 'crisis' was simply no longer good enough.

The state of the global economy in the first half of 2008 made it a prime candidate for the 'perfect storm' thesis. Nor was it merely a craze among the 'end of the world brigade'. As the chief economist of the International Monetary Fund, Simon Johnson is hardly one for apocalyptic visions of the future, but in November 2007 he popped up to warn of a 'perfect storm' caused by the interaction of turmoil on the financial markets and the spiralling cost of energy. 'The combination of

the credit crunch and high oil prices could bring a big reduction in international trade from which no one would be
immune,' he said. It says something about the febrile mood in
that autumn that only a month previously, Mr Johnson had
unveiled half-yearly forecasts for the global economy in which
the Fund said it barely expected growth to miss a beat in 2008,
edging down from 5.2 per cent to 4.8 per cent.

Robert Kuttner, editor of *The American Prospect*, was another
convinced that 2008 would see a witches' brew of bad news.
Writing in the *Boston Globe* (December 21 2007), he said:
'America now faces an economic perfect storm: a weakened
financial system, diminished consumer purchasing power, a
swooning dollar, and rising inflation. Ours is a resilient nation.
The eventual recovery will require a repudiation of free-market
economics, as bold as the New Deal. But like so much else
about the Bush legacy, recovery will be far more agonizing
than it had to be.'

While avoiding use of the phrase, Joseph Stiglitz, the Nobel
Prize winner and former chairman of the council of
economic advisers under Bill Clinton whom we came across
earlier in this book, had a message similar to Mr Kuttner's.
A tax code weighted in favour of the rich, a 70 per cent rise
in the budget deficit, a near $850 billion trade deficit; record
oil prices; a depreciating dollar; a dearth of investment in
education, science and research: all this, according to
Professor Stiglitz, made George Bush a candidate to seize
the unenvied mantle of America's worst president from
Herbert Hoover, someone with hands-on experience of a
perfect economic storm.

*Whoever moves into the White House in January 2009 will face an un-
enviable set of economic circumstances. Extricating the country from Iraq will
be the bloodier task, but putting America's economic house in order will be
wrenching and take years.*

*What is required is in some ways simple to describe: it amounts to
ceasing our current behaviour and doing exactly the opposite. It means not
spending money that we don't have, increasing taxes on the rich, reducing*

corporate welfare, strengthening the safety net for the less well off, and making greater investment in education, technology, and infrastructure.

Inevitably newspapers embraced the new soundbite. 'The storm clouds are gathering over the jobs market; the climate on the high street is growing distinctly chilly; a typhoon of bad debt is buffeting the banks,' the *Independent* noted. On December 5 2007. 'Could a "perfect storm" be about to hit the British economy?' A month later, the *Guardian* asked, 'Is This the Big One?', adding: 'It is 15 years since Britain last suffered a recession. But now the housing market is slumping, oil prices are soaring and a credit crisis paralysing the banking world. Are the conditions right for a "perfect economic storm"?' (January 3 2008) It should be admitted at this point that the author of that piece was also the co-author of this book.

In many cases, the use of the phrase the perfect storm was inappropriate; a reduction in America's growth rate to around 2 per cent in the light of the subprime crisis did not merit the description. Nor did forecasts from City of London economists that Britain was about to have its toughest year since the early 1990s but still avoid suffering a single quarter of falling output. In previous eras, such outcomes would have been described as the stop phase of a stop-go cycle or a soft landing. It appeared, however, that a long period of rapid growth – the five-year period from 2003 to 2007 marked the strongest performance by the global economy since the climax of the post-war boom in the late 1960s and 1970s – had made commentators forget what tough times were really like, and they lurched into hyperbole at the first hint of trouble.

So let us be clear. We do not consider it to be a 'perfect storm' should British house prices fall by 5 per cent while simultaneously a weaker pound makes it less appealing for British consumers to increase their carbon footprint with a weekend shopping trip to Manhattan. Nor do we consider it to be a perfect storm should higher oil prices occasion two or three years of belt-tightening in the US that result in weaker corporate profits and smaller bonuses for Wall Street traders.

If it is to justify the nomenclature, a perfect storm has to meet a far tougher test; a concatenation of events, serious enough in themselves, that taken together ensure an outcome that is bad, perhaps worse, than any informed commentator could envisage. Our view is that some of the headwinds facing the global economy – the financial losses sustained as a result of the US subprime crisis, for example – are serious enough to cause quite significant damage to growth and living standards over the coming years, but that the outcome would be far more serious were the problems of injudicious lending to be amplified by energy shortages, environmental disaster, policy error, rising inflation, terrorism and tension between the United States and China. The arrival of all of these horrors at once would be akin to Odysseus being left at the mercy of the elements after the crew on his ship opened the bag of winds presented to him by King Aeolus.

Before describing what a genuine perfect storm might look like, it is worth noting that the next few years may see the status quo restored: Odysseus may be able to get all the winds back into the bag bar the West Wind drifting him gently home to Ithaca. More often than not, the worst does not happen. Despite the scare stories, the world's computers did not all malfunction as a result of a Millennium Bug when the clock struck midnight on December 31 1999; the West's population had, at the time of writing, remained unaffected by SARS or Asian bird flu; the record of the past quarter of a century has been that every setback to the global economy – from the Latin American debt crisis to the terrorist attacks on New York and Washington in September 2001 – had been shrugged off.

The philosopher Karl Popper always insisted on making the best possible case for his opponents before seeking to refute it; doing so, he said, made his argument all the stronger. Popper would have little trouble constructing a case for business as usual over the coming years; a market-based system has withstood anything and everything that has been thrown at it over the past 250 years, and a graph of global output since the middle of the 18th century shows a steady upward trend, with

even the Great Depression registering as an almost impercep-
tible downward blip. Capitalism has proved itself to be
malleable and adaptable; the profit motive has emerged, albeit
sometimes battered, from world wars, hyper-inflation, speculative manias, crashes and depressions. It has found a home
in states run by economic liberals, social democrats and
communists. The system has learned how to bend with the
wind (the current vogue for environmentally friendly forms
of production being a prime example of firms knowing when
and how to give ground to the prevailing political orthodoxy),
how to co-opt its critics, how to keep a low profile when necessary and, most importantly of all, how to learn from its
mistakes.

Policy makers learn from past experience. Nobody would
seriously suggest today, for example, that finance ministries
should seek to balance budgets during economic downturns,
as was the accepted wisdom at the time of the Wall Street
Crash of 1929. Ben Bernanke, the current chairman of the
Federal Reserve Board, was an academic before he was a
central banker, and made his reputation for his work on the
causes of the Great Depression. More than anyone in early
2008, Mr Bernanke was alive to the risk of repeating the policy
errors that turned a stock-market crash into a slump – leaving
interest rates too high for too long, and raising taxes or cutting
spending in a misguided belief that the budget needs to be
balanced even when the economy is in freefall.

As a governor of the Fed under Alan Greenspan, Mr
Bernanke outlined his thinking in a speech in 2002 ('Deflation:
Making Sure "It" Doesn't Happen Here'; National Economists
Club, Washington, November 21 2002). The Fed, he said, would
'take whatever means necessary' to prevent the US from
repeating the deflationary experience of Japan in the 1990s.
Coping with the threat of a period of falling prices was straightforward; the Fed and the US Treasury had the means to do
the job, and although the best cure for deflation was to make
sure it did not appear in the first place, Mr Bernanke made it
clear that he would be prepared to crank up the printing presses.

'By increasing the number of US dollars in circulation, or even by credibly threatening to do so, the US government can also reduce the value of a dollar in terms of goods and services, which is equivalent to raising the prices in dollars of those goods and services. We conclude that, under a paper-money system, a determined government can always generate higher spending and hence positive inflation.' This speech won Mr Bernanke the nickname 'Helicopter Ben', since the assumption was that in a deflationary crisis the Fed would, figuratively speaking, take to the skies and dump wads of dollar bills on the economy, a policy response first raised by Milton Friedman. By 2008, the theories of 'Helicopter Ben' had ceased to be academic. While he was cutting interest rates, the White House was suggesting a tax cut worth 1 per cent of American GDP – $140 billion – to encourage spending.

Again, this owed much to the post-mortem examination of the Great Depression. In the jargon of the profession, politicians now allow the economic stabilisers to work in recessions; they accept lower tax revenues and higher public spending even if the inevitable consequence is that budget deficits increase. The government thereby leans against the wind, supporting economic activity until, as Lord Keynes said, the animal spirits of the private sector revive.

And revive they do, eventually. Britain could be said to have suffered two perfect storms under the long period of Conservative control from 1979 to 1997; the recession that wiped out a quarter of the country's manufacturing capacity in the early 1980s and a downturn of almost equal severity that laid low the property market a decade later. In the early 1980s, industry was faced with inflation at 20 per cent, a doubling of oil prices, interest rates of 17 per cent and a pound artificially boosted in value by the arrival in the late 1970s of North Sea oil. At a time when global demand was weak, UK companies were internationally uncompetitive and they went out of business in droves, pushing unemployment to levels not seen since the 1930s. Within five years of the economic trough in 1981, however, the economy was growing strongly again. Oil prices were below $10 a barrel, the pound had collapsed, interest rates had been cut, inflation was just above 2 per cent.

Five years later, Britain was back in recession. The recovery of the mid-1980s turned into a wild, speculative boom in 1988 that necessitated interest rates of 15 per cent to bring it under control. Inflation picked up once more, hitting almost 11 per cent and – despairing of finding a domestic solution to rising prices – the Conservative government pegged the pound to the Deutschmark in the hope that it could import some anti-inflationary rigour from Germany. Two extra ingredients made up the perfect storm: rising oil prices as a result of the first Gulf War and German reunification. The latter triggered a surge in inflation, prompting the German central bank – the Bundesbank – to keep interest rates high. That had knock-on effects for other European countries, including Britain, because they too were required to keep interest rates high in order to maintain the value of their currencies against the mark. In Britain, high interest rates led to a rapid cooling of the economy and a doubling of unemployment, which returned to almost three million. People who had bought their homes at the top of the market in 1988 found that they could no longer keep up the mortgage payments. Home repossessions and bankruptcies rose to record levels; house prices entered a six-year period of decline.

Again, however, recovery was relatively swift. Britain ceased to peg its currency against the mark and the pound dropped in value by 30 per cent, making exports cheaper on world markets. Without the need to defend the pound, interest rates were cut from 10 per cent to 6 per cent in four months. Oil prices again tumbled once the short war against Saddam Hussein was over. The years immediately after Black Wednesday were not easy for consumers, since taxes were raised aggressively as the government sought to repair the damage to the public finances caused by the recession, and even with interest rates at 6 per cent rather than 15 per cent house prices did not start to rise again until 1995. Even so, by the time Tony Blair took office in May 1997, the economy was growing strongly, consumer spending was buoyant, and exports from a more competitive manufacturing sector meant Britain's trade gap with the rest of the world had been closed.

Periods such as the early 1980s and the early 1990s are the exception rather than the rule. In only five years since the Second World War has Britain experienced years when gross domestic product (GDP) – the yardstick for measuring growth – has declined. That is, perhaps, not entirely surprising since technological advance and improvements in working practices mean that historically the economy has grown by 2.5 per cent on average for the past six decades. Years when output is actually falling indicate that the economy is performing a long way below its potential.

It is for that reason – and not just innate optimism – that economic forecasters rarely see recessions coming. J.K. Galbraith had enormous fun at the expense of American economic pundits in *The Great Crash* (Penguin Books; originally published 1954, current edition first published 1992), a book peppered with bitter-sweet examples of how the great and the good failed to see the stock-market crash coming, predicted that the fall in share prices would be a short-lived affair and completely failed to realise that America was facing the biggest depression in its history, even when factories were closing and the dole queues were lengthening.

Most of the time, those who take a cautious approach to forecasting are proved right. Economies tend to operate at around their potential growth rate – in Britain's case GDP tends to expand in the range of 2–3 per cent each year. Those who habitually say that the economy is about to plunge into recession are sometimes right, but so are stopped clocks.

At the start of 2008, the prevailing view was that both the US and the UK were going to have a year of sub-trend growth, and that while there was a risk that America would have a brief recession Britain would grow at between 1.5 and 2 per cent. Even the most bullish of forecasters did not expect developed economies to escape unscathed from the financial crisis prompted by the souring of subprime loans, but it remained a possibility – albeit a slim one – that aggressive cuts in interest rates coupled with co-ordinated central bank action to unfreeze financial markets might allow the global economy to continue serenely on its way.

Anatole Kaletsky, the distinguished commentator at *The Times* newspaper, was one who was confident that things would turn out better than the Cassandras were predicting. In an article called 'Goodbye to all that: the worst is over for the global credit crunch' (*The Times*; January 14 2008), Kaletsky said there would be no recession in the US and that stock markets would rise in 2008. 'I believe that the global credit crisis, far from taking a turn for the worse, is now almost over,' he added. This was minority view, even in the City and on Wall Street, two geographical locations not normally known for their rampant pessimism. Goldman Sachs, Merrill Lynch, Citigroup, Morgan Stanley, just about every big beast of the US investment banking world had, by the end of 2007 or the start of 2008, pencilled in a recession for America in 2008 and a pronounced slowdown for Britain and the rest of Europe. This was not desperately surprising given that most of these self-same banks were reporting record quarterly losses as a result of their exposure to subprime securities; the gloom spread downwards from the boardroom to the analysts.

That said, there was still a chance that Kaletsky would be proved right. Although there was more and more news coming in to refute the Fed's confident assertion in early 2007 that subprime would be contained and cause problems only to the real estate market, not all the news was gloomy. Consumers still appeared to be spending money; unemployment had picked up, but at 5 per cent the jobless rate was much lower than it had been in previous downturns, and lower than in continental Europe. It was the same story in the UK. The last set of figures from the labour market in 2007 showed a quarterly rise in employment of 175,000 and the 15th successive monthly fall in the number of people out of work and claiming benefit. So, as we seek to assess the impact of the financial turmoil, the starting point is that there might not be even a shower or squall let alone a storm, but merely a gust of wind.

In the past, this has certainly been the case. The Warwick University economist Andrew Oswald has noted that every sharp increase in the oil price in the past 35 years – 1973–1974, 1979–1980 and 1990–1991 – has prompted a global recession. 'The single best cyclical indicator for the world economy is the price of oil,' he told the *New York Times* as the American-led coalition prepared to invade Iraq in early 2003 ('Jump in price of oil puts new strains on the economy'; March 2 2003). Far from flooding the global energy market with cheap crude, the defeat of Saddam Hussein was the catalyst for a long and pronounced increase in the cost of oil, and every time it hit a new benchmark – first $40, then $50, then $60 and finally $100 a barrel – there were predictions of impending recession. But as noted earlier in this chapter, the fivefold increase in the cost of crude failed to prevent the global economy from having its best period of growth since the days of Edward Heath and Richard Nixon. Indeed, one explanation for the rising cost of energy was that the rapid expansion of the global economy had led to the voracious demand of newly industrialising countries such as China and India outstripping supply.

Even so, there were few takers for the Kaletsky view of the world in the first few months of 2008, not least because those running developed economies – and the Federal Reserve in particular – had ceased to be confident that the problems from the subprime crisis would be contained. Instead, there was a recognition that there were already contagion effects. In late 2007, Bill Gross, the managing director of the fund manager Pimco, predicted a further 10 per cent fall in US house prices and said the only real question was how bad 2008 would be. 'The 2008 outlook for housing prices will be a function of whether the Fed can cut off a worst-case scenario, but we think continued weakness in housing and slower economic growth are already baked into the cake for next year' (Pimco Spotlight; December 2007). US growth, Mr Gross added, would slow to 1 per cent – a view shared by the leading Wall Street investment banks, where the consensus view was that the US would suffer two quarters of negative growth – the technical definition of recession.

In the UK, the Royal Institution of Chartered Surveyors, the body that represents estate agents, produced its gloomiest survey in 16 years in January 2008 against a backdrop of credit becoming more expensive and less easily available. The number of mortgage products on the market was sharply down, one eighth of first-time buyers had to pay 7 per cent or more to obtain a mortgage. In May 2007, less than 1 per cent had been forced to pay such expensive rates. House prices in Greater London, the centre of the boom in the property market over the previous 10 years, were down more than 6 per cent in the final three months of 2007 (Halifax regional house price index; January 19 2008).

One piece of good news was that the actions by the Bank of England, the Fed and the European Central Bank to pump funds into the financial markets had helped to make it cheaper and easier for banks to borrow from each other. The bad news, however, was that a belated mood of caution and the need to repair balance sheets damaged by losses on 'toxic waste' securities meant that these benefits were not being passed on to the banks' customers. Michael Saunders, UK economist at Citibank, summed up the mood when he said it would be wrong to assume that easing strains in money markets meant the crisis was over. 'The economic slowdown has barely begun. Most of the bad news – in terms of soft consumer spending, job losses, cuts to profit forecasts, and falling property values – still lies ahead' ('Still Getting Worse'; *Citigroup Sterling Weekly*; January 18 2008). Admittedly the Saunders missive did appear in the week that Citigroup was left contemplating a near-$20 billion write-off on subprime debt, a 42 per cent cut in its dividend and a record quarterly loss was the most expensive last waltz in history. But Mr Saunders was by no means alone. Nor was his the most gloomy prognostication for the UK economy.

Mainstream City thinking went like this. With the US

housing market still declining, banks were likely to have to own up to much bigger losses on their speculative activities. In addition, tighter credit conditions would expose some other examples of excess which the markets had conveniently ignored during the good years. Britain's commercial property sector, for example, received far less attention than its residential counterpart, but had experienced a boom of equivalent size. Billions of pounds had been invested in property funds; as with real estate, securitised derivatives and the global economy the feeling was that the only way was up. By the early months of 2008, property prices were plunging, prompting hefty selling by small investors. Aware that their cash balances were inadequate in the event of a Northern Rock-style run, the property funds responded by putting a freeze on withdrawals.

Nervous attention was also being paid to the companies that guaranteed bonds – the so-called monoline insurers. As with almost everything else in the world of modern financial markets, the mundanity of the name disguised what these companies were up to, and how their possible collapse could add a fresh leg to the subprime crisis. When banks in the US and Europe bought CDOs they insured themselves with monoline insurers, highly leveraged by AAA-rated firms that ostensibly specialise in taking the risk out of risky investments. Like any insurance operation, this was a good business to be in when the number of claims was small; as it became evident that most of the bonds guaranteed by the monoline insurers were worthless their losses mounted and their credit ratings were cut. This raised the possibility that they would have to sell assets to meet their commitments or, even worse, collapse. Merrill Lynch, nursing its own $16.7 billion of losses on virtually worthless subprime debt announced in January 2008 that it was putting aside $3.1 billion connected to mortgage-backed securities that it had thought were off its books.

Indeed, the monolines were in a highly exposed position. They had guaranteed $150 billion of derivatives backed by subprime mortgages and as much as $1.5 trillion in municipal bonds. They had very little actual capital and were leveraged 100-1 – similar to the hedge fund Long Term Capital Management in 1998. By early 2008, some monoline insurers were on the brink of insolvency and the US government was trying to piece together a rescue package. Investment sage Warren Buffet said he was interested in taking over the parts of the business that dealt with municipal bonds but did not want the subprime arm (hardly surprising since Mr Buffet once famously called derivatives 'financial instruments of mass destruction' (Barkshire Hathaway chairman's letter 2002).

What the banks feared was that the monolines would lose their Triple-A rating, which would mean that they could not meet their commitments to insure the big banks for subprime exposure and would prompt an estimated further $150 billion in write-downs. That, in turn, would lead to a further tightening of credit conditions and lead to both a deeper recession and further downward pressure on share prices.

While Gordon Brown was seeking at every opportunity to stress Britain's ability to shrug off a crisis that had started in the US, City analysts were far less sanguine. 'To a very large extent, the risks to the UK are the same as those in the US, though they are arguably even more severe,' said Rob Camell of ING in London ('2008 – where could it all go wrong'; ING; January 11 2008). 'The UK housing market has risen faster and further than that in the US, though without the same supply imbalance, and perhaps with greater fundamental support. Nevertheless, household balance sheets in the UK are more stretched relative to the US in terms of household debt to disposable income. And government finances are in much poorer shape to help the economy, should that be needed.'

Britain, it was argued, could have a mini-perfect storm all of its own. Firstly, there was no guarantee that the collapse of Northern Rock would be the last should the UK suffer the sort of residential property crash that had been seen in the US. As the City firm Kleinwort Dresdner noted (in December 2007 conversations with the authors) there had been three previous booms in British house prices in the post-Second

World War era; after each there had been a subsequent 30 per cent fall in prices when adjusted for inflation. Secondly, there were warnings that years of consumer profligacy followed by a period of negative equity and tougher criteria for borrowers could lead to a rising number of bankruptcies and mortgage delinquencies, thereby putting even more stress on the UK banking system. Thirdly, the Bank of England's ability to respond to a slowing economy was constrained by rising infla- tion, which meant the chances of deep cuts in interest rates was less likely in the UK than in the US. Finally, the govern- ment was in no position to take up the slack through tax cuts or spending increases, as had happened in the first few years of the decade when Britain avoided the recession that affected the US, Germany, France and Japan by spending its way out of trouble. Budget deficits usually come down when economies are growing fast and by the start of 2008 the UK had been growing at an annual rate of 3 per cent or more for almost two years. Yet far from getting better, the budget deficit continued to rise, forcing the government to cut back the rate of spending growth and to impose below inflation pay rises on the public sector. The title of a report on the global economy from HSBC summed up the mood. 'Goodbye to all that' (December 2007).

We have much sympathy with this analysis. In our previous book (*Fantasy Island*; Constable; 2007) we argued that Britain's economy had been over-reliant on debt and that the chronic tendency to spend more than we earned and consume more than we produce would, sooner or later, come back to haunt policy makers. Labour's decade in power had been marked by a continuation of the decline in manufacturing, leaving the economy flying on three engines; the City of London, the housing market and the public sector. In 2008, all three were in danger of stalling.

It is our contention, nevertheless, that this would still not constitute a perfect storm, or anything like it. The most pessimistic City analysts were still predicting a moderation in UK growth rather than a recession; their counterparts on Wall

Street believed that by the end of 2008 cheaper money and tax cuts from the US Treasury would ensure that the American economy was expanding once more.

Our view is that the phrase 'perfect storm' is rendered meaningless without a more stringent test and that this will require more than a slowdown in the UK turning into a recession and a short recession in the US becoming a more prolonged hard landing. As has no doubt become clear in the earlier chapters of this book, we have some sympathy with those like Albert Edwards at Société Générale who wonder whether there is not going to be a much higher price to be paid for the years of living dangerously. 'The debate is shifting from whether the US economy will go into recession, to how long and how deep it will be. Strangely, no one seems to be contemplating a deep recession. I'm not sure why, given the unprecedented consumer debt excess that could easily unwind. As profits slump, investors are relying on equity cheapness to limit any bear market. They should not' ('Is the penny finally dropping?'; Société Générale; January 8 2008).

The debt-soaked economies of the US and the UK may indeed be the Ponzi schemes that Mr Edwards considers them to be. He may also be right in doubting whether the Great Moderation attributed to central banks is no such thing if the periods of strong, stable growth with shallow recessions have been deliberately 'bought' at the cost of successive credit and asset bubbles. But even if all that is true, it would merely be one of the ingredients – albeit a vital one – for a perfect storm. Worryingly, the other ingredients appear to be readily available.

HIGH ANXIETY: OIL, HURRICANES, RUMOURS OF WARS

Excessive levels of debt and financial stress provide necessary but not sufficient conditions for a perfect storm. It would, for example, have been unimaginable for policy makers in the

1950s and 1960s to contemplate a period of loose credit leading to a freezing up of global credit markets. For one thing, credit markets were domestic not global; but more importantly, the activities of the financial sector were carefully monitored following the debacle of the late 1920s and any suggestion that borrowing conditions were becoming too loose was met with the imposition of credit controls. The globalisation of finance, the abandonment of the policy instruments used to control speculation, the increasing importance of finance in domestic economies and the complacency engendered by a long period of low-inflationary growth have all made the economics of the UK and the US more vulnerable to a crisis. But not every slowdown turns into a recession and not every recession turns into a slump.

One current danger is the re-emergence of inflationary pressures. Even as the economies were slowing in the winter of 2008, there was unmistakable evidence of rising fuel and food prices. Some of these increases were beyond the control of policy makers in London or Washington; one reason, for example, that butter prices in UK supermarkets were up by 50 per cent in a year was that the growing prosperity of Chinese consumers meant that for the first time they could afford refrigerators in which to store dairy products.

The effects of rising prices were starting to be felt beyond the West. The UN Food Programme said in February 2008 that the rising cost of food meant it no longer had the money to keep malnutrition at bay in the world's poorest countries. Josette Sheeran, head of the programme, called it: 'The new face of hunger.'

Central banks responded to this pressure in different ways. The European Central Bank, still dominated by memories of marks being carried around in wheelbarrows in the Germany of 1923, discussed whether it should raise interest rates to combat inflationary pressure. The Bank of England adopted a middle-way approach; having expressed concern in the first half of 2007 about the cost of living in the UK it first shelved plans for dearer borrowing and then cut rates modestly. It stressed, however, that it was still concerned that the higher cost of energy and food might be the start of a wage-price spiral. The Federal Reserve, despite presiding over the economy with the highest inflation, had no such reservations; the Fed had no wish to be blamed for a second Great Depression (or even, in an presidential election year, a common or garden recession) and it cut rates quickly and deeply.

Unless the conditions facing the three central banks were wildly different, at least two of them were making a policy error. Either they were worried about an inflation problem that didn't exist, leaving themselves open to the charge of failing to spot the risk of a downturn until it was too late. If so, they were guilty of the mistake made by the Fed after the 1929 crash. Alternatively, they were playing with inflationary fire and by pumping cheap money into the economy would simply put off the reckoning to another day. Graham Turner, an expert on the Japanese economy, said from the early days of the crisis that the Fed needed to act quickly and decisively. 'Until the Fed recognises the seriousness of the US housing market crisis and starts cutting, equity markets will continue to correct lower, increasing the risks of recession in 2008' ('Leverage, Contagion and Stocks'; GFC Economics; August 15 2007).

Stephen Lewis was in the opposite camp. He compared Mr Bernanke with Bill Miller, the chairman of the Federal Reserve who in the late 1970s ignored inflationary warning signs in an attempt to reflate the economy. Lewis said that while Mr Bernanke might not be the growth 'nutter' that Mr Miller had been, he had precious little to say about the risks of rising prices.

Bernanke gave the impression he had been unnerved by the scale of the problem facing US financial institutions. In assessing the prospects for the economy, he hardly got beyond the subprime market and the financial turmoil. If, in the past, market participants have complained that the Fed has not heard what they are saying about their distress, they could hardly maintain that charge after yesterday's speech (in which Bernanke said he

stood ready to continue cutting interest rates). The Fed chairman at least
is 100 per cent focused on the financial sector's woes. ('Economic Insights',
from financial services company Insinger de Beaufort January 11 2008)

Mr Lewis made the point that after Mr Miller had allowed
inflation to spiral to 13.5 per cent in 1980 it took draconian
action from his successor, Paul Volcker, to bring it back under
control. It involved pushing the Fed Funds rate back up to 21
per cent. The underlying inflationary backdrop was less threatening than in the late 1970s and early 1980s, but US households
were far better able to withstand tough anti-inflation medicine
from the Fed under Bernanke than they had been under Volcker
or than they would be today, because mortgages were almost
exclusively fixed rate in the late 1970s and early 1980s. 'A similar
loss of confidence in today's circumstances would bring on the
kind of crisis in household finances that Bernanke is trying to
avoid.'

Wall Street and the City retained a tender, almost touching,
faith in policy makers even as it became clearer and clearer
that they were no longer fully in control of events. Every
utterance was greeted with reverence, although the impact
on the markets seemed to grow weaker and weaker as the
months went by. The belief that the Fed, the Bank of England
and the ECB knew what they were doing and could steer a
path between the Scylla of recession and the Charybdis of
inflation was strong. A soft landing was, however, one of only
three possibilities; the others were that cutting interest rates
(and it was assumed that eventually the Bank of England and
the ECB would follow the Fed's lead) would be the equivalent of a 'fix' for the world's debt junkies, the effects of which
would wear off even more quickly than they had in the past.
Alternatively, there was the risk that cutting interest rates
would have no effect on borrowers long overdue for a period
of cold turkey.

The oil market provided an added complication. Historically,
periods of slow economic growth have led to a drop in the
price of crude, with falling demand for energy leading to lower

prices. In 2008, there was no guarantee that this pattern would be repeated, in part because the bigger developing economies – China and India – were still growing fast. Even with demand in the West threatening to slow, there were doubts about whether there was enough supply capacity to cope – the legacy of a long period in which there had been scant investment in new refining capacity. More importantly, there was the question of whether the days of cheap oil were over.

There have been no major new discoveries of crude since 2002 and – as with food – rising demand has been pushing up prices. In the mid-1950s, M. King Hubbert accurately predicted that oil production in the US would peak at the start of the 1970s and then start declining. Many oil experts believe that peak oil for the world is now rapidly approaching, if it has not already arrived, for cheap crude that is easy to extract. Colin Campbell, former chief geologist at a number of major oil companies, put it this way: 'It's quite a simple theory and one any beer drinker understands. The glass starts full and ends empty and the faster you drink it the quicker it's gone' (*Independent on Sunday*; June 14 2007). The green movement has latched on to peak oil since it believes the projected doubling of demand for oil from 80 million barrels a day to 160 million barrels per day would be disastrous for the environment, pushing the world over the edge of runaway climate change. It is not only environmentalists who believe peak oil is a reality, however. Matthew Simmons, who worked as an energy adviser to George W Bush, believes that $100 oil prices are the inevitable consequence of demand outstripping supply.

'The world expects several decades of growing supplies of generally affordable oil,' said the energy economist Jeremy Leggett in a published note ('The Trouble with Oil'; December 2007). 'Every corporate and ministerial plan is geared to this assumption. Beyond the peak of global oil production the world will face shrinking supplies of increasingly expensive oil. That is a manageable proposition if the peak is several decades away. It is a major problem if the peak is imminent.

Growing numbers of people well qualified to offer an opinion fear that it is indeed imminent.'

Global production of oil currently stands at around 85 million barrels per day. By 2030, projected demand is expected to be 116 million barrels per day, a figure the oil cartel OPEC, the International Energy Agency and the leading oil companies believe will be almost impossible to meet on current trends. If the world is really close to, or at, the moment of peak oil, prices will not just remain at $100 a barrel but could easily rise further. In April 2005, Jim Rogers, who founded the Quantum hedge fund with George Soros, predicted that crude could cost $150 a barrel within ten years (Hedge Funds Global Opportunities Conference in New York); a forecast that looked far less fanciful three years later.

Mr Rogers said: 'The question on oil will be how high the price goes and stays, because there may be vast amounts of oil in the world but no one has discovered a great oilfield in over 35 years.

'The Alaskan and Mexican fields are in decline, and while the North Sea has made the UK one of the great oil exporters in the last 20 years, within the decade the UK will be a net importer.'

Optimists argue that the date for peak oil has constantly been pushed back and that with global prices high there will be an incentive to find and develop fields in the more inhospitable parts of the world. Leggett says the optimists are in denial; fewer and fewer giant oil fields are being discovered, large portions of supposedly proved reserves might not exist, while it is an illusion that large amounts of crude can be extracted from Canadian tar sands. The cold wastes of Alberta are unlikely to rival the deserts of the Middle East; the oil from the tar sands is hard to get at, expensive to extract and will provide little more than 2.5 million barrels per day by 2015 (Leggett; *ibid*).

The very real prospect is that oil prices continue to be high. And while it is certainly true that the shift in production in developed economies from manufacturing to services means that each unit of output is now less energy intensive, oil is still vital for the West. Higher crude prices mean higher costs for business and lower disposable incomes for consumers. In the short run, the impact is inflationary but in the longer run the squeeze on corporate profits and consumer spending is deflationary. The fact that the world economy continued to grow strongly in the five years during which oil prices rose from $20 a barrel in early 2003 to $100 a barrel in early 2008 does not mean that the impact of dearer energy can be permanently shrugged off.

Painful though this would be for Western economies, the impact would be far more grievous in the event of oil supplies being cut off for any reason. One possible cause of shortages would be environmental disaster of the sort that was wrought to US production in the Gulf of Mexico by Hurricane Katrina in August 2005. The other threat stems from geo-political risk.

Climate change experts say that the risk of environmental disaster as a result of climate change is growing, noting that there has been a correlation since 1970 between sea temperature and the increased frequency of cyclones. The year 2005 saw the most destructive hurricane season on record, culminating in the loss of more than 2,000 lives and an estimated $125 billion worth of damage in the violent storm that flooded large parts on New Orleans. Even more violent hurricanes, with larger peak wind speeds and heavier rainfall are predicted for the future ('Hurricanes: a compendium of hurricane information'; US Global Change Research Programme; June 2007). The global insurance industry, faced by the prospect of ever-larger claims has, unsurprisingly perhaps, been in the vanguard of attempts to persuade policy makers to take climate change more seriously.

Global political developments provide the final piece of the jigsaw. At one level, the threat is obvious: the attacks on New York and Washington on September 11 2001 had an immediate impact on Western economies; Wall Street was shut for several days and when it reopened share prices fell abruptly; consumer confidence collapsed; certain sectors of the economy – airlines especially – suffered considerable commercial damage. Any repetition of 9/11 at a time when financial markets are feeling the effects of the credit crunch, falls in house prices and dearer energy would amplify the impact of any downturn.

But there are two more geo-political threats. The first arises from the fact that large quantities of the global reserves of oil and natural gas are in countries that are either politically unstable (the Middle East) or controlled by regimes prepared to use energy as a strategic weapon in international relations (Russia). With Western governments acutely aware of how vulnerable they are to regime change in Saudi Arabia, terrorist attacks on oil installations in Iraq, religious fundamentalism in Iran and sabre-rattling in Moscow, energy security has moved up the policy agenda and is one reason why the British government has, in the face of considerable domestic opposition, supported the building of a new generation of nuclear reactors.

All this is happening against the background of profound changes to the international balance of power, mirroring changes seen a century ago; changes that made the world a far more dangerous place in the years 1890 to 1945 than it had been in the previous three-quarters of a century.

There were no major wars involving all the great powers between Waterloo and 1914; a period of peace that historians attribute to the fact that the then global hegemon, Britain, was committed to the peaceful exploitation of its largely maritime interests and that there was a balance of power between the other great powers. From the late 19th century, this balance of power was affected by the rise of some powers – the United States, Germany, Japan, Russia – and the decline of others, Austria-Hungary, the Ottoman empire. Britain became involved in two costly world wars for the reasons it had always reluctantly involved itself in continental adventures, to prevent one continental power achieving dominance. The Cambridge historian Harry Hinsley wrote in the early 1960s (*Power and the Pursuit of Peace*; Cambridge University Press; 1963) that the balance of power was restored in 1945 when neither the United States nor the Soviet Union could normally consider invading each other or letting loose their nuclear weapons, the 1962 Cuban missile crisis and the 1983 'hot autumn' being exceptional and highly dangerous moments in history. This did not prevent the two great powers from fighting proxy wars in other parts of the world – in Asia, Africa and Latin America – but it did mean that there was no chance of a third world war. Mr Hinsley dates the challenge to the 19th-century balance of power as 1890, and future historians may date 1990 as the moment when the post-Second World War balance of power started to come apart. This was the year when the reunification of Germany heralded the end of Moscow's dominance in Eastern Europe and the break-up of the Soviet Union. In Asia, there were signs that the pro-market reforms introduced by Beijing in the late 1970s were turning China into an industrial power of real clout; India was a year away from introducing its own attempt at moving away from a command economy.

And just as the tensions from the break-up of the 19th-century balance of power quickly became evident, so the period of tranquillity that followed America's elevation to unrivalled global superpower was also brief. The emergence of the new Asian powers – not just China but also a Russia re-invigorated by the economic strength it attained by virtue of its considerable reserves of ever more valuable oil and gas – posed a discernible threat to American hegemony. And, as Paul Kennedy stressed in his seminal work on the link between economic and political power, the US should not assume that it would remain unchallenged for ever.

Although the United States is at present still in a class of its own econom-ically and perhaps even militarily, it cannot avoid confronting the two great tests which challenge the longevity of every major power that occu-pies the 'number one' position in world affairs: whether, in the military/strategical realm, it can preserve a reasonable balance between the nation's perceived defence requirements and the means it possesses to maintain those commitments; and whether, as an intimately related point,

it can preserve the technological and economics bases of its power from
relative erosion in the face of the ever-shifting patterns of global produc-
tion.' (The Rise and Fall of the Great Powers; Fontana; 1988)

What Professor Kennedy did not realise, perhaps, was just
how quickly these political changes could occur. Writing in
1988, he failed to spot that the Soviet Union was atrophying
economically and on the point of collapse.

So how could this threat to the US materialise? One theory
is that America's international creditors – China and the Gulf
States – will put the sort of pressure on Washington that
Washington put on Britain and France at the time of the Suez
crisis in 1956. Flynt Leverett, writing in the *National Interest*
magazine (number 93, January/February 2008), said the US
was now facing an 'axis of oil' – a loose and shifting coalition
of energy-exporting and importing states, anchored by Russia
and China. 'The ability of such a coalition to resist American
hegemony is now compounded by the vulnerability of the
United States to financial and monetary pressure by its major
international creditors – most of which are at least putative
members of the axis of oil.' Should China and Russia choose
to do so, they have the power to put co-ordinated financial
and monetary pressure on the US for strategic ends.

Most importantly, there is the question of how the US
would cope should the dollar cease to be the 'world's money'.
At the time of the Asian crisis in 1997 and 1998 such a suggestion would have been unthinkable; since then US trade
deficits have grown bigger, China has grown rapidly, the euro
has appeared as a rival reserve currency and the US-led invasion of Iraq has led to increased tension in the Middle East.
The Chinese have financed the American trade deficit by
buying vast quantities of US Treasury bonds and have quietly
made it plain that they would be prepared to make life difficult for Washington by selling assets should the White House
continue to threaten the imposition of trade sanctions. In
the Middle East, the Iranian government has openly
suggested pricing oil in euros rather than dollars, while even

the traditionally pro-Washington Saudi government has culti-
vated a strategic partnership with Beijing.

A true perfect storm, therefore, might look like this. In
October 2008, on the 35th anniversary of the start of the Yom
Kippur War, George Bush finally loses patience with Teheran
and, in the last big decision of his presidency, launches air
strikes against Iran's nuclear capability. The Iranians retaliate
by shutting off supplies to the West and, in a further blow to
crude supplies, militants in Saudi Arabia launch a coup attempt
against the royal family. On the same day, just as the citizens
of Louisiana, Mississippi and Texas think they have seen the
last of the stormiest summers on record, a category five hurricane sweeps across the Gulf of Mexico and shuts down half
of America's oil refining capacity.

The combination of military action in the Middle East
and natural disaster sends the price of oil – already close to
record levels – shooting up to $150 a barrel, pushing up infla-
tion in all Western economies. Central banks, fearful of
another 1970s-style surge in the cost of living, raise interest
rates, intensifying the effects of the worst economic downturn seen since the 1980s. Financial markets suffer a spasm
of selling. Banks stop lending and as businesses fail in their
droves lengthening dole queues prompt a meltdown in the
housing market. No part of the world is left untouched by
the turmoil, although the impact is severest on the country
that was the root of the problem – the United States. China
does not fall into recession, but finds that it is hit by the curse
that often afflicts countries that host the Olympics. With the
games over, Beijing cuts back on investment and takes action
to curb inflation just at the time that exports to the US are
being choked off. China's growth rate halves to 5 per cent
and there is a domino effect through the rest of the Asia. A
bill imposing trade sanctions on Beijing for its refusal to
revalue its currency is passed by Congress; China responds
by dumping a quarter of its dollar assets, sending the US
currency and global markets into freefall.

In the recent past, predicting doom and gloom has been

a game for losers, the financial markets equivalent of the boy who cried wolf. There is good reason for this; policy makers act to stop recessions developing; when times are tough businesses cut prices in order to keep consumers spending; at a global level there is no obvious reason why the Chinese or the Saudis would want to cripple the American economy since to do so would cost them hundreds of billions of dollars in lost exports. The perfect storm may never happen.

Yet, ultimately, the message of the tale of the boy who cried wolf was that there was indeed a wolf. Consider the following facts: debt in America stands at 300 per cent of GDP and the last time it was at this level hundreds of banks were going bust in the Great Depression; credit has been expanding in the US at more than double the rate it was in the 1920s; banks in the US, Britain and Europe are nursing as yet unknown losses as a result of subprime mortgages; Britain has seen the first run on a high street bank in almost a century and a half; real wages in Britain and the US have been squeezed; oil prices have quintupled in the past five years; the Middle East from Gaza in the west to Afghanistan in the east is in political and economic turmoil; China is becoming relatively stronger and is seeking to expand its influence in the Pacific; the US is becoming relatively weaker; a series of environmental disasters has highlighted the risk of climate change to the global economy.

None of which means there is going to be a perfect storm, let alone that there is the economic equivalent of Britain's Meteorological Office that can precisely time its arrival. Yet the sky is growing darker not just with storm clouds but with chickens coming home to roost. There is a very real risk that economies already enfeebled by a borrowing binge and untrammelled speculation will be further weakened by policy error, higher oil prices, environmental collapse and rising geo-political tension. Should that occur – as it might within the next five years – three things will happen. There will be an economic crisis the like of which has not been seen since the 1930s. The gods that have failed will be pilloried in a new era of populism. And there will be a hunger for new and better ways of doing things. It is to the policies for a saner world that we turn in the last chapter of this book.

10

After the Gold Rush:

How the New Populism makes the financial system safer, gives ordinary people a bigger slice of the cake and puts the New Olympians back in their cage

Faced by failure of credit they have proposed only the lending of more money. Stripped of the lure of profit by which to induce our people to follow their false leadership, they have resorted to exhortations, pleading tearfully for restored confidence. They know only the rules of a generation of self-seekers.

> – Franklin Roosevelt; inaugural address; March 1933

Ultimately what one loves about life are the things that *last*, because those who care, see to it that they do.

> – Steven Bach; *Final Cut*; Faber and Faber edition; 1986

'If the creation of wealth itself destroys and wastes humanity, that wealth, however vast, will never suffice to repair the ravages it has wrought'.

> – Jeremy Seabrook; *The Race for Riches*; Marshall Pickering; 1988

With the world reeling from a global financial crisis, Gordon Brown flew to Japan to spell out a few home truths to both his hosts and to other leaders of the main economic powers. Mr Brown stressed the need for the Group of Seven club of rich nations to work together to restore international stability and renewed growth.

'But this is only possible if the industrialised world provides the engine for growth by sustaining demand in the world economy,' Mr Brown wisely added.

'All industrialised countries – in Europe and Japan as well as North America – must bear their share of that adjustment. No one country can either escape its responsibility to play its part in sustaining global demand or be required to bear the whole burden and thereby encourage protectionist sentiment.'

In an impressive *tour d'horizon*, Mr Brown added that fears of the dumping of cheap Asian products must not lead to the West closing its markets, and reaffirmed there could be no relaxation of the British government's tough anti-inflationary policy.

Finally, and unsurprisingly, he rejected claims from Britain's Tory opposition that the government was responsible.

A freehand summary of Mr Brown's remarks to the international summit held in Japan in early February 2008? It could be read in that way. But it is actually a résumé of a more youthful Gordon Brown's opinions as expressed on September 16 1998 during a trip to Tokyo in the wake of turmoil caused by the currency crises in the Far East and the Russian decision the previous month to default on some of its external debt. In 1998 and 1999, Gordon Brown urged the G7, the International Monetary Fund and pretty much any gathering of either finance ministers or central bankers, or both, to bolster the international financial system against future crises by improving surveillance of cross-border money flows, by establishing early warning systems that would whistle like a boiling kettle when ill-conceived economic policy in one country threatened to 'spill over' and create problems for other countries, by improving the 'transparency' of financial markets to ensure nobody would have the chance to make a killing out of others' general market ignorance and generally to establish a new 'world financial architecture' that would allow everybody to enjoy the full benefits of financial globalisation while ensuring that all the risks were safely encased in an intergovernmental version of the sort of concrete tomb used for the storage of radioactive nuclear waste.

Does any of this ring a faint bell? Having read the earlier sections of this book, does the notion that all rewards can be preserved while all risks can be parked somewhere out of sight and out of mind sound eerily familiar? It is, we would argue, merely the political version of the financial market fantasy that suggests ever more complex 'instruments' can be used to disperse risk while allowing banks, hedge funds and others to hang on to the rewards.

As the current storm broke upon the leading economies, there was every sign that Mr Brown, now prime minister, remained committed to the notion that large-scale problems in large-scale financial markets among large-scale participants required a large-scale political response from the G7, the IMF and any other worthy international forum that wishes to get involved. Key to this is the notion that markets will become less volatile if they can only be made more transparent. Mr Brown has been pushing this notion with regard to the oil market since at least the autumn of 2004, and has set up an information gathering initiative to that end with the Saudi Arabian authorities. Since the autumn of 2004, the price per barrel for the North Sea's Brent crude has soared from about $46 to smash through the $100 a barrel level, suggesting Mr Brown's 'transparency' may not be all it is cracked up to be.

As 2008 dawned, however, the old song book was dusted down as Mr Brown and his colleagues tried to find a way out of the encircling gloom. As ten years earlier, the first reaction was always to huddle together with other G7 ministers and officials and work on a communiqué. Perhaps the subconscious hope is that even if the assembled big-wigs produce wrong-headed answers, this will matter less if blame for these 'solutions' can be spread over a number of different countries. Again, there is an echo here of the financial engineers' belief that risk, if smashed into sufficiently tiny pieces and dispersed among a great range of institutions and other investors, had effectively ceased to be risky. That this notion was wrong by about 180 degrees was amply demonstrated in the global market crisis that first struck in the summer of 2007. Far from making markets less risky, by spreading risk the wizards in the banks had managed to globalise the consequences of reckless lending in specific markets.

Thus on January 17 2008, Alistair Darling flew to Paris for talks with the finance ministers of the three other G7 members of the European Union: France, Germany and Italy. The chancellor was keen to get agreement on the need for better market surveillance from the IMF and the G7's Financial Stability Forum ahead of the meeting of the Group of Eight in Tokyo early the following month (the G8 is the political version of the G7, at which Britain is represented by the prime minister rather than the chancellor and which comprises all the G7 members plus Russia). The UK's faith in the efficacy of 'better market surveillance' was especially touching in light of the fact that the FSF was set up in April 1999 in the wake of the Asian and Russian financial crises precisely to ensure such shocks could not recur. That they did so, with much greater force, from mid-2007 onwards suggests the FSF has not fulfilled its promise.

Watching Messrs Brown and Darling flying to international meetings, calling for greater surveillance and transparency and suggesting new ways of 'tackling imbalances' and 'reducing volatility', the private citizen may well conclude, with the former baseball player and manager Yogi Berra, that: 'This is like déjà vu all over again.' Or perhaps Mr Darling's performance has been reminiscent of that of a former Archbishop of Canterbury, Robert Runcie, whose globe-trotting method of operation was described thus by the writer A.N. Wilson: 'He has said bland things to the Pope. He said bland things to the Lutherans. He is saying bland things now he is home again' (quoted in *The Young Fogey Handbook;* Javelin Books; 1985).

Another figure with good reason to feel much the same way would be the New Olympian hedge fund manager, speculator or investment banker. At gatherings of the G7, the IMF, or EU finance ministers and so forth, they would quickly have established that, despite the chaos they had unleashed on the world economy, nobody was really gunning for them. At the first sight of the popping flashbulbs at ministerial press conferences, of delegates reaching for the translation headsets, of the trolleys of coffee and pastries wheeled by waiters or waitresses dressed in dark trousers or skirts and trim green waistcoats, of the barcoded conference security passes whose efficacy seems predicated on the idea that any terrorist will have the decency to give his real name, of the police helicopter overhead, of the ranks of official Lincoln Town Cars clogging up central Washington, they will assume that, whatever their current business problems, they have nothing to worry about from politicians and regulators. And on present showing they will be right.

We do not need any more New Olympian institutions to 'monitor' world markets and to give 'early warning' of the next crisis. Those that we already have did little good in heading off the present debacle. Nor do we need endless meetings of the type described in the last paragraph, bulging with the Terracotta Army of look-alike and think-alike ministers, central bankers and bureaucrats. But we had better resign ourselves to the prospect of international conferences galore. None is likely to get to the root of the problem. They will resemble gatherings of liberal schoolmasters who, bewildered by the destructive consequences of having allowed 'the kids' to 'express themselves', wring their hands as they survey the devastation, unwilling to contemplate the admission that they were horribly, utterly wrong and fearful, anyway, that it may be far too late to take any meaningful action.

*   *   *

Such toothless gatherings, we shall be told, will produce 'codes of conduct' for hedge funds, and 'tough new standards' for accounting and for prudential banking standards. Their existence will be predicated on the concept that finance is now an affair of huge, multinational entities, thus only huge global governmental get-togethers have the slightest chance of bringing even a semblance of order to the activities of these entities. This idea reaches back at least until the 1970s, and was adumbrated in a hugely enjoyable, very well-written and (in our view) quite mistaken book by journalist and writer Axel Madsen (*Private Power*; Abacus; 1981).

Madsen declared multinationals enjoy 'power beyond flag and country', adding: 'Of the 100 wealthiest entities on the international scene, well over half are corporations.' The argument that for a private entity to be wealthier than a political entity somehow damages the legitimacy or potency of the latter is reminiscent of the fuss in Britain in the early 1960s after it emerged in that the pop singer Adam Faith earned more than the prime minister. That Mr Faith's earnings and the prime minister's authority had no connection whatever with one another was, it seems, in sore need of being forcefully pointed out.

Indeed, elsewhere in Mr Madsen's book, the cat is very nearly let out of the bag by none other than Sir David Orr, then chairman of consumer goods multinational Unilever. Here was someone who clearly did not believe that huge multinationals somehow had the nation state at their mercy:

If anyone asks him if it isn't true that that polyglot companies are largely beyond the control of any single government, Orr smiles and says that's, of course, true, 'but only because we come under the control of all the governments of the countries in which we operate for everything over which those governments exercise jurisdiction. Our problem is to ensure any given action is only controlled by one government; and, quite often, especially in tax matters, we fail.

It is worth noting, in passing, that Sir David's comments cast a new light on the creation of entities such as the European Union – far from such large entities being essential in order to exercise some sort of control over large companies, they look rather more like being essential to the simplification of large companies' dealings with political authorities.

One final excerpt from *Private Power* discloses a rather more sinister side to the much-touted New Olympian myth that the nation state has a strictly truncated future in the brave new world of global finance. Mr Madsen quotes journalist Norman Macrae on the question of worker participation in industry. We are not expressing a view one way or another on this issue, but are deeply concerned by the rationale behind Mr Macrae's objection to it. The passage runs as follows:

> *To the proponents of worker participation who say that the arguments for it are the same as those for universal suffrage in the 19th Century, Macrae says: 'Exactly, the arguments for it belong entirely to this land of look-behind. Voter control of anything in the 20th Century, like monarchy in the 19th Century, is where the world is coming from, but not where it is going to.'*

Mr Macrae's words quoted here were taken from a piece in *The Economist* entitled 'The Coming Entrepreneurial Revolution: a survey'. It was published in the early days of the New Olympian revolution, on December 25 1976. But then, the idea of the mobile and ungovernable corporation appeals to politicians who prefer the patronage of the super-rich to the tedious work of public administration. Increasingly they see their job as providing public relations expertise to 'the big end of town' – they sell the 'inevitable' erosion of pension rights, the 'inevitable' decline of public services, and the 'necessity' of yet more privatisation through the full range of market research and 'perception management' techniques.

In exchange for their services they are flattered by the plutocratically inclined media, and they get to experience the jet-set life of the super-rich. Key to the New Olympian project has been the notion that mere mortals and their governments need the Olympians a lot more than the Olympians need them. It is extraordinary to see how successful has been this piece of propaganda, across the decades, across the continents and across political party lines. Even after the current crisis saw Big Finance whining like druggies facing cold turkey for public bail-outs and state-supplied cheap credit, the illusion, amazingly, persists, a feat of mass hallucination worthy of the classical gods of antiquity.

We believe that only when this illusion is dispelled can work really begin on creating a robust post-crises financial structure.

A DEMEANING DEPENDENCY CULTURE: BIG FINANCE AND BIG BUSINESS TODAY

With all due respect to Mr Macrae, our inspiration for understanding the respective roles of government on the one hand and large-scale business, finance and industry on the other is Theodore Roosevelt, US president from 1901 to 1909 and cousin of Franklin Roosevelt, whom we quote at the head of this chapter. 'Teddy' Roosevelt – a Republican and an imperialist – was about as far from being a dangerous leftist as it is possible to be, but he had this to say:

The vast individual and corporate fortunes, the vast combinations of capital which have marked the development of our industrial system, create new conditions and necessitate a change from the old attitude of the state and the nation toward property . . . More and more it is evident that the state, and if necessary the nation, has got to possess the right of supervision and control as regards the great corporations which are its creatures. [Our emphasis] (Quoted by Edmund Morris in Theodore Rex; *Random House; 2001)*

In his presidential message to Congress on December 3 1901, Roosevelt declared: 'It is no limitation upon property rights or freedom of contract to require that when they receive from the government the privilege of doing business under corporate form . . . they shall do so upon absolutely truthful representations . . . *Great corporations exist only because they are created and safeguarded by our institutions* and it is therefore our right and duty to see that they work in harmony with those institutions' [Our italics] (quoted in Morris; *ibid*).

In other words, we made you – we can break you. And it is in that spirit that we offer our suggestions, not in the spirit of establishing yet another international quango sitting in agreeable premises in New York, or Geneva or Paris, monitoring, consulting, surveilling and early-warning, headed by the very able chap who used to be deputy to another very able chap who has been tipped as the next head of the Bank for International Settlements, or the IMF, or similar. Britain's New Olympians, in particular, are never happier than when comparing themselves to the salty merchant-adventures of the nation's past, and no after-dinner speech in the City or glossy magazine article about London's dominance as a financial centre is complete without some reference to the swashbuckling traders whose galleons plied the seven seas and whose DNA has somehow been passed down to the bankers, dealers and asset-strippers of the modern Square Mile. The reality is that the investment banks, hedge funds and others are creatures of our law, incapable of existence without life support from our legal system, entirely dependent on the juridical and political systems they effect to despise, just as the moon astronauts were utterly dependent for life itself on the items they had brought with them from earth, to which they were effectively attached by a sort of invisible umbilical cord.

It is we, through our elected representatives, who have created the limited liability company (which allows corporations to enjoy all the rewards of their successful activities while being able to pass on much of the losses of their failed ones on to society at large), the fractional reserve bank (which allows banks to create new money out of thin air) and the trust (which conveniently allows assets to 'own themselves').

The limited company is not only an extraordinary mechanism for privatising profit and socialising losses, but allows shareholders and executives to escape much of any bad consequences of their behaviour:

In Britain, corporate signatures end in 'ltd', that means 'limited liability'. The Latins are more poetic and descriptive: they use 'SA' – Sociedad Anonima, or Society of the Nameless. It all adds up to the same thing: when the cops come, there's nobody home . . . This legal anomaly has led to all sorts of aberrant corporate behaviour. (Robert Townsend; Up The Organisation; Coronet Books edition; 1971)

Fractional reserve banking, as we saw in the chapter 'Never Break the Chain', allows banks to behave in a way that would be considered fraudulent in any other walk of life – to lend out money that does not exist and, by doing so, to bring into existence the great majority of money in use in the economy. Those with loans or overdrafts may imagine their borrowings are made up of money belonging to savers. Almost all of it is not; it is bank-created imaginary money, legally spun out of thin air by the bank in the form of loans, and when banks create too much of it, generating inflation, they put up interest rates, which increases their return on their loans. Furthermore, central banks will usually step in to rescue any bank that has recklessly abused its credit-creation ability.

Trusts, the slightly mysterious third sibling in this trio, perform one very simple task; they allow assets to be parked, away from any named owner. One iron law of finance is that every asset is ultimately owned by individuals – companies, banks, partnerships and investment funds are merely 'intermediate', artificial entities. Trusts are the one exception to this rule; they can be owners in their own right, without any immediate human beneficiary. The potential advantages of keeping assets for a time off any person's books in terms of tax planning and many other manouevres are obvious.

This trio – limited companies, fractional-reserve banks and trusts – are all creatures of law, creations of the political system. Their existence renders unintentionally amusing the following entry in a dictionary of economics published in 2000:

Law and economics: . . . The economics of law and economics is firmly in the liberal economics camp, favouring free markets and arguing that regulation often does more harm than good (Matthew Bishop; *Pocket Economist*; The Economist Books).

Show us a real-life merchant adventurer who abjures these three vital legal props and instead hazards his own fortune, day in and day out, in the pursuit of business and we will be lusty in our demands that the state get off his back. We may even help him aboard his galleon and wave him off from the quayside. But we will offer long odds on his ever appearing.

This, then, must be the starting point of reform – nothing more nor less than saying 'boo' to the New Olympians, to breaking their spell and telling them that we are well within our rights to bring their activities back under democratic control.

But by 'under democratic control' we do not mean, as at present, under the oversight of the New Olympians' technocratic opposite numbers in unelected national and trans-national bodies, whether Britain's Financial Services Authority or the International Monetary Fund. These Olympian officials exist precisely to promote the financial Olympians' agendas; their answer to every systemic problem is more 'competition', freer trade, a smoother functioning of the very machine that has caused the trouble in the first place. On the contrary, we would argue that the New Olympians have hollowed out the democratic process precisely by removing more and more powers from political control and handing them over to this cadre of technocrats. The result in the first decade of the 21st century was, at best, the view among voters that it was not worth voting because their views were never listened to and, at worst, the rise of extreme parties eager to exploit grievances about job insecurity and stagnant real incomes. Action to redress the democratic deficit would have been necessary even were it the case that rule by the New Olympians had ensured a permanent economic nirvana. As it is, we are all in the happy position that the entirely benign project of bringing the Olympians to account for their economic misdemeanours will have the wholly desirable effect of reviving democracy.

But having asserted our right to control the private sector New Olympians and to give instructions to the public sector Olympians, rather than take instructions from them, what sort of control ought to be asserted and what sort of instructions ought to be issued?

Not the sort that have proved so ineffectual in the past. As we said above, the last thing we need is another monitoring forum, another code of conduct, another 'information exchange and transparency initiative' or another 'benchmark of best practice'. These and similar proposals are rooted in the assumption that there is nothing much wrong with the New Olympian system that cannot be put right by either some mild admonition and oversight or by actually removing obstacles to the better functioning of the Olympian system itself. This is the world view of the Institute of Economic Affairs, of the Adam Smith Institute, of the business schools and the financial section of many newspapers. The 'asset' – be it a landholding, a shareholding or a business enterprise – exists in some state of nature. Then politicians or state employees come along with their laws and their taxes and 'distort' it.

All true enough, in the sense of personal private property: a car, a home, a piece of jewellery. Property brought into being and guaranteed by the state and by law, however, cannot, as Theodore Roosevelt explained, be seen in the same light or treated in the same way. It is partly because we have allowed ourselves to be persuaded that the two types of property are identical that we are in the current position. It will be objected that we, society, already ask a great deal from the financial and big business interest in return for privileges such as limited liability and credit creation. Do we not insist that they treat their employees fairly, that they comply with reams of business principles and that that they disburse assorted state benefits

through pay packets? True enough. Moneybags Bank is regulated as an employer, as a potential polluter, as a potential
discriminator, as a subject of anti-money laundering regulations and as a possessor of large amounts of personal data. It
is regulated as almost everything, *but it is not regulated as a
bank*. Its actual business is entirely deregulated. Irresponsible
lending, dangerous speculation, investment in toxic securities
– there is practically no limit to the use the bank is allowed
to make of the government-guaranteed product in which it
is allowed to traffic: money. Much the same goes for the large
limited liability public company, required to show what passes
for virtue in the modern world in every aspect of its activities – except its business. Takeovers, lay-offs, outsourcing . . .
the pursuit of 'shareholder value' is over-riding.

As with the hollowing-out of democracy, these abuses of
legal privileges would be obnoxious in principle even had they
produced permanent stability and prosperity. That they have
not should make it easier to get to grips with them.

LOVE OF THE COMMON PEOPLE: ROOSEVELT, ATTLEE AND CONTI-NENTAL SOCIAL DEMOCRACY

So we propose, first and foremost, root and branch reform of
the financial system. We eschew the word 'radical' as it has
become too all-encompassing in its application to have real
meaning – Nigel Lawson was a self-styled 'Tory radical'.

To help define our terms, it may be useful to examine
what happened last time a new generation of leaders came
to grips with the wreckage of a speculative financial system
run riot. The most notable example, and the most lustrous,
after all these years, was the accession to power of the man
whose quotation heads this chapter – President Franklin
Roosevelt.

As he took office in March 1933, amid a chronic slump that
closed almost all of the nation's banks and brought its

economic life to a halt, the new president's mixture of dynamism and self-confidence excited even those not his natural admirers, such as Churchill:

A single man, whom accident, destiny or Providence, has placed at the head of one hundred and twenty millions of active, educated, excitable and harassed people, has set out upon this momentous expedition. Many doubt if he will succeed. Some hope he will fail. Although the policies of President Roosevelt are conceived in many respects from a narrow view of American self-interest, the courage, the power and the scale of his effort must enlist the ardent sympathy of every country, and his success could not fail to lift the whole world forward into the sunlight of an easier and more genial age. (Great Contemporaries; 1937)

At a distance, Roosevelt's New Deal seems a many-tentacled beast, whose aspects range from arts funding and job creation schemes to the foundations of a rudimentary welfare state. But for simplicity's sake, it may be easiest to regard the New Deal as having had five main pillars: reflation of the economy, public works programmes (such as the electrification of the Tennessee Valley), strict control of banking and finance, improved welfare for the very poor and pro-trade unionism (this latter aspect receiving comparatively little attention these days). There is certainly a left-wing case against President Roosevelt as someone who patched up American capitalism after its reckless driving had resulted in a spectacular crash, but who had achieved little else. Anthony J. Badger, of Newcastle University, states that case:

The deficiencies of the New Deal were glaring. As the nine million unemployed in 1939 testified, the policies for industrial recovery did not work . . . The commitment to deficit spending was belated and half-hearted. Neither through taxation nor through anti-trust prosecution was the Roosevelt administration able to break up the economic power of large corporations or to redistribute wealth . . . The ambitious plans to resolve the problems of rural poverty were largely stillborn. Spending on direct relief was always inadequate . . . Too often relief perpetuated traditional and degrading attitudes towards welfare recipients. Work relief never reached more than 40 per cent of the unemployed.

But Badger continues:

It is equally easy to replace this bleak catalogue of New Deal failure with a positive achievement of its success – the more so when New Deal activism is contrasted to the inaction of the federal government under [Herbert] Hoover [the previous president].

In contrast to Hoover's vain exhortations to keep wages up . . . [Mr Roosevelt] put a statutory floor under wages, checked the downwards deflationary spiral, and halted the relentless erosion of labour standards. Together with direct federal public works expenditure, the NRA [National Recovery Administration, a government body] seemed to prevent matters from getting worse and, through 1936, government intervention in the economy paralleled, if it did not cause, modest but definite recovery. A stabilised banking and securities system, eventual deficit spending, and protected labour standards gave hope for ultimately orderly recovery. (The New Deal; Macmillan; 1989)

The programmes of the Labour administrations of 1945–1951 displayed almost as many differences from the New Deal as similarities, the most obvious being that it occurred after the Second World War rather than before. Indeed, it is arguable (although this is not the place in which to make the argument) that the war was to Britain what the Great Depression had been to the United States – a defining national moment after which the ordinary people, having suffered so much, would be invited to society's high table, never to be turned away again.

Public works were a far smaller feature of Clement Attlee's 'New Jerusalem', as it has become known, than of President Roosevelt's New Deal, for the simple reason that large-scale job creation was a less pressing need in a post-war command economy. Similarly, publicly financed farm support was less totemic in post-war Britain that in pre-war America; *The Grapes of Wrath* was set in California, not Shropshire. And one of the great reforms of the Attlee years – the granting of independence to India and Pakistan – had no echo of any kind in the US. Neither did another, the large-scale national-isation of mining, transport, health care and other activities.

That said, the similarities are striking, in particular the intertwining of more generous welfare benefits with an inter-ventionist and reflationary economic policy. On both sides of the Atlantic, the emphasis was on very much greater personal and social security, to be sustained by a mightily productive economic base, working at full stretch at all times, from which depression and recession would be banished.

As with President Roosevelt, Mr Attlee's legacy has been criticised from the liberal left:

The Labour Government of 1945–51, whatever its reformist aspirations, was never really a group of social radicals. They adhered to the empire; many of them believed in white supremacy; they, or most of them, upheld the extreme penalty of the rope; they refused to upset the miners by abolish-ing fox hunting (popular in some mining areas at this time) or other traditional rural pursuits such as hare coursing.' (Kenneth O. Morgan; The People's Peace; Oxford University Press; 1992 edition)

One may argue that treating economic security as a higher priority than stopping people from hunting foxes was one of the great strengths of the Attlee governments. Certainly, the way its accession to office was greeted suggests many people would have agreed. This is former *Picture Post* editor Tom Hopkinson:

In 1943 . . . [our proprietor Edward Hulton] published a book – The New Age *– which Tom Clarke, former editor of the* News Chronicle, *described in a review as '. . . a brave and eager book, a refreshing adventure among ideas'. It called for 'a change of heart and a new spiritual and social urge', and the reviewer described the Utopia it envisaged: 'There will be no Stock Exchange . . . no speculations in shares, no genuflexions before an obsolete gold standard. No money "talking" as if it were a commodity. Business will be more controlled, internationally and internally, in an economic system combining nationalization and private enterprise.' The mood* *continued into August 1945, when Hulton wrote a resounding welcome to Mr Attlee's new Labour Government.*

'The great victory of the Labour Party at the General Election was a surprise to everybody, to Labour people almost as much as to anyone else. We now have, for the first time in British history, a Labour Government in power with a large majority. Wise men have long realised that Labour must some day come to power; and it is well that it should do so unfettered. More will be relieved that the form of Conservatism represented by Lord Beaverbrook, and aided and abetted by Mr Churchill in his latest phase, has been flung indignantly overboard . . .

'I am not personally a Socialist . . . still less am I a materialist. Yet I rejoice that latter-day Conservatism has been overthrown.' (Picture Post 1938–50; Allen Lane; The Penguin Press; 1970)

Images of the 1945 Labour government's economic reforms are dominated, for some, by the plaques placed at the entrance of every British coal mine on January 1 1947, declaring: 'This colliery is now managed by the National Coal Board on behalf of the People', for others by hazier images of idealistic young doctors welcoming their first National Health Service patients. Yet the Attlee government's policies towards finance and the City were every bit as far-reaching as those pursued in the United States under the New Deal. While nationalisation of the Bank of England in 1946 made little practical difference, it was hugely symbolic, parking an enormous tank on the front lawn of the City. Henceforth, banking, insurance and finance would be subordinated to national economic policy. Unlike in post-Depression America, there was no immediate need to separate stockbroking, market making and commercial banking from one another – the City's own closed-shop rules did that already. All that was needed was to ensure the rules were properly enforced, that brokers and market makers would remain as separate, relatively small partnerships, that merchant banks would be grouped under the Accepting Houses Committee, where an eye could be kept on them, that the discounted bill market would transmit the Treasury's interest rate decisions to the wider world and that the Bank governor would, as the cliché has it, raise an eyebrow at any untoward speculative activity. The Bank would police exchange controls, and the Stock Exchange would decline in relevance as key industries were taken into public ownership.

Across the Channel, post-war social democracy took different forms in different countries. France had a large public sector, West Germany's was relatively smaller. Italy maintained some of the large state holding companies inherited from the fascist era. Swedish social democracy relied on the need to compete in export markets to discipline large companies and keep the economy in trim. France preferred to devalue the franc early and often, confident that French people would buy French cars, eat and drink French produce and take their holidays in France, thus shielding themselves from the inflationary effects of a weaker currency while gaining competitive advantage overseas.

All that said, there are a number of common themes in continental post-war social democracy running through most of the economies of what was then 'Western Europe'. '[In] the late 1950s and 1960s another Europe appeared. This was a Europe which put emphasis on unity, on creating a great centre of production, on being modern and progressive, on establishing uniform systems of justice and welfare, on giving an example of international co-operation' (Richard Hoggart and Douglas Johnson; An Idea of Europe; Chatto & Windus; 1987).

The first theme was a stress on peaceful labour relations and partnership between capital and labour. This was obviously more successful in some countries (Germany, for example) than others (such as France). But everywhere it was a theme.

The second was a stress on creating national and, later, European 'champion' companies in different industries, under the guidance of national governments.

The third relates to social cohesion and the compression of income differences. Ostentation was frowned on, glaring inequality was thought impermissible and progressive taxation bit significantly into the top slice of higher-earners' incomes. West Germany, for all its powerhouse status, never produced a breed of super-rich tycoons – leading industrialists were expected to live comfortably, not luxuriously.

A fourth theme was the relative insignificance of banking and finance, even in countries such as the Netherlands in which the financial sector had traditionally been strong. In some countries, parts of the banking system were in public ownership. Germany's lavishly praised central bank, the Bundesbank, pursued hard money policies for political and social reasons, not to foster a large financial sector with an international reach. On the continent, only Switzerland provided an echo to the pre-1945 and post-1976 British obsession with a strong currency linked to a powerful banking sector, and Switzerland was rather more successful in this endeavour, at least in terms of keeping the Swiss franc as a hard currency.

And the fifth theme of European social democracy was a stress on competitive markets to deliver higher living standards. This may seem to jar with the first four themes, but it does not. After all, the Common Market was *the* post-war European institution. Competition between European businesses would, it was believed, raise productivity – indeed, productivity may almost be seen as a separate theme in its own right. The *quid pro quo* for the higher pay and shorter hours enjoyed by continental European workers was a constant rise in output per person. In tripartite Europe, the company supplied the best machinery, the workers operated it to the limit of its potential and the government redistributed some of the company's profits back to the workers in social benefits.

It was a far cry from much of British industry, bedevilled by restrictive practices, 'go slow'-type industrial action and 'who does what' demarcation disputes. Indeed, it is worth noting that the notion of continental Europe as an intrinsically more social democratic, welfarist, left-of-centre sort of place in contrast to the savage Anglo-Saxon capitalism of modern Britain did not take root in the UK until the late 1980s. For most of the post-war period, the continent's more vocal

British admirers were on the right and in business circles, where the 'responsible' trade unions of West Germany, in particular, were highly regarded.

He [Edward Heath] had been deeply impressed by the German success in co-operation between government, employers and trade unions which enabled their workers to produce more and to live so much more prosperously than British workers. On one occasion, as Heath was taking his leave after a visit to Bonn, Chancellor Willy Brandt mentioned the people waiting for his next appointment: 'There are 16 union leaders out there. They are the men I run Germany with.' (Richard Clutterbuck; Britain in Agony; *Penguin Books; 1980*)

But as right-of-centre British admirers of the continental approach were to find out from the late 1980s onwards, the European notion of an open market was not the free-fire zone of the Anglo-Saxon model, but a social construct to be carefully supervised by institutions such as the European Commission, in the years before it became as enthusiastic about untrammelled trade and capital movements as it is today, and the European Court of Justice.

BACK TO THE FUTURE: SOME POINTERS FOR THE PRESENT

What can be drawn from this brief historical exploration of economic and social policy in the mid-20th century? In place of the New Olympianism we propose a New Populism, a creed that puts ravenous finance back into its cage and concentrates on a real-world agenda of jobs, living standards and security in retirement instead of the Olympian agenda of free trade, free capital movements and the primacy of finance. The New Populism we envisage would rest on a number of principles.

First and foremost, we would argue, however separated in time and place, these mid-20th-century policies all stressed *the subordination of finance.* From Washington in the 1930s to London in the 1940s to Paris and Bonn in the 1950s and 1960s, financial sector activities were kept on a tight rein, their destructive potential fully realised and their proper, auxillary role in relation to the real economy kept firmly in focus. Banks and other large corporations are creatures of law, and it is the public's right and duty to supervise them. Furthermore, they, the financial New Olympians, have had their chance. The result of letting them off the leash has been a disaster. This, then, is our first and possibly most important principle.

The second is *personal and social security*, the principle that society should insure its members against misfortune, protect their savings and make proper provision for their old age. This is what we tried to do in the past, and, in Britain, are trying again to do, with very mixed results, using a range of entitlements of frequently baffling complexity. The loss of a person's job ought to be a problem, not a cosmic disaster. Savings in approved schemes ought to be guaranteed. Why are the sort of high-quality pensions on offer in the post-war period now 'unaffordable' and why did that unaffordability mysteriously emerge only once the Soviet Union and its allies had disappeared? It would rightly be thought extraordinary were policy makers to agonise today over the difficulties of ensuring the average family could buy an Austin Cambridge car and a black and white television – our society is greatly wealthier than it was 40 years ago, and very much improved cars and consumer goods are relatively much less expensive. Why retirement schemes should be any different is not clear.

A third principle is *accountability*, or 'democracy', to put it slightly differently. The leeching away of powers from national parliaments to the New Olympians' mandarin allies in bodies such as the IMF, the World Trade Organisation, independent central banks and the European Commission (these days a far more pro-finance and pro-free trade organisation than in the early decades of the European Economic Community), is, we stated earlier, the Olympians' anti-democratic project. It would be obnoxious even without the

economic and financial turmoil that it has created. So great
is the democratic deficit that people increasingly either do
not bother to vote or vote for non-mainstream parties. The
answer from left-of-centre parties, terrified of crossing
the Olympian orthodoxy, has been more of the same. Thus
the UK's Labour Party is losing votes to the British National
Party and the Irish Labour Party is losing votes to Sinn
Fein. The response of both parties has been to cede more
powers to Brussels and to insist on the need for another
world trade agreement that will transfer more authority to
the WTO.

There have been suggestions in the UK that Gordon Brown
is planning a bill reasserting the primacy of British over EU
law. That would be a most welcome blow against the Olympian
system, but we fear it is unlikely to be proposed by Mr Brown,
a fundamentally conformist person with an apparent yearning
for respectability.

A fourth principle is *the undersirability of a semi-detached
super-rich class*. Not only does such a class pull money values
completely out of shape, in the housing market for example,
but it tends to be the *fons et origo* of the horrendous errors
from which the world economy is now reeling. It was super-
rich investment bankers and derivatives traders who dreamed
up collateralised debt obligations and exotic derivative products. It was the super-rich who have demanded cheap money
for most of the last decade and cheered on the inflating of
the credit bubble.

This leads to our fifth principle, *the protection and strengthening of an independent middle class*. The super-rich and their
political allies are destroying the middle class – that is a major
part of the theme of this book. Lawyers and doctors are to
be faced with a stark choice between corporate employment
and unemployment, while de-skilling and outsourcing are
eating into occupations such as accountancy, journalism and
technical design. Much of this is attributed to 'market forces'
when in fact it stems from legislative changes designed to tear
down time-honoured protection for professionals. But even

were the market to be driving all these changes, we believe the value of a professional middle class, independent of both the state and of corporate power, greatly outweighs any efficiency losses and that the market ought to be curbed. Besides, professions exist to offset market failures caused by inequalities of information – a deregulated market for health care would be a free-for-all for entrepreneurs offering a glittering array of 'choice' to 'consumers', many of whom would of course end up dead. Professions must be subject to public scrutiny – they should be subject to sensible independent regulation, too. But they cannot be adequately replaced by corporate forms of employment.

Which leads neatly to our sixth principle: *social stability and tranquillity are more important than market efficiency or shareholder value.* In other words, to the specific protections from the market for the professions ought to be added a general protection for everybody. If market forces dictate the concreting over of the south of England, or the obliteration of British manufacturing, or the closure of the rural Post Office network, then they should be resisted. This is, of course, an impeccably conservative as well as a centre-left position. This is T.E. Utley, writing in the *Daily Telegraph* on January 10 1977:

I simply do not believe that if society decides that some evil produced by the spontaneous forces of competition (i.e. mass unemployment in an area like Ulster, afflicted by civil disturbance, or the destruction of the farming industry) calls stridently for governmental action to temper it, that action is bound to prove disastrous, however prudently and deliberately it is conceived and carried out.

Our seventh and final principle may surprise some readers: *liberty of the person.* Hang on, you may say. You propose all sorts of controls on financial and business activity. It is a bit late in the day for you to start banging on about individual freedom.

Not at all. The New Olympians have been keen to assert that their right to move colossal sums around the world, to speculate and to generate credit, is indivisible from the right of humbler folk to live their lives as they choose, but we argue otherwise. The Olympians are in receipt of huge legal and other support from the state; ordinary people, including the self-employed and those running small businesses, are not. Limited liability and fractional reserve banking mean nothing to them. And yet, as the financial interest has been progressively freed over recent decades, the liberty of the person has been increasingly restricted. Spot-tested at work for drugs, monitored by closed-circuit television, subject to rules prohibiting 'inappropriate' language, soon, if a government programme proceeds to its original conclusion, to be burdened with a national identity card, the individual is having a thin time of it. It is time to restore privacy and autonomy to the private citizen.

Much is made of the need to make trade-offs between liberty and security in the age of terrorism. We are told that we must face restrictions on our liberty to prevent terrorist attacks, and few object to sensible restrictions in this respect. But the New Olympians must concede the same point. They have been merrily transporting the financial equivalent of fissile material around the world for several years now, and the result is widespread contamination of the financial system. Irresponsible lending has caused genuine suffering

So yes, our principles would give rise to much greater control of finance and big business. The 'liberty' of the Olympians' institutions would be severely restricted. And this in turn gives rise to the suggestion that such controls would be ineffective, because, 'in a globalised world', there is nothing much that can be done to control the investment banks, hedge funds and others. This deprecation of 'old-fashioned controls' has been the orthodoxy for at least 20 years. It depicts interventionist governments as hopelessly flailing about, trying to get a grip on capital movements, an exercise as futile as trying to control the wind. This notion is not new. Addressing the Massachusetts legislature in 1867, writer and lawyer Richard Henry Dana spoke of the undesirability of passing laws against usury: 'The market of the world moves with the irresistible power of ocean tides' (quoted in *The Gift*, by Lewis Hyde; Random House; 1979).

The notion is, however, quite misleading, for two reasons. First, the technology that makes possible almost instantaneous money transfers round the world and split-second dealings in cash and securities makes possible also the tracking of such funds by national authorities. Indeed, large financial movements are tracked already, in the name of 'anti-money laundering measures'. No one suggests this is a pointless activity. Should some form of capital controls be thought desirable, the surveillance and enforcement machinery should not be impossibly difficult to bring into existence. As we noted, the technology is already there.

Second, there is a low-tech reinforcement for this high-tech equipment. Contracts or deals entered into in offshore jurisdictions, or anywhere else, in defiance of financial controls could be declared void in British law. This 'negative enforcement' is highly attractive. It requires no police; it relies simply on British courts *not* doing something, i.e. recognising and enforcing financial arrangements made without authorisation.

Both these methods of enforcement also give the lie to the objection that financial controls can work only with international agreement. In some cases, the objector is genuine and really hopes for every country in the world to sign up to a grand treaty on controlling speculative activity. In others, the objection is a ploy from those with no desire to see finance put back in its cage, rather like the child who declares he is only too happy to tidy up his bedroom but only when his left thumb stops hurting.

Not that international agreements are to be despised, provided two things are kept in mind. First, that, as things stand, such agreements are likely to be drawn up and enforced by the New Olympians' political and bureaucratic allies. Second, even when drawn up in good faith, such agreements tend to represent the minimum that all countries can sign up to. Individual nations serious about dismantling the New Olympian system will find they need to go it alone, at least to begin with.

So given the above-mentioned principles, and given that, contrary to myth, measures can be enforced, what ought those measures to be, in practical detail? In our limited experience, it is when critical commentators put forward their own 'ten-point plan' that they get shot down. To vary the metaphor, we ended our last book in true professional boxer fashion, presenting the smallest possible target to our opponents. A two-point plan confined itself to suggesting the UK ought to curb its enormous borrowings and stop destroying the natural environment. We are prepared to be a little more expansive this time.

First, we suggest very much tighter controls on lending and on the generation of credit. Linked to this is a second suggestion, for the forced demerger of large banking and finance groups, splitting retail banking from both corporate finance (merchant banking) and from securities dealing. This would echo the Glass-Steagall legislation of inter-war America, which separated retail and investment banking and which was repealed in the 1990s.

Third, even the remaining demerged units are likely, in many cases, to be large entities. We would suggest breaking them up into smaller banks, on the principle that mega banks make mega mistakes that affect us all. Instead of institutions that are 'too big to fail', we should aim for institutions that are small enough to fail without creating problems for depositors and the wider public

Fourth, we would suggest subjecting all derivative products and other exotic instruments to official inspection. Only those approved would be permitted to be traded. Anyone trying to circumvent the rules by going offshore or on to the internet would face the 'negative enforcement' mentioned above – their contracts would be unenforceable in law.

Fifth, we would seek to offer the same protection for our remaining top-class industrial companies as is routine in France or the United States – and perhaps go further. Ultimately, the aim must be an orderly downsizing of the financial sector, much as post-war France and Italy sought an orderly move of employment from agriculture to industry. More of the engineers and technical experts from our best universities would end up making things. Some of the famed 'rocket scientists' who spend their days in the City cooking up ever more abstract financial entities may even end up making . . . rockets.

Certainly, at a moment when the survival of human life of the planet might depend on our finding new technologies to generate energy and reduce our disruptive impact on natural systems, it seems perverse to the point of madness to corral our brightest and best technicians on to open-plan trading floors in air-conditioned skyscrapers.

Sixth, we would sharply increase taxes on the hedge fund operators and private equity partners, to ensure at the very least that they pay the same rate of tax as their cleaners. The loophole whereby income can be disguised as a capital gain and thus taxed at a lower rate was closed by a previous Labour government in the mid-1960s, only, bizarrely, to be reopened by Labour more than three decades later. It is time to close it again.

Seventh, we would suggest deregulating genuinely private businesses and the self-employed (frequently the two are synonymous). One by-product of the Olympian myth that vast financial institutions are part of the 'enterprise culture' has been the imposition on genuine enterprises of the sort of employment and other legislation used to extract at least some payback from the New Olympians for the benefits of limited liability and other privileges. The self-employed and small firms ought to be regulated only with regard to their activities (e.g. a jam maker would have to obey the food and hygiene laws) and not as businesses. Indeed, by greatly enhancing the attractiveness of the partnership or the small firm, such deregulation may divert many talented people from the pursuit of Olympian status to gentler, more rewarding and more socially useful business careers.

None of this will be easy. Some of it may involve abro-
gating Britain's signature to various international treaties, those
enshrining New Olympian objectives, not least the various
European treaties. Nor does much of this New Populism
appear to be immediately in prospect, despite the darkening
clouds over the world economy. And whereas it could move
rapidly on to the agenda should the crisis worsen markedly
and suddenly, it is possible also that it will take time to piece
together a Populist coalition.

We have touched already on some of the elements that
may join such an alliance: small business people and farmers
(if there are any left); independent middle-class professionals
and shopkeepers. Then there are those filling the basic supervisory roles that ought to be the backbone of society: railway
station managers and their equivalents in bus depots and
motorway service stations, police sergeants, prison officers,
high street store managers, non-commissioned officers in the
forces and similar. We would seek to add two significant
blocks of members: manufacturing and export businesses
and trade union members. Industry and those working in it
have been the biggest losers from the Olympian experiment
as productive capacity has been destroyed and millions of
manufacturing jobs wiped out. Those owning, running and
working in industry know better than anyone the virulence
with which New Olympianism has blighted the economy.
Both union members and managers have much to gain from
a more sensible attitude to industry.

And those within such a coalition will always have the
inestimable advantage of the fact that, beneath the shiny
packaging, the Olympians' creed is and always has been the
reverse of their own. It is Unpopulism, the belief system
that sacrifices jobs and productive assets on the altar of
deal-making, that demands schools and Post Offices be
'rationalised' (i.e. closed), that insists on lower tax rates for
the rich than for their domestic servants, that has created a
vast debt bubble and chronic global instability and which,
even at this late hour, has the effrontery to suggest that the

answer to the crisis lies in the even more enthusiastic application of New Olympian ideas in terms of untrammelled
free-market activity.

Unpopulism ought to make the selling of the New Populism
a lot easier. But there is likely to be plenty of work to do in
terms of spreading the word. The independent professionals
need to grasp the dangers of being assimilated by commercial entities and to cease to regard Corporate Britain as an
essentially friendly place, respectful of the status of lawyers,
accountants and the rest. Similarly, liberal writers, artists, senior
left-leaning white-collar personnel – those that tend, lazily,
although not entirely inaccurately, to be labelled with the
names of their presumed favourite newspapers or with
the London boroughs where they like to live, need to be made
aware of the urgent need to build alliances with the remnants
of organised labour. Export-orientated business needs to
agitate for a state system that supports them rationally and
effectively, in terms of financial support, trade policy and the
exchange rate. State employees need to recognise that the
notion of a 'public sector' as traditionally understood is under
attack, from New Labour as much as from the right. Rather
than support either 'market reforms' (which often mean worse
services provided by lavishly rewarded private contractors) or
the bloated social-engineering sector (which seems designed,
in part at least, to soak up many of the additional graduates
generated by the breakneck expansion of higher education),
public sector workers should call for more democratic accountability and the re-establishment of incorrupt, cost-effective and
competent public services, provided on clear and, as far as
possible, non-discretionary premises on the straightforward
basis of entitlement.

This may sound like hard, dusty work. Certainly it does
not offer the excitement of revolutionary agitation. But it is
a political response to the current situation that offers some
chance of success. And if those who met on Mont Pèlerin all
those years ago were not daunted, and neither should we be.

Beyond all this we would hope for a cultural shift, towards

decency, fairness and social stability, away from the demented pursuit of 'shareholder value' and 'yield'. There are signs of a reaction to the excesses of the past two decades and the chaos they have wrought. In Britain, there has been a greater emphasis on thrift, on not throwing perfectly good food away and on cutting out conspicuous waste.

Symptoms of a new mood of disgust at the excesses appeared in various places and for various reasons. There was the groundswell of discontent at plans for yet further expansion of Heathrow Airport. On January 29 2008, Chris Blackhurst, city editor of the *Evening Standard*, summed up the mood of many: 'BAA [the airport's operator] wants to build a third runway and a sixth terminal . . . Why not put a plea in now for a fifth runway and an eighth terminal? In fact why not do away with planning restraints completely and bulldoze chunks of west London to give BAA the model it seeks?'

There was an article entitled 'Confessions of a graduating MBA student' in the *Financial Times* on December 24 2008 from recent INSEAD graduate Neil Courtis: 'Overconfident, overpaid and everywhere – the 2007 vintage of MBAs [Masters of Business Administration, a mis-named bachelor degree in business]. Last year Ben Bernanke, the chairman of the US Federal Reserve, earned $183,500. With bonuses included, this is almost exactly what a graduate MBA now expects to be paid to create PowerPoint slides for a bank or consulting firm . . . No wonder recruiters think we are arrogant.'

He added: 'Perhaps this is simply evidence of the euphoria of the last few inches of the upswing.'

Yes, quite.

There was a seasonal article by business journalist and former banker Martin Vander Weyer in the *Daily Telegraph* on December 28 2007 ('Philanthropy is good: remorse is better'), comparing the hedge fund and private equity millionaires of today unfavourably with Charles Dickens's Scrooge. The latter, he pointed out, did not merely give to charity; he repented of his ways. 'When the hedge fund boys get together for a black-tie charity auction and raise casual millions, there is something distasteful about it all . . . we should ask whether the trend towards business philanthropy is disguising another trend, towards social damage caused by market excess.'

It had been a long time since anyone had suggested the New Olympians might have anything about which to feel remorseful. Meanwhile, for ordinary mortals, the financial crisis and the credit crunch gave an added urgency to a revival of prudence and saving. But these pressures aside, there seemed to be a yearning for a less frantic and greedy way of life, one less geared to the needs of a plutocracy and less in awe of it.

We opened with a quote from one of the bleaker of Graham Greene's characters, the black-marketeer Harry Lime. As we draw close to the end of our narrative, perhaps we can now redress the balance by turning to one of Greene's more uplifting tales.

In his 1955 novel *Loser Takes All* (Heinemann), Graham Greene's narrator, Bertram, is a recently married lowly white-collar employee who finds himself with his wife in Monte Carlo. Stony broke after a few days, Bertram then devises an apparently successful system for winning at roulette. He is, briefly, fabulously rich. He jousts among the three Olympians – Dreuther, Blixon and Bowles – who own the firm for which he works. For a very brief moment, he himself controls the firm, having lent one of the Olympians money against a crucial packet of shares. His marriage falls apart, as his wife tells him:

'"I didn't marry a well-off man. I married a man I met in the bar of the Volunteer – someone who liked cold sausages and travelled by bus because taxis were too expensive."'

The novel closes with the couple reunited in a cabin on board ship, leaving the Olympian playground of Monaco behind them:

'"We shan't be rich," I added quickly . . . I got up and took the great system out of my jacket pocket and tore it in little pieces and threw them through the porthole – the white scraps blew back in our wake.'

The gods promised us paradise if only we would obey and pamper their hero-servants and allow their strange titans and monsters to flourish. We did as they asked, and have placidly swallowed the prescriptions of the lavishly rewarded bankers, central bankers, hedge fund managers and private equity tycoons, while turning a blind eye to the rampaging of the exotic derivatives, the offshore trusts and the toxic financial instruments. Had they delivered, there would, at least, be a debate to be held as to whether the price was too high, in terms of the loss of democratic control and widening social inequality. But they have not. Chronic financial instability and the prospect of, at the best, years of sluggish economic activity as we pay off borrowings of a debt-burdened society are the fruits of their guidance.

These gods have failed. It is time to live without them.

Afterword

Shortly after completing the main manuscript for this book, we travelled to Washington to report for our respective papers' meetings of the Group of Seven rich nations, the International Monetary Fund and the World Bank.

For as long as anyone could remember, the mood among finance ministers and central bankers had been relentlessly upbeat, bordering on the euphoric. With the regularity of Big Ben heralding the six o'clock radio news, the G7 and IMF communiqués would declare that: 'The fundamentals of the world economy are sound.'

This time, the message was very different. The IMF called the crisis that had erupted the previous August 'the largest financial shock since the Great Depression, inflicting heavy damage on markets and institutions at the core of the financial system.'

Growth forecasts were slashed and Donald Kohn, vice-chairman of the Federal Reserve Board, the US central bank, said: 'It isn't over yet.'

Leading bankers from institutions, including Citigroup, Barclays, Deutsche Bank and Credit Suisse, were invited to the G7 dinner on April 11 to explain just how they had managed to get the world economy into this mess. Alistair Darling, Britain's Chancellor, was said to have been profoundly un-impressed. Hardly surprising, given that back in the UK he and fellow MPs were acutely aware of a rising tide of anger among mortgage holders.

They had tumbled to the fact that they were being made to pay for the banks' mistakes not merely as taxpayers required to bail out the financial system but as customers now facing more expensive mortgages and less easily available credit.

Not surprisingly, tighter homeloans threatened to burst the bubble in the housing market. In the week of the IMF meeting, the Halifax bank's house-price index reported a 2.5 per cent monthly fall, the biggest since the wave of repossessions in the early Nineties.

Clearly, this was no ordinary crisis. Indeed, for those with long memories it evoked nothing so much as the 1978/1979 'winter of discontent', when Britain's trade unions, after weeks of often bitter strike action, smashed through a Government pay limit. In place of the mounds of uncollected rubbish on the streets there were the mounds of suddenly-worthless securities that nobody wanted to buy. For the trade unions who believed their size and membership made them too big to ignore, there were the banks and brokerages that were, apparently, too big to fail. For the flying pickets, there were the financiers in pinstriped suits informing one and all that the failure of taxpayers to bail them out of the consequences of their huge mistakes would threaten a 'systemic crisis'.

The tables were turned on organised labour after the late Seventies, in both Britain and America. Just how successful this three-decade war had been was highlighted during the week of the IMF meeting, when the Washington Post reported that nine porters at Boston's Logan airport had seen their incomes drop dramatically after the airline for which they worked decided to charge passengers for bag check-in. This diverted money previously paid direct to the porters in tips to the company instead.

Capital's winter (and spring) of discontent provided both a challenge and an opportunity. Would elected governments seize the chance fundamentally to reform an economic system shattered by the excesses of the New Olympians?

With even the banks themselves admitting their mistakes (while pleading nevertheless to be spared re-regulation), no more promising moment for such reform had presented itself for more than half a century.

Will this chance be grabbed with both hands? At the time of writing, the question remains open, But, hearteningly, there are signs that it will be. In Washington, policymakers from around the world seemed emboldened by the scale of the crisis to contemplate measures to rein in the turbo-charged financial interest and to prevent it from any repeat of its reckless orgy of speculation.

Such measures had not been mentioned in polite society for a quarter of a century or more. That they were returning to common official parlance was a measure of radically changed times, and a sign of hope.

Larry Elliott and Dan Atkinson
Washington, April 2008

Index

Abbey National, 24, 48, 101–2
Accepting Houses Committee, 295
Adam Smith Institute, 290
Africa, 274
Alaska, 271
Alberta, 271
Ali, Tariq, 76
Alliance & Leicester, 61, 62, 71
Amazon, 141
American Prospect, The, 253
Amis, Martin, 135
Amsterdam, 190
Anderson, Adam, 190
Anderson, Lindsay, 76
Applegarth, Adam, 42, 48, 49, 50, 51–2, 53, 56, 57–8, 59, 71
Argentina, 247
Arizona, 232
Arthur, Terry, 100
Asda, 138
Ashford, 152
Asia, 126, 127–9, 130, 158, 180, 212, 274, 276, 282 *see also* names of countries
Asian Monetary Fund, 127–8
Atradius, 124

Attlee, Clement, 92, 293–5
Australia, 105, 210, 243

BAA, 308
Baader-Meinhof gang, 77
Bach, Steven, 279
Badger, Anthony J., 292–3
Baker, Dean, 233
Balls, Ed, 171
Bangladesh, 120
Bank of England, 2, 21, 39, 43, 45, 54, 64, 74, 111, 163, 183, 197, 209, 262, 269, 295–6
  banking supervision taken away from, 55, 70
  and BP affair, 109, 110, 169
  and Competition & Credit Control, 87
  deputy-governor post suggested, 70
  Financial Stability Reviews (2007), 54, 217–18
  and inflation, 118–19, 161, 162, 265, 267–8
  and interest rates, 55, 87, 118–19, 131, 160–2, 164, 168, 174, 265
  Monetary Policy Committee, 98, 160, 161, 162

and Northern Rock affair, 29, 46, 47, 50, 51, 52, 55–6, 58, 59, 60, 61, 62, 63, 66, 67, 68
Bank for International Settlements (BIS), 131–3
Bank of Japan, 208
Banque de France, 32
Barclays Bank, 1–2, 59, 74, 109
Barclays Capital, 21, 49
Barclays' Equity Gilt Study, 197
Barings Bank, 32, 137
Barroso, Manuel, 212–13
BBC, 43, 57, 84, 85, 90
Bear Stearns, 2, 7, 20, 23, 112, 217, 223, 241
Beatles, The, 76
Beaverbrook, Lord, 295
Berle, Adolph, 93
Berlin, 91
Bernanke, Ben, 30, 224–5, 234, 240, 241–2, 256–7, 268–9, 308
Bernard, Elaine, 249
Berra, Yogi, 282
Bevan, Aneurin, 85
Beveridge, Lord, 78
Beveridge report, 92
BIS (Bank for International Settlements), 131–3
Bishop, Matthew, 289
Black, Dame Carol, 1
Blackburn, Robin, 76
Blackhurst, Chris, 308
Black Wednesday, 118, 173, 258
Blair, Tony, 1, 3, 4, 6, 7, 44, 46, 119, 130, 149, 178, 179, 259
Bloomberg, 141, 234
BNP Paribas, 7, 14, 15, 20, 57
Bonn, 299
Booker, Christopher, 83
Borio, Claudio, 132
Boston Globe, 252, 253

Bowie, David, 85, 202, 221
BP see British Petroleum
Bradbury, Malcolm, 73, 79
Bradford & Bingley, 61, 62
Braine, John, 152
Brandt, Willy, 98, 298
Branson, Sir Richard, 46, 65, 138
Brenner, Robert, 80
Bretton Woods system, 78, 79, 91, 214
Britannia Arrow, 64
British Aerospace, 43
British Air Line Pilots Association, 146
British Airways, 5
British Gas, 146, 155
British Leyland, 43, 147
British Medical Association, 138
British National Party, 300
British Petroleum (BP), 109–10, 169
British Rail, 148
British Shipbuilding, 43
British Telecom, 146
Broughton, Martin, 5–6
Brown, Gordon, 1, 2, 6, 15, 22, 44, 142, 148, 149, 164, 171, 177, 178, 264, 280–1, 282, 300
    and Capital Gains Tax, 34–5
    and casinos, 3, 4
    code for fiscal stability, 68
    compared with Nigel Lawson, 166–9
    financial regulations (1997), 55, 70
    'golden rule', 174–5
    joke about chancellors, 7, 224
    New Year message (2008), 251
    and Northern Rock, 63, 67, 82
    opposes bill about workplace rights, 21
    speech to CBI (1999), 173–4
    Spending Review (2004), 36

Brussels, 60, 68, 213, 300
Bryan, William Jennings, 247
Buffet, Warren, 231–2, 264
Building Societies Association, 101
Bundesbank, 258, 297
Bush, President George W., 130,
     240, 244, 253, 270, 276
Bush administration, 242, 245
Business, The, 141

Cable, Vince, 33–4, 67
Cahoot, 24
California, 14
Camell, Rob, 264
Cameron, David, 63
Campbell, Colin, 270
Canada, 249, 271
Cancun, 214
Cannes, 152
Capital Economics, 171–2
Capital Radio, 155
Carter, President Jimmy, 79, 100
Casablanca (film), 211
Castle, Barbara, 84
Cayne, James, 223, 224
CBI (Confederation of British
     Industry), 5, 174
Centre for Economic and Policy
     Research, 233
Centre for Economic Policy
     Research, 226–7
Center for Responsible Lending,
     226, 227
Chartered Institute of Purchasing
     and Supply, 160
Chicago Times, 252
China, 7, 112, 120, 127, 130, 179, 180,
     196, 210, 212, 214, 239, 255,
     261, 267, 270, 274, 275, 276,
     277
Choyleva, Diana, 229
Churchill, Winston, 80, 91–2, 95,
     292, 295

Cioffi, Ralph, 23
Citibank, 15, 262
Citi Financial, 27
Citigroup, 20, 24, 26–7, 28, 29, 126,
     133, 134, 260, 262
Clarke, Peter, 73
Clarke, Tom, 294
Clinton, President Bill, 79, 127,
     248–9, 253
Clinton, Hillary, 248, 252
Clutterbuck, Richard, 298
CNBC, 111
Cockett, Richard, 92
Cohen, Nick, 105, 106
CoHSE, 90
Common Market, 297
Confederation of British Industry
     (CBI), 5, 174
Congress, 55, 191, 192, 201, 249,
     286
Conservatives (Tories), 18, 81–2, 84,
     91, 109, 140, 146, 149, 196–7,
     257, 258
   Central Office, 135, 146
   see also names of politicians
ContactPoint, 181, 182
Cooper, Yvette, 5–6
Co-operative Bank, 24
Council for Mortgage Lenders,
     162
Countrywide, 20–1, 52
Courtis, Neil, 308
Coutts, Ken, 177
Cramer, Jim, 111
Crosland, Anthony, 37
Crossrail, 6
Cuban missile crisis, 246, 274

Daily Mirror, 101
Daily Telegraph, 111, 112, 140, 142,
     154–5, 186, 301, 308
Dall, Bob, 201
Dana, Richard Henry, 302–3

Darling, Alistair, 22, 29–30, 33, 34, 35, 43, 46, 61, 62, 63–4, 65, 66, 69, 70, 71, 158, 171, 175, 176, 177, 181–2, 282
Davos, 20, 116, 213
Defoe, Daniel, 189
Dell'Ariccia, Giovanni, 227
Democratic Party, 79, 99, 247, 248, 249 see also names of Democrat politicians
Department for Children, Schools and Families (formerly Department of Education and Skills), 142
Department of Health, 155
Detroit, 77
Diamond, Bob, 21, 74
Dickens, Charles, 189
Direct Line, 143
Doggett, Peter, 77–8
Doha Round, 116
Donovan, Lord, 84
Dow Jones, 13
Downing, David, 79
Dubček, Alexander, 80
Du Cann, Edward, 87
Dukakis, Michael, 79
Dylan, Bob, 76

Ealing borough council, 153
ECB see European Central Bank
Eccles, Marriner, 94
Economist, The, 53, 162, 218, 237, 285
Economist Intelligence Unit, 244
Edwards, Albert, 266
Edwards, John, 135, 247, 248
Egg, 24–9
Eisenhower, President Dwight, 79–80
EMI, 252
Enron, 55
Ernst & Young, 184

Essex University: Institute for Social and Economic Research, 144
Europe, 232–3, 296–7, 298 see also names of European institutions
European Central Bank (ECB), 13, 21, 116, 242, 262, 267, 269
European Commission, 5, 16, 68, 102, 115, 212–13, 298, 299
European Community, 86
European Court of Justice, 298
European Economic Community, 299
European Union (EU), 68, 71, 140, 150, 181, 233, 234, 282, 283, 285, 300
Evans-Pritchard, Ambrose, 112
Evening Standard, 108, 139, 308

Far East, 173, 280
Faux, Jeff, 245–6, 249–50
Federal Deposit Insurance Corporation, 94
Federal Home Loan Mortgage Corporation, 241
Federal Reserve Board (the Fed), 3, 13, 14, 21, 30–1, 111, 131, 192, 224–5, 230, 236, 240, 241–2, 243, 244, 245, 256–7, 260, 261, 262, 268–9
and Bear Stearns, 2–3
and Long Term Capital Management (LTCM), 110, 209
see also Bernanke, Ben; Eccles, Marriner; Greenspan, Alan; Miller, Bill
Financial Services Authority (FSA), 42, 45, 46, 53, 54–5, 56–7, 58, 59, 60–1, 62, 63, 70, 151–2, 289

Financial Stability Forum, 282
Financial Times, 32, 33, 137, 141, 159, 242, 252, 308
First Boston, 202
First Direct, 143
Fisher, Professor Irving, 251
Fitzgerald, F. Scott, 11, 12
Fleckenstein, William, 23
Fleming, Ian, 116, 158
Flybe, 139
Food Standards Agency, 154
Foot, Paul, 83
Ford, Gerald, 106
France, 14, 31–3, 77, 234, 243, 265, 282, 296, 304, 305
Franklin, Benjamin, 93
Fraser, Steve, 93
Friedman, Milton, 74, 99, 257
FSA see Financial Services Authority
FTSE 100, 48, 49
Furedi, Frank, 155
Future Mortgages, 27

G7 see Group of Seven
G8 see Group of Eight
Galbraith, J.K., 246–7, 259
Gates, Bill, 116
George, Lord, 55, 128
Germany, 77, 117, 210, 214, 232, 243, 247, 258, 265, 267, 273, 274, 282, 296, 297, 298
Gieve, Sir John, 55–6
Glass-Steagal Act, 94, 236, 304
Glyn, Andrew, 125, 177
Goldman Sachs, 16, 45, 46, 65, 66, 75, 126, 260
Goodheart, Charles, 50
Gosforth, 48
Gotcha! (play), 85–6
Government Communications Headquarters, 169
Graham, David, 73

Granite, 50–1, 56
Great Depression, 76, 92, 95, 236, 248, 256, 257, 277
Greece, 210
Greene, Graham, 6, 309
Greenspan, Alan, 23, 39, 99, 100, 114, 122, 128, 130, 131, 191 192, 197, 221, 224–5, 236, 237, 238, 241–2, 256
Griffiths, Katherine, 25, 27
Griffiths, Trevor, 106
Gross, Bill, 261
Group of Eight (G8), 282
Group of Seven (G7), 212, 213, 215, 280, 281, 282, 283
Guardian, The, 13, 57, 139, 254
Gulf of Mexico, 272, 276
Gulf States, 275
Gunther, Max, 160

Hailey, Arthur, 101
Halifax, 48, 53, 123, 160, 162, 164, 262
Hamburg, 190
Hands, Guy, 252
Hanson, Pauline, 105
Hausmann, Ricardo, 238
Hayek, Friedrich von, 74, 91, 92, 95, 96, 99, 100
HBOS, 1–2, 59
Healey, Denis, 37
Heart of Birmingham Primary Care Trust, 138
Heath, Edward, 81, 82, 83, 84, 86, 89, 90, 97, 98, 106, 169, 298
Heathrow Airport, 308
Henry, Brian, 119
Hines, Barry, 85
Hinsley, Harry, 273–4
Hitler, Adolph, 91, 92
HM Revenue and Customs (HMRC), 35–6, 181

Hoather, Tracy, 184, 186–7
Hoggart, Richard, 296
Home Office, 154–5
Hoover, Herbert, 253
Hopkinson, Tom, 294–5
Howard, John, 105, 106
Howe, Sir Geoffrey, 169
HSBC, 2, 59, 231, 265
Hubbert, M. King, 270
Hulton, Edward, 294–5
Hunt, H.L., 79
Hunter, Dr Philip, 142
Hurd, Douglas, 81, 90–1
Hurricane Katrina, 272
Hussein, Saddam, 130, 258, 261

If (film), 76
IFS (Institute for Fiscal Studies),
    36, 37
Igan, Deniz, 227
IMF see International Monetary
    Fund
Independent, 254
Independent on Sunday, The, 42,
    270
India, 7, 120, 127, 130, 179, 214, 239,
    261, 270, 274, 294
Indonesia, 126
Industrial Relations Bill, 169
ING, 264
In Place of Strife (White Paper),
    84
Insolvency Service, 184
Institute of Economic Affairs,
    290
Institute for Fiscal Studies (IFS),
    36, 37
Insull, Samuel, 93–4
Intelligence Capital, 111
International Court of Justice,
    115
International Energy Agency,
    271

International Monetary Fund
    (IMF), 5, 16, 115, 126–7, 149,
    194–5, 196, 202, 207, 210, 211,
    213, 214, 218, 226, 229–31,
    252–3, 280, 281, 282, 283, 289,
    299
Iran, 273, 275, 276
Iran–Iraq war, 130
Iraq, 130, 261, 273, 275
Ireland, Republic of, 210, 234
Irish Labour Party, 300
Irving, Washington, 188
Italy, 77, 282, 296, 305
Item forecasting club, 184

Jagger, Mick, 78
James, Clive, 103
Japan, 133, 191, 196, 214, 215, 232,
    242, 256, 265, 273, 280
Jarrow March, 85
JC Flowers, 65
Jersey, 50
John, Elton, 85, 222
Johnson, Douglas, 296
Johnson, President Lyndon, 78,
    99–100
Johnson, Paul, 37
Johnson, Simon, 252–3
Johnson Matthew Bankers (JMB),
    64
Johnston, Philip, 139–40
Jones, Alfred Winslow, 208
Joshi, Dhaval, 164
JP Morgan Chase, 2, 75, 223

Kaletsky, Anatole, 260, 261
Keefe, Barry, 85, 86
Kennedy, Senator Edward, 100
Kennedy, President John F., 246
Kennedy, Paul, 274–5
Kerr, Ian, 27
Kerrigan, Gene, 111
Kerry, John, 79

Kerviel, Jerome, 32
Kes (film), 85
Keynes, John Maynard, 9, 78, 94–5, 95–6, 257
Kindle, 141
King, Mervyn, 2, 21, 52, 55, 57, 58, 59, 60, 61, 62, 74, 118, 119, 126
Kingston-upon-Thames, Royal Borough of, 154
Kitson, Michael, 177–8, 185–6
Kleinwort Dresdner, 264–5
Krugman, Paul, 75
Kuttner, Robert, 253

Labour, 1, 7, 22, 37, 38, 43, 44, 45, 46, 70, 84, 88–9, 92, 97, 137, 139, 141, 149, 151, 152, 153, 166, 173–8, 182, 185–6, 265, 293–5, 300, 305, 307 *see also* names of Labour politicians
Laeven, Luc, 227
Laker, Sir Freddie, 101
Lamy, Pascal, 116
Larkin, Philip, 112
Latin America, 126, 255, 274
Law Lords, 102
Lawson, Nigel, 110, 166–7, 168–70, 174, 291
Leach, Graeme, 107
Leeson, Nick, 31–2, 137
Legal & General Investment Management, 65
Leggett, Jeremy, 270–1
Lennon, John, 76, 82
Letwin, Oliver, 107
Leverett, Flynt, 275
Levin, Bernard, 1, 83
Levy Institute, 235
Lewis, Michael, 201
Lewis, Stephen, 268–9
Liberal Democrats, 33, 67

Libertarian Books, 100
Likely Lads, The (TV programme), 84
Lisbon, 190
Lloyd's of London, 20
Lloyds TSB, 2, 59, 60, 61, 62
Lodge, David, 102, 188
Lomax, Rachel, 39
Lombard Street Research, 128, 203–4, 216, 229
London, 5, 7, 13, 15, 17, 21, 22, 55, 74, 77, 110, 129, 147, 148, 155–6, 180, 215, 262, 299
Long Term Capital Management (LTCM), 8, 110, 129–30, 208, 209, 242, 243, 264
Los Angeles, 14, 76
Los Angeles Times, 252
Lowenstein, Prince Rupert, 78
Loynes, Jonathan, 171–2
LTCM *see* Long Term Capital Management
Lucas, Maya, 28

Macau, 78
McCarthy, Callum, 62
McClintock, Harry, 114
McDonald's, 139
McFall, John, 42
Mackenzie, Lee, 11
Macmillan, Harold, Earl of Stockton, 102
Macrea, Norman, 285
Madsen, Axel, 284–5
Mail on Sunday, The, 34, 183
Major, John, 148
Major administration, 159
Malawi, 214
Malaysia, 127, 191, 210–11
Manchester, 3
Manson, Charles, 78
Marcuse, Herbert, 105
Mellon, Andrew, 225, 251

Merrill Lynch, 16, 20, 49, 223–4, 260, 263
Merton, Robert, 129–30
Metronet, 151
Mexico, 126, 249, 271
Michigan, 232
Middle East, 130, 271, 273, 275–6, 277 *see also* names of countries
Miller, Bill, 268, 269
Ministry of Justice, 154
Minsky, Hyman, 235, 236
Mises, Ludwig von, 74
Mitterand, François, 14
Mondale, Walter, 79
Monetary Policy Committee (MPC), 98, 160, 161, 162
Mont Pèlerin society, 74, 75, 91, 92, 95, 121
Morgan, Kenneth O., 294
Morgan, Roger, 182
Morgan Stanley, 126, 202, 260
Morley, Dr Robert, 138
Mosimann's, 151–2
Mozilo, Angelo, 21
Mpasu, Sam, 214
MPC *see* Monetary Policy Committee
Munkhammar, Johnny, 156–7
Murdoch, Iris, 158

NAFTA (North American Free Trade Agreement), 249
National Coal Board, 295
National Giro (later National Girobank), 71
National Health Service (NHS), 95, 138, 144, 150, 151, 181, 182, 295
National Interest, 275
National Recovery Administration (NRA), 293
Nationwide, 48, 71, 164

Nationwide (TV programme), 90
Neal, Larry, 192
Netherlands, 117, 190, 210, 297
Network Rail, 139
Newcastle Chronicle, 49
Newcastle United, 48–9
New Deal, 75, 236, 292–3
New Hampshire, 252
New Left Review, 80
New Orleans, 272
New Republic, 126
News International, 147
News of the World, 147
News on Sunday, 101
Newton, Isaac, 189
New York, 6, 15, 55, 129, 196, 222, 239, 255, 272
New York Times, 261
New Zealand, 133, 156–7, 210, 215
NHS *see* National Health Service
Niemeyer, Otto, 95
Nixon, President Richard, 79, 98
Nono, Luigi, 103
North American Free Trade Association (NAFTA), 249
Northern Ireland, 105
Northern Rock, 29–30, 38, 42–72, 74, 82, 87, 110, 112, 138, 152, 159, 264
North Sea, 271, 281
Norway, 212
NRA (National Recovery Administration), 293

Obama, Barack, 248, 252
Observer, The, 103
Office of Fair Trading, 70, 88
Office for National Statistics, 67, 150, 159, 180
Office for Standards in Education, Children's Services and Skills (Ofsted), 182

Ohio, 232
Olivant, 65
Ono, Yoko, 82
Olympic Games, 151
O'Neal, Stanley, 223–4, 234
OPEC (Organisation of Petroleum
    Exporting Countries), 95,
    271
Open Market Committee, 131
Operation Robot, 97
Organisation of Petroleum
    Exporting Countries see
    OPEC
Ormerod, Paul, 119
Orr, Sir David, 284
Orwell, George, 135
O'Sullivan, John, 248
Oswald, Andrew, 261
Overend and Gurney, 47–8

Pacific Rim, 121
Pahl, Ray, 144
Paisley, Ian, 105
Pakistan, 294
Palley, Thomas, 17, 195
Palme, Olaf, 98
Paris, 76, 77, 180, 190, 282, 299
Partnoy, Frank, 202–3, 219
Paulson, Henry, 62, 112, 234, 240,
    242
Peloton Partners, 39
Persaud, Avinash, 111, 239–40,
    244–5
Peston, Robert, 43
Picture Post, 294–5
Pillar Trust, 28
Pimco, 261
Pitman, Sir Brian, 65
Pliny the Younger, 11
Poole, Bill, 111
Popper, Karl, 74, 255
Portugal, 210
Post Office, 71, 139–40, 301

Prague, 80
Price, Alan, 85
PriceWaterhouseCooper, 16
Prince, Chuck, 26, 28, 133, 134
Prudential, 24, 25

Quantum, 271

RAB Capital, 65, 66
Ramsay, Robin, 86, 87, 88, 170
Rand, Ayn, 99–100
Randall, Jeff, 186
Ranieri, Lewis, 201
Reading, Brian, 128, 238
Reagan, Ronald, 73, 105
Red Brigades, 77
Red Mole, 76
Redwood, John, 146, 148
Reform, 106–7, 150–1
Reid, Margaret, 73
Republicans, 79 see also names of
    Republican politicians
Republic of Ireland, 210, 234
Restrictive Practices Act, 88
Reuters, 141
Revel, Jean-François, 98
Ricardo, David, 17
Ridley, Matt, 58
Rodrik, Professor Dani, 214–15
Rogers, Jim, 271
Rolling Stones, The, 76, 77, 78,
    222
Rolls Royce, 45, 82
Roosevelt, President Franklin D.,
    9, 75–6, 92–4, 95–6, 279, 286,
    291–3
Roosevelt, President Theodore,
    286–7, 290
Rose, David, 144
Roubini, Professor Nouriel,
    242–3
Rowthorn, Bob, 177
Royal Bank of Scotland, 2, 160

Royal Institution of Chartered Surveyors, 262
Royal Mail, 140
Runcie, Robert, 282–3
Russia, 92, 129, 173, 208, 211, 212, 213, 273, 275, 280, 282

Sachs, Samuel, 201
St Albans, 108
Salomon Brothers, 200–1
Sameday, 184
Sanchez, Abe Walking Bear, 123–4
Sandler, Ron, 71
Sants, Hector, 54–5, 60
Sarbanes-Oxley Act, 55
Saudi Arabia, 130, 211, 213, 273, 276, 281
Saunders, Michael, 159, 262
Schmitt, John, 233–4
Scholes, Myron, 129–30
Schumpeter, Joseph, 183
Schwed, Fred, 19
Scott, Professor Ira, 73
Seabrook, Jeremy, 147, 279
Securities and Exchange Act, 94
Securities and Exchange Commission, 20, 94
Sexton, David, 108
Shanghai, 14
Sheeran, Josette, 267
Simmons, Matthew, 270
Singapore, 211, 230
Single European Act, 102
Sinn Fein, 300
Skene, Leigh, 203–4, 215
Slade, 85
Slater Walker, 64
Slaughter & May, 65
Small Business Research Trust, 184
Smile, 24
Smith, Adam, 17

Société Générale, 31–3, 164, 266
Softly, Softly (TV programme), 84
Soros, George, 4, 18, 271
South East Development Agency, 152
South Korea, 191
South Sea bubble, 189, 190, 192
Soviet Union, 120, 274, 275
Spain, 210, 234
Spectator, The, 248
Spencer, Liz, 144
Spencer, Professor Peter, 184, 186
Springsteen, Bruce, 232
SRM Global, 65, 66
Stiglitz, Joseph, 126–7, 253–4
Stockton, Harold Macmillan, Earl of, 102
Stourton, Ed, 57
Straw, Jack, 155
Sturzenegger, Frederico, 238
Summers, Larry, 126, 213
Sun, The, 138, 147
Sunday Independent, 111
Sunday Telegraph, The, 25, 136
Sunday Times, The, 28, 63, 82, 147
Sweden, 296
Swiss Re, 20
Switzerland, 72, 74, 91, 116, 117, 297

Taiwan, 179, 211
Tangier, 78
Tebbit, Norman, 105, 146
Tesco, 136, 137, 138, 142
Tet offensive, 78
Texas, 232
Thailand, 126, 127, 191
Thatcher, Margaret, 73, 98, 105, 122, 123, 145, 167, 196
Thomas Cook, 89

Thompson, Paul, 65
Thornton, Clive, 101
Times, The, 83, 147, 260
Today programme, 57, 62, 90
Tokyo, 191, 215, 280
Townsend, Robert, 288
Trades Union Congress, 89
Trading Places (film), 221–2, 240
Transport for London, 155
Travis, Merle, 26
Treasury, British, 3, 5, 6, 33, 34, 37,
    45, 46, 54, 60, 61, 62, 63, 65,
    66, 67–8, 68–9, 118, 152, 159,
    175, 181, 295
  Select Committee, 42, 55, 70
Treasury, US, 126–7, 209, 214,
    225, 234, 236, 238, 248, 256,
    266
Trichet, Jean-Claude, 116
Tricks, Henry, 208
Truman, Harry, 247–8
Trustee Savings Bank, 102
Turner, Adair, 233
Turner, Graham, 268

UBS, 20, 49
UCS (Upper Clyde Shipbuilders),
    82
UN Food Programme, 267
Unilever, 284
Union of Post Office Workers,
    82
United Craft Organisation, 147
United Health Europe, 139
Upper Clyde Shipbuilders (UCS),
    82
US Global Change Research
    Programme, 272
Utley, T.E., 301

Varley, John, 109
Vietnam, 120
  War, 76, 77, 79, 99

Virgin, 65, 66,138
Virgin Money, 65
Volcker, Paul, 239, 269
Voltaire, 114

Wachtel, Howard, 93, 94
Wallace, George, 105, 106
Wall Street Crash, 190, 225, 229,
    248, 256
Wall Street Journal, The, 141
Walpole, Robert, 189
Wanless, Derek, 57
Wapping, 147
Warburton, Peter, 124
Warnock, Francis, 239
Warnock, Veronica, 239
Washington, 196, 212, 255, 272, 299
  Consensus, 127, 214
Washington Post, 239
Waugh, Auberon, 105
WEO *see World Economic Outlook*
Wesker, Arnold, 82
Westpac, 64
Weyer, Martin Van der, 308–9
*Whatever Happened to the Likely
    Lads?* (TV programme),
    85
White, Bill, 131–2
Whitehall, 151, 153, 154
Whitman, Walt, 222
Wilkinson, Frank, 175, 177–8,
    185–6
Williams, Shirley, 98
Wilson, A.N., 282–3
Wilson, Harold, 81, 88, 96
Woodward, Bob, 23
World Bank, 5, 16, 115, 126, 127,
    214
Worldcom, 55
World Economic Forum, 20, 116,
    213
World Economic Outlook (WEO),
    195, 207, 210, 229–30, 231

World Trade Organisation
(WTO), 5, 15–16, 115, 116,
214, 299, 300
Wray, Randall, 235–6
Wriston, Walter, 15

WTO *see* World Trade Organisation

Yes, Minister (TV programme), 88

Z Cars (TV programme), 84